17 Drives

College Football's 2015 Season, One Game At A Time

MARK SCHOFIELD

To Owen and Simone, words cannot express what you both mean to me.

To Rachelle, to whom I owe so much. All I can say is that you continue to be the most impressive person I'll ever know. Thank you for saying yes.

CONTENTS

ACKNOWLEDGMENTS

I used to believe that playing football was the greatest team effort I had ever experienced. Then I helped start a website writing about the sport, which was a more impressive group effort.

Then I wrote a book.

This would not have been possible without the incredible help and support from everyone at Inside the Pylon, from all of the editors and writers. In particular I want to thank Craig Craker, Pete Hodges, Philip Kibbey, Chuck Zodda, Andy Wiborg, and John Harrington for their assistance in editing and formatting. Of course, this entire endeavor would not have been possible without the help from ITP's Editor in Chief, David R. McCullough, who has been a driving force behind everything our site has put together. Without the help, guidance and support from all of these folks – and everyone at ITP – this never would have been accomplished.

I want to thank the countless – and there are countless – football fans and writers out there who challenge me every day in how I think about this game I love. There are truly too many to thank. But three in particular stand out: Alex Kirby, who has also taken to book form to bring Xs and Os to readers, and is an inspiration in this field; Dan Hatman, who has given me his time to help me understand this game, and the importance of context; and, Matt Waldman, who is a genius at both player evaluation and the written word.

I also have to thank my family. My parents have been so supportive throughout my life, and my career change, as have my in-laws. My brother, one of my first teammates, continues to be one of my biggest fans. It also helps to have the greatest team at home supporting me, with my wife Rachelle and our two children, Owen and Simone.

INTRODUCTION

Trailing by three points with a little less than seven minutes remaining in Super Bowl XLIX, Tom Brady stepped into the New England Patriots' offensive huddle and delivered a clear message to his teammates:

"OK fellas, we need a championship drive."

The veteran quarterback didn't shout about winning the game, or about running the football down the throats of the Seattle defense. He calmly told his offensive teammates that what was needed was a drive: successful plays strung together resulting in a score. Brady needed a drive to potentially deliver another Super Bowl victory to New England. And his teammates responded.

Every football game is a Shakespearean drama played out over the course of 60 minutes, with peaks and valleys, good plays and bad plays, in front of thousands – if not millions – of eyes. But in each game there are turning points: moments when the balance of power shifts from one team to the other. They can occur early in a game, in the third quarter, or in the final seconds These moments are often part of a single drive, coming as an offense puts together a string of plays that change the course of a game. These are moments when 11 players, bonded together, see the fruits of their hard work in the spring and summer pay off.

The 2015 college football season contained many highs and lows – big upsets, stunning performances, and thrilling games that came down to the final seconds. In this book we examine 17 of these game-changing drives, an unconventional week-by-week recap of the season. These drives reveal not only how their particular contest turned out, but when viewed collectively, tell the story of a season and provide a glimpse into how the game is being played across the college football landscape. The season-long story gives us a window into the schemes, plays and designs that teams are using on the field, and what teams call upon when the biggest play is needed.

Each one of the 17 moments contained herein are, in their own way, championship drives. Some, like the Week 4 game-winning drive by the Memphis Tigers against the Cincinnati Bearcats, showed off a potential NFL star like Tigers QB Paxton Lynch, who marched his team down the field in 2 minutes. Others, like Stanford's short but clutch drive against the Notre Dame Fighting Irish, dashed one team's College Football Playoff hopes. And one – a classic 9-minute, 22-play, 82-yard drive, led by Michigan State's Connor Cook against undefeated Iowa in the Big 10 Championship Game – helps define the term championship drive. Finally, the CFB playoffs, and Alabama's execution resulting in the crowning of a National Champion.

This book has something for everyone, from the casual football fans looking to relive their team's big drive, to the coach studying the X's and O's of a top college program. I hope you enjoy reading this as much as we did putting it together. Enjoy the games.

CHAPTER ONE

ALABAMA BUILDS ITS LEAD OVER WISCONSIN

The 2015 college football season kicked off with a number of interesting non-conference Week 1 matchups, but the marquee game of the week, the Kickoff Classic, was between Alabama and Wisconsin in the House That Jerry Jones Built, aka AT&T Stadium in Arlington, Texas. The Badgers entered the game hoping to kick off their season with a huge upset, while the Crimson Tide needed the victory to begin building a playoff resume.

Only one team would get its wish. This third quarter drive from Alabama told the story of the night.

Following a Wisconsin punt, the Crimson Tide take over possession at their own 33-yard line, with 7:27 remaining in the third quarter. They line up with 21 offensive personnel (two running backs, two wide receivers, and one tight end) on the field, with quarterback Jake Coker (#14) in the shotgun. Future Heisman-winning running back Derrick Henry (#2) stands to the left of the QB in the backfield. Alabama uses slot formation on the right, with running back Kenyan Drake (#17) the inside receiver, and a wing-slot formation to the left, with tight end O.J. Howard in a wing alignment next to the left tackle. The Badgers have a 3-3-5 sub package on the field, showing Cover 6. Cornerback Darius Hillary (#5) is down in the box in a linebacker's alignment, shaded to the slot formation side of the field, while outside linebacker Jack Cichy (#48) stands on the line of scrimmage shaded over the TE:

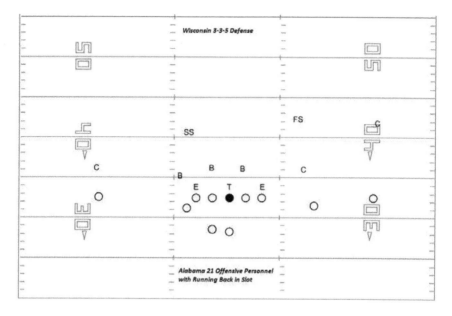

Prior to the snap, Drake comes in jet motion toward the quarterback. The only adjustment the defense makes is having Hillary slide to the inside:

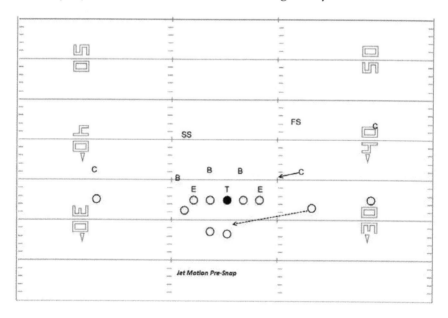

The Crimson Tide run an outside zone lead play here, with Drake taking the short flip from the quarterback and aiming for the left edge while Henry leads him toward the outside. In unison, the offensive line fires out toward this side as well:

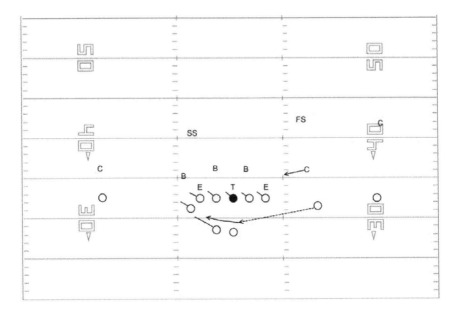

The tight end Howard (#88) throws the key block at the point of attack. Off the snap the linebacker Cichy bursts upfield into the backfield, and the tight end uses the defender's speed against him, giving him depth initially before driving him to the outside:

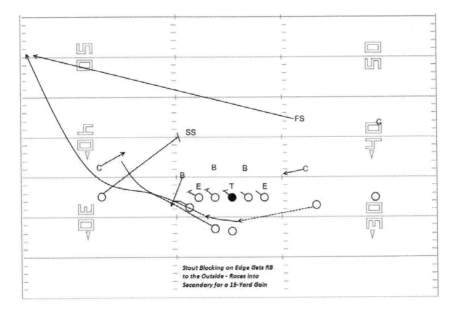

Stout Blocking on Edge Gets RB to the Outside - Races into Secondary for a 15-Yard Gain

Drake cuts into the hole created along the edge and turns upfield before being knocked out of bounds by free safety Leo Musso (#19) after a 15-yard gain.

On the second play of the drive Alabama runs Drake on an inside zone play for no gain, but left tackle Cam Robinson (#74) is flagged for a holding penalty. Alabama now faces a 1st and 20 on its own 38-yard line. The offense lines up with Coker in pistol formation, Henry behind him, two receivers and a tight end on the right, and a single receiver split to the left. The Badgers stay with their 3-3-5 package, with Cichy again on the line of scrimmage to the weakside of the offense, showing Cover 6 in the secondary. The press cornerback is matched up over the single receiver split wide to the left:

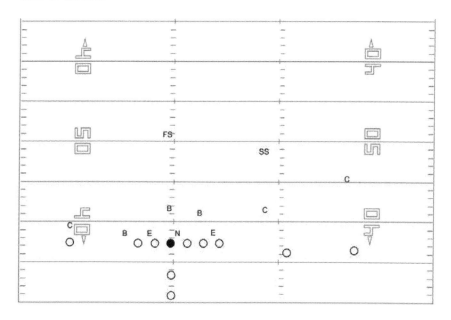

At the snap, the Badgers send Hillary on the corner blitz from the trips side of the formation, and roll their coverage into Cover 4. The blitz calls for the two remaining linebackers to widen into underneath zones at the snap. This plays right into the package play the Crimson Tide employ here:

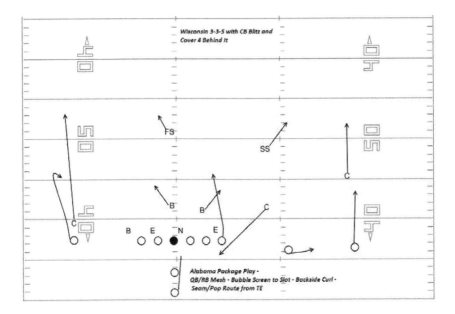

As Henry and Coker meet at the mesh point, the quarterback reads the linebackers: He has the option of giving the football to Henry, throwing the bubble screen to the outside, or finding Howard on the seam route. Hillary's blitz gives the defender an angle on the running back should Coker hand off the ball. But the blitz also opens up the seam route for Howard. Coker pulls the football out of the running back's belly and makes a quick throw to his tight end on the seam route:

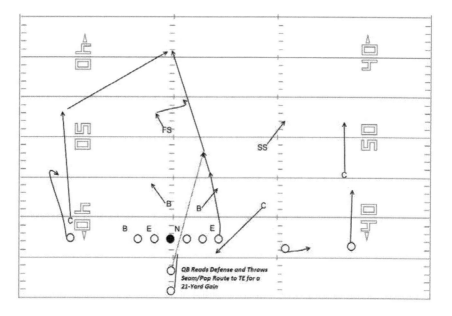

QB Reads Defense and Throws Seam/Pop Route to TE for a 21-Yard Gain

Howard pulls in the throw 9 yards downfield, and after securing the reception is able to cut toward the sideline and avoid a diving tackle attempt from Musso. He picks up 21 yards, giving the Crimson Tide another first down.

Now in Badger territory, the Crimson Tide set up for the next play with the same one running back, three wide receiver, one tight end package on the field. Coker is in the pistol formation with Henry behind him. Robert Foster (#8) is the single receiver split to the left, while Howard aligns as an upback behind the right tackle, and Alabama uses a tight inverted slot formation on the right. The Badgers stay with their 3-3-5 package, this time sliding Hillary down near the line of scrimmage over the inverted slot alignment while showing Cover 4:

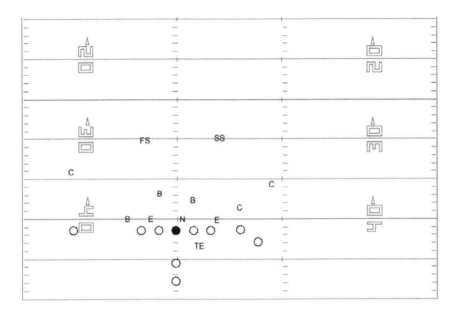

After a play-action fake, the Crimson Tide run a spot concept to the right: Howard releases to the flat while wide receiver Richard Mullaney (#16) runs a corner route. Fellow WR ArDarius Stewart (#13) runs a snag route, cutting inside:

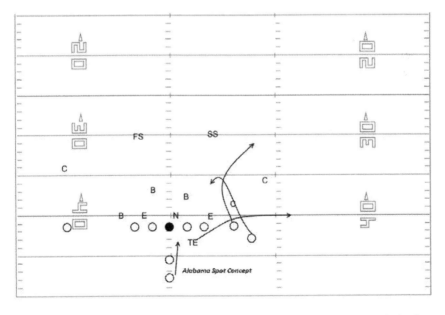

As this play develops, Hillary gets an initial jam on Howard, before staying with him on the flat route. Both the playside cornerback Sojourn Shelton (#8) and safety D'Cota Dixon (#14) drop deep in response to the corner route from Mullaney. This opens up the underneath area of the field for Stewart's snag route:

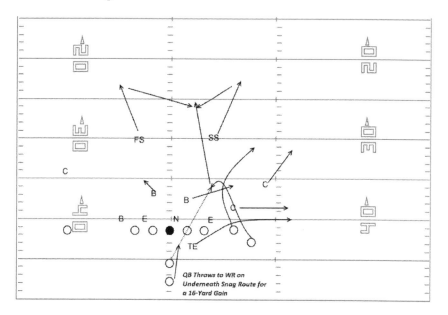

QB Throws to WR on
Underneath Snag Route for
a 16-Yard Gain

After hauling in the pass from Coker, Stewart bangs his way down to the Wisconsin 25-yard line, with a 16-yard gain and another Alabama first down.

For this next play, Alabama makes a personnel adjustment and brings on an extra tight end. The Crimson Tide line up using two tight ends in a wing alignment on the left and two receivers in inverted slot formation on the right. Coker is in the pistol formation with Drake behind him. The Badgers adjust their defense as well, reverting to their base 3-4 defense with outside linebacker Vince Biegel (#47) on the line of scrimmage over the dual tight ends. Wisconsin shows a Cover 4 look in the secondary before the play:

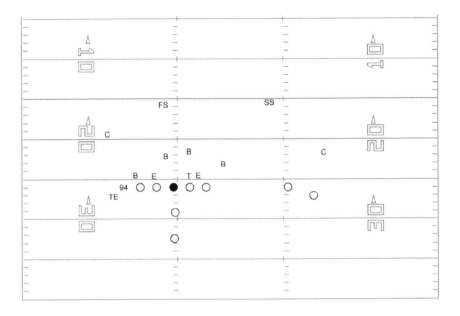

Alabama runs a split-zone play. Howard blocks across the formation and takes on Cichy, now lined up as an outside linebacker off the ball. Meanwhile the rest of the offensive line – and reserve tight end/defensive lineman Dakota Ball (#94) – block in unison to the left on the zone action:

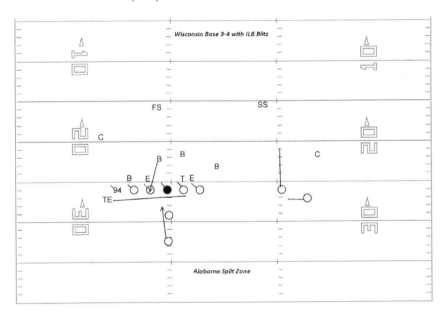

As you can see, inside linebacker T.J. Edwards (#53), shaded toward the two tight ends, blitzes at the snap. His momentum allows him to knock left guard Ross Pierschbacher (#71) into the backfield. Drake takes the snap and heads for the left side, but the penetration – and the reeling guard – forces him to make his bend read and cut backside, behind Howard, who is executing the split zone block on the right edge:

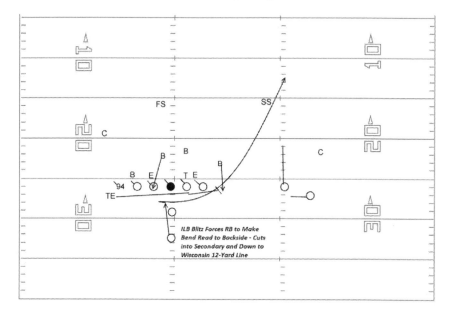

Howard gets a strong block on Cichy, enabling Drake to circle around the outside linebacker and cut upfield for a 12-yard gain, and another Alabama first down.

On the next play, the Crimson Tide return to the spot concept, using the same formation and design from earlier in the drive. They set up with Coker in the pistol and Henry behind him, with Bell now aligned as the upback in place of Howard, and the tight inverted slot on the right. The Badgers keep their 3-4 defense on the field, employing Cover 4 again:

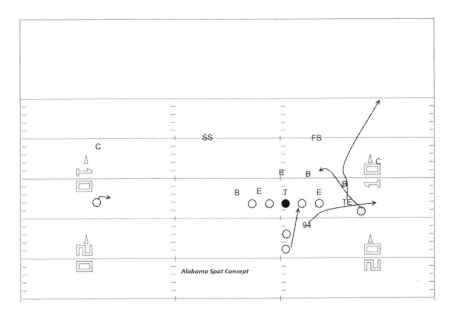

Alabama Spot Concept

This time, the Badgers cover the spot concept well. Cichy gets a jam on Bell as the tight end tries to release to the flat, and then stays with the tight end the entire route. Both the playside cornerback and safety rotate under the corner route. The difference this time is the Badgers have an extra linebacker underneath, Edwards, sitting on the snag route. Coker tries to jam in a throw to Stewart, but the inside linebacker is there to deflect the pass to the turf:

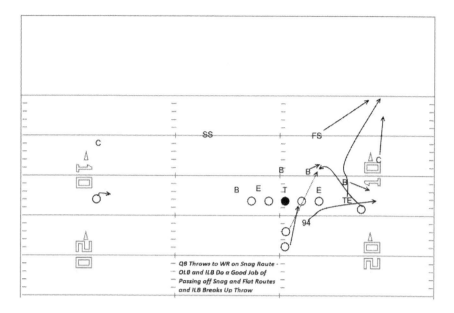

Amazingly, this is the first time Alabama has reached second down on the drive. The Tide line up with three receivers, a tight end, and Coker in the pistol formation, with Henry behind him. The offense has dual slot formations, with a stack-slot look on the right and a tight end wing slot look on the left, with reserve tight end Ty Flournoy-Smith (#83) lined up just outside the left tackle. The Badgers stay with their 3-4 defense, and show Cover 2:

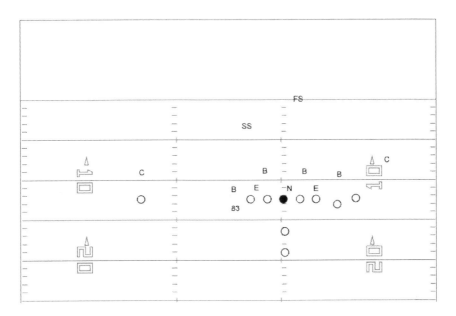

Prior to the snap of the ball, Mullaney comes in jet motion from the stack slot to the quarterback. He is a decoy here, as the Crimson Tide add a slight twist to another play previously used on the drive, a split-zone run:

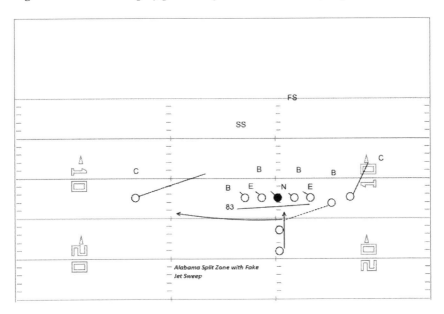

After taking the snap, Coker shows a quick fake to the WR and then hands the ball to Henry, heading up the middle. But as the big runner nears the left A gap, both defensive end Arthur Goldberg (#95) and Edwards are waiting for him. Somehow, Henry cuts on a dime to the outside, deftly avoiding the tackle attempts of the two defenders:

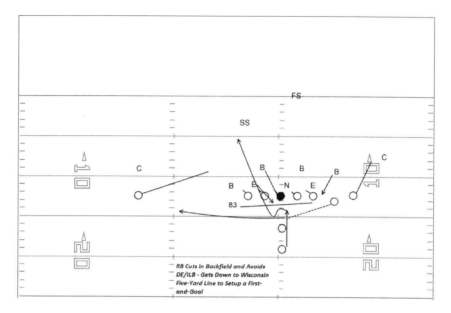

RB Cuts in Backfield and Avoids
DE/ILB - Gets Down to Wisconsin
Five-Yard Line to Setup a First-
and-Goal

He then cuts upfield and races inside the 5-yard line, where he is finally dragged down at the 2. The nifty cut and acceleration set up the Crimson Tide with a first down and goal.

On the next play, Henry finishes the drive with this short touchdown run on the same exact play:

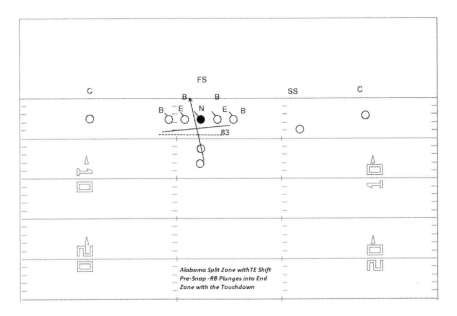

Alabama Split Zone with TE Shift
Pre-Snap -RB Plunges into End
Zone with the Touchdown

The efficient seven-play scoring drive that featured just one second-down play gave Alabama a 28-7 lead, and the Crimson Tide did not look back en route to a 35-17 victory. The win gave the SEC school an impressive non-conference win in its season opener, and put the rest of the country on notice.

CHAPTER TWO

OKLAHOMA TIES IT LATE

Week 2 of the 2015 college football season saw the then-19th-ranked Oklahoma Sooners travel east to take on the 23rd-ranked Tennessee Volunteers in a Big 12-SEC clash. The Volunteers got the better of play early, primarily due to two interceptions thrown by Sooners quarterback Baker Mayfield, and the hosts enjoyed a 17-3 lead at the half. However, Oklahoma was stubborn and got a touchdown back before forcing a Tennessee punt with just six minutes remaining, trailing 17-10.

After Sterling Shepard (#3) returned the punt to the Oklahoma 40-yard line, the Sooners set up their offense with Mayfield in the shotgun and three receivers, one tight end, and one running back on the field. Tight end Mark Andrews (#81) aligns in the slot to the right with wide receiver Durron Neal (#5) on the outside. Shepard and Dede Westbrook (#11) set up in a slot alignment on the left, with Westbrook to the outside. Samaje Perine (#32) stands to the right of the quarterback in the backfield. The Volunteers have a 4-2-5 nickel defense in the game, showing Cover 6 in the secondary:

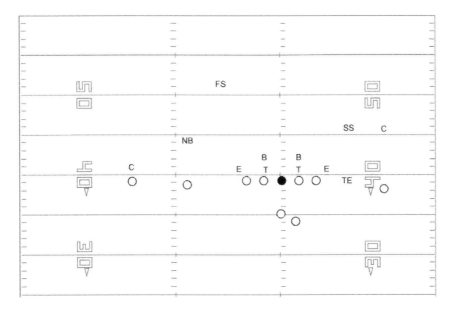

The Sooners run the ball, with Perine and Mayfield meeting at the mesh point and the running back pointed at the left side. The offensive line flows to the left, leaving defensive end Corey Vereen (#50) unblocked. The quarterback reads the defensive end, with the choice to either hand the ball off or keep it depending on how Vereen reacts:

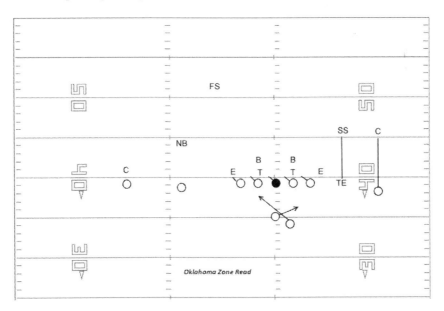

Oklahoma Zone Read

The DE slides down the line a few steps in response to the fake to Perine, and Mayfield chooses to keep the football. Given a slight one-step advantage, the quarterback is able to gain the edge and head outside, where Andrews and Neal are blocking:

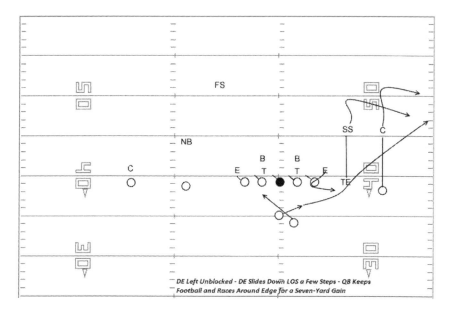

DE Left Unblocked - DE Slides Down LOS a Few Steps - QB Keeps Football and Races Around Edge for a Seven-Yard Gain

Mayfield picks up a 7-yard gain before being forced out of bounds.

Facing 2nd and 3 at their own 47-yard line, the offense hurries to the line without a huddle. Mayfield sets in the pistol with Perine behind him. They use an unbalanced line, moving right tackle Josiah St. John (#55) to the left side and placing the tight end Andrews in a traditional right tackle alignment. The Volunteers show Cover 2 in the secondary, bringing Emmanuel Moseley (#12) down over Neal in press alignment:

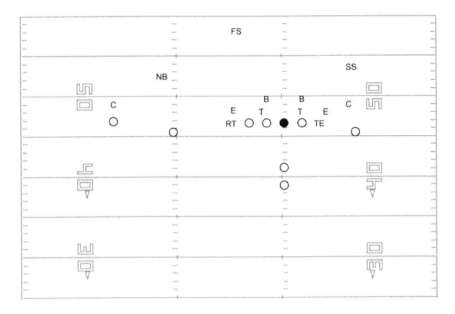

Oklahoma runs an outside zone play to the left. Mayfield takes the snap and turns to his left while Perine cuts behind him to receive the handoff and the offensive line flows in unison to the left side of the field. To add an element of misdirection, Westbrook circles into the backfield behind Perine, faking a reverse to the right:

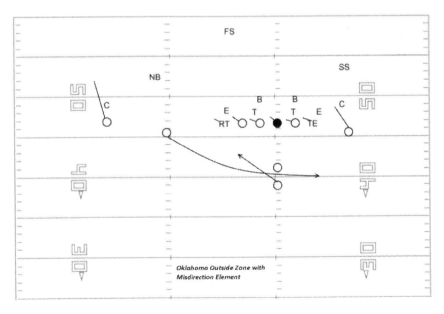

Oklahoma Outside Zone with Misdirection Element

As Perine flows to the outside, he spots a tiny crease between center Ty Darlington (#56) and right guard Nila Kasitati (#54). The running back cuts hard in the backfield as he makes his bend read, back to the right:

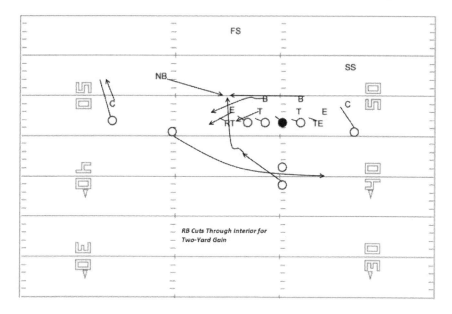

Nose tackle Kendal Vickers (#39) tries to chase Perine down by scraping down the line, but the ball carrier accelerates through the narrow crease and plunges forward. However, he is tripped up in the hole by the duo of defensive tackle Owen Williams (#58) and linebacker Jalen Reeves-Maybin (#21) after a short 2-yard gain.

With the clock running, the Sooners return to the line of scrimmage for this critical 3rd and 1 play with under 6 minutes remaining. Again they set up with their 11 personnel group, but exchange Andrews for fellow tight end Connor Knight (#89), who aligns on the end of the line outside left tackle Orlando Brown (#78). Westbrook lines up as a flanker while Neal and Shepard align in an inverted slot on the right, with the latter receiver on the inside. Tennessee stays with its 4-2-5, shows Cover 1 and brings safety Todd Kelly Jr. (#6) down into the box, where he stands to the outside of the TE:

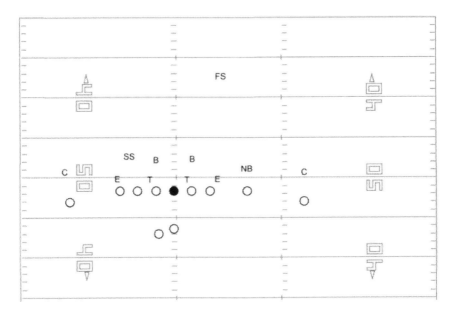

The Sooners send Perine on an inside zone run:

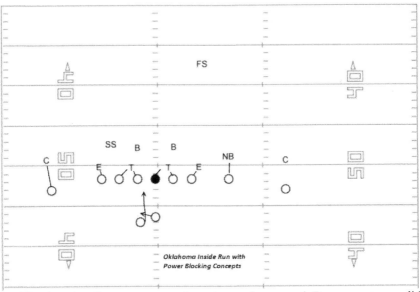

Oklahoma Inside Run with Power Blocking Concepts

The interior line gets a good push up front, and Brown gets a solid down block on the defensive tackle. Knight is tasked with blocking defensive end Derek Barnett (#9) and sealing the edge, which allows Perine to bend this run to the left a bit:

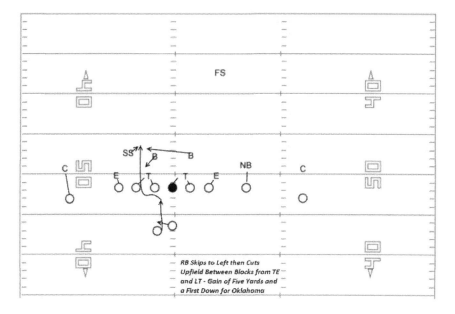

RB Skips to Left then Cuts
Upfield Between Blocks from TE
and LT - Gain of Five Yards and
a First Down for Oklahoma

The back then plunges forward for a 5-yard gain. Kelly makes the tackle, but the Sooners have converted the third down and advanced into Tennessee territory.

With a fresh set of downs, the Sooners get the ball on the left hashmark and deploy a trips formation to that side. Knight stays in the game, this time aligning next to right tackle Dru Samia (#75). Mayfield stands in the shotgun with Perine to his right. The Volunteers stay with Cover 1, putting three defensive backs over the trips formation and aligning Moseley with the linebackers just outside the tight end:

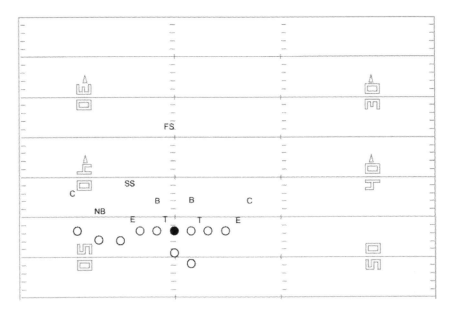

Oklahoma runs a bubble screen to the trips side, delivering the ball to Jarvis Baxter (#1), who has both Neal and Westbrook looking to block:

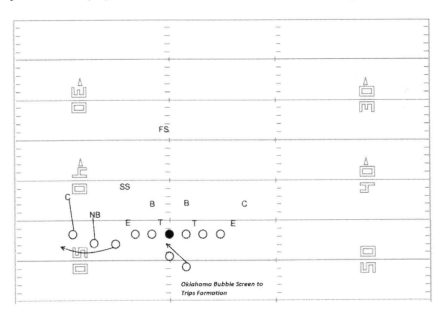

However, Baxter takes his eye off the football for a split second trying to scan the downfield blocking. The football caroms off his hands and lands on the turf incomplete.

On second down, the Sooners adjust their personnel and line up with four wide receivers and a running back (10 personnel). Mayfield stands in the shotgun with Perine to his left. The offense uses a 2x2 alignment, deploying slot formations to each side of the field. The Volunteers adjust as well, switching to a 3-3-5 defense and bringing on linebacker Chris Weatherd (#42). They show blitz with all three linebackers standing on the line of scrimmage:

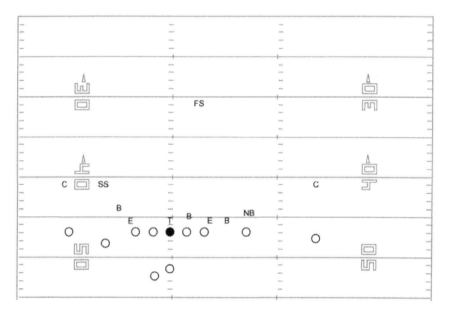

Only one linebacker blitzes, Colton Jumper (#53), but he is joined on the rush by three linemen and another blitzer – nickelback Malik Foreman (#13). Meanwhile, the offense sends both slot receivers on seam routes, while the outside receivers run short in-cuts:

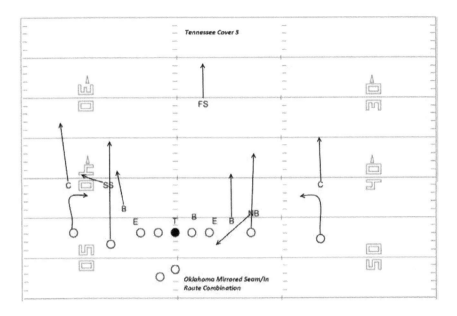

As Mayfield drops to throw, he sees a crease open between the right guard and right tackle. With green grass to that side of the field, he tucks the football and escapes the pocket:

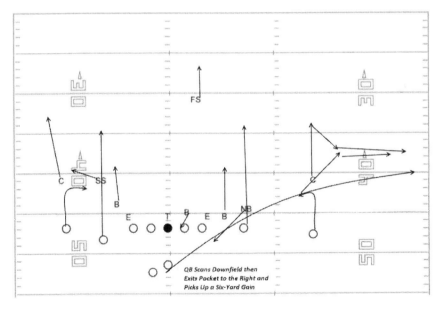

The QB angles for the sideline and ducks out of bounds after picking up 6 yards.

Oklahoma needs 4 yards to extend the drive on third down. The Sooners set up with the same 10 personnel group on the field and the ball on the right hashmark. They put trips to the wide side and leave Shepard alone on the right side of the formation. The Volunteers stay with their 3-3-5 defense, again putting all three linebackers in blitz posture. The secondary shows Cover 1 before the play, with the two inside cornerbacks aligned over the two inside trips receivers in off-man technique, while the outside CBs are in press coverage:

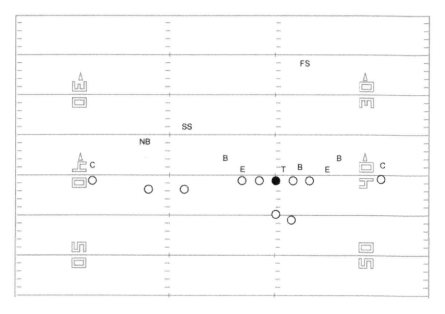

The Sooners look to throw, with Shepard cutting to the inside on a slant before breaking vertically outside. Westbrook runs a curl from the outside along with Neal, the middle trips receiver. Baxter, the inside trips receiver, runs a vertical route bending outside:

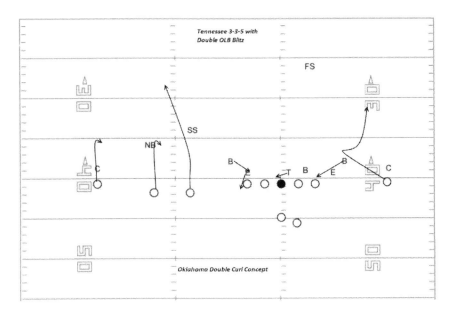

But as Mayfield drops, the pocket begins to collapse around him. In addition to both outside linebackers blitzing, Barnett uses a speed move on Brown and dips around the left tackle. The quarterback feels the pressure tries to escape the pocket to his right:

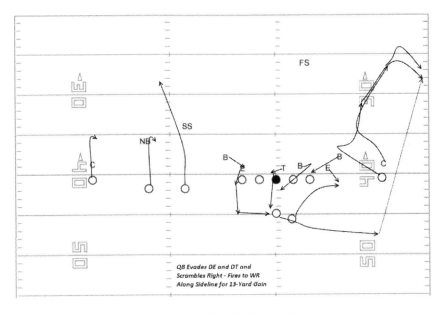

After evading Barnett, Mayfield again looks downfield but cannot find anyone open. While moving to his right, the signal caller is nearly tripped up on a diving attempt by Williams, but somehow Mayfield stays upright and spots Shepard scooting along the sideline. The receiver snares the football out of the sky, gets a foot down and crashes to the turf cradling the ball. After a booth review, the catch was confirmed for a gain of 13 yards, down to the Volunteers' 27-yard line.

When play resumes, Oklahoma sets up with the same four receivers and Perine to the right of Mayfield in the backfield. Westbrook, Neal and Baxter deploy as trips left, with Shepard again a single receiver to the opposite side. Tennessee stays with its 3-3-5 nickel, but only one linebacker, Weatherd, is showing blitz pre-snap. Meanwhile, the secondary shows a soft two-high safety look:

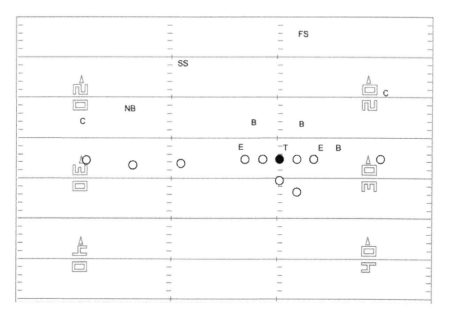

The Sooners attempt to set up a screen to Perine on the right, but Reeves-Maybin diagnoses the play quickly:

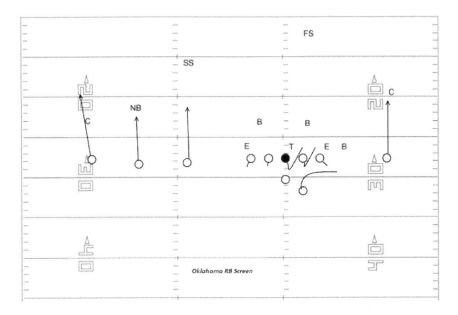

Oklahoma RB Screen

As Mayfield retreats in the pocket, the center and right guard look to release in front of the RB. But because of quick pressure off the ball from the defensive linemen, Vickers and Vereen, the two lead blockers are slow to release. This allows Reeves-Maybin to explode forward, splitting the blockers:

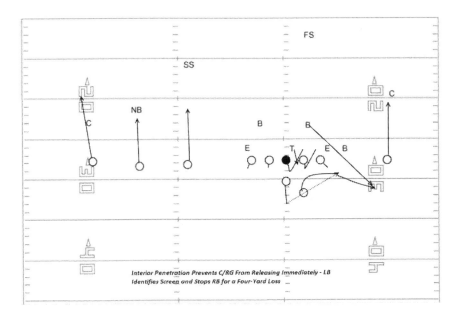

Interior Penetration Prevents C/RG From Releasing Immediately - LB Identifies Screen and Stops RB for a Four-Yard Loss

Reeves-Maybin puts his helmet squarely into the chest of Perine and drives the runner to the turf for a loss of 4 yards.

Now facing second and long, both teams line up with the same personnel as the previous play. However, the Volunteers do not show a blitz alignment and instead drop all three linebackers off the line of scrimmage. Mayfield stands in the shotgun with Perine to his right, with the secondary showing Cover 1:

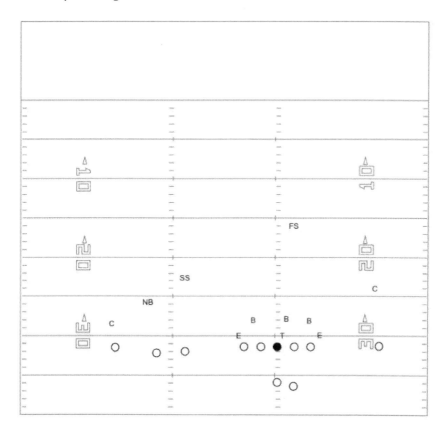

Oklahoma wants to attack vertically, with Shepard running a straight go route on the right. From the trips side, the inside receiver Baxter runs a deep slant while Dahu Green (#18) runs an out pattern from his outside alignment. The middle trips receiver, A.D. Miller (#13), runs a vertical seam route. The Volunteers stick with Cover 1, with Reeves-Maybin blitzing:

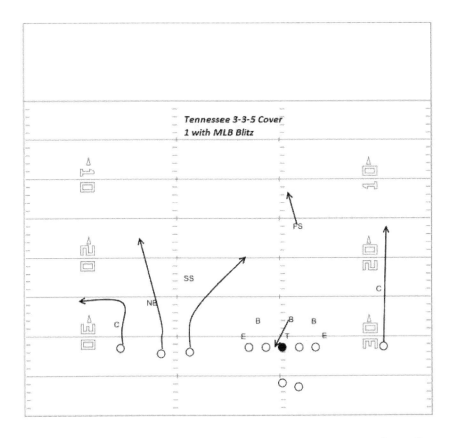

Tennessee 3-3-5 Cover 1 with MLB Blitz

The A gap blitz from the middle linebacker generates immediate pressure, flushing Mayfield to his left where he narrowly escapes the clutches of Barnett. Scrambling, the signal caller spots Miller with a step on the cornerback near the goalline, and heaves a throw toward the back of the end zone:

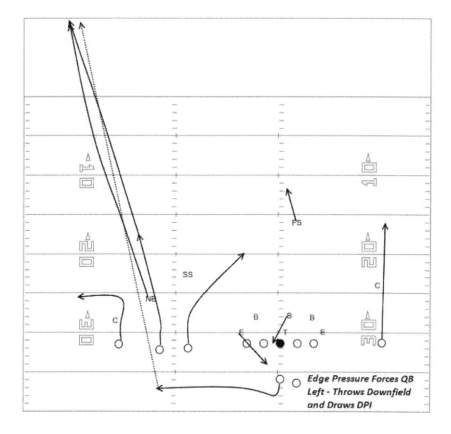

Edge Pressure Forces QB Left - Throws Downfield and Draws DPI

The pass sails out of bounds, well over the head of Miller. However, the receiver is prevented from making a play because the nickelback shoves him out of bounds, causing the referees to throw flags and call pass interference.

Thanks to the penalty, Oklahoma lines up for the next play on the 16-yard line. Here, the Sooners use two running backs and three wide receivers, putting Mayfield in the shotgun with Joe Mixon (#25) to his left and Perine on his right. They set up an inverted slot formation to the wide side of the field, with Shepard split wide to the right. The defense adjusts as well, returning to its 4-2-5 scheme and showing Cover 1 in the secondary, with safety Brian Randolph (#37) in the box, standing over the right tackle and shading Perine:

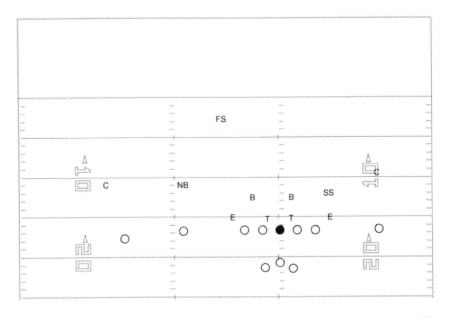

On the weak side of the formation, Shepard runs a slant route while Perine executes a wheel route up the right sideline. On the left the trips formation uses a spot concept: Mixon runs a flat route, Neal runs a corner pattern, and the wide man, Westbrook, comes underneath on the snag route:

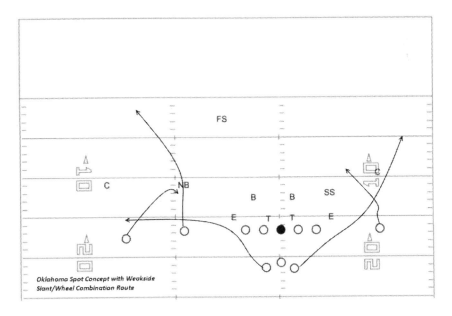

Oklahoma Spot Concept with Weakside
Slant/Wheel Combination Route

Mayfield drops to throw and Westbrook comes open underneath. The quarterback makes a quick and accurate throw and the receiver makes the catch, turns upfield, and avoids a tackle attempt from cornerback Cameron Sutton (#7):

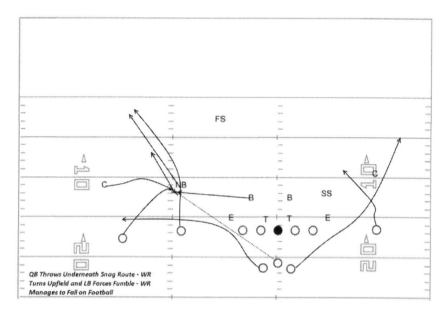

But Reeves-Martin makes a huge play: Working back to the football, the LB wraps up the receiver and punches the ball free. FUMBLE!

Luckily for Oklahoma, Westbrook is able to secure the football before Kelly pounces on the free ball. The Sooners maintain possession, while the Volunteers are forced to regroup after nearly ending the drive.

Needing only a single yard to extend their drive, the Sooners turn to the ground once more. They line up in Wildcat formation, with Mixon set to take the snap and Perine standing next to him. They split Mayfield wide toward the right sideline with Shepard to the inside, putting Westbrook and Green to the left side of the field in a slot alignment. The Volunteers stay with their 4-2-5 defense and show straight man coverage:

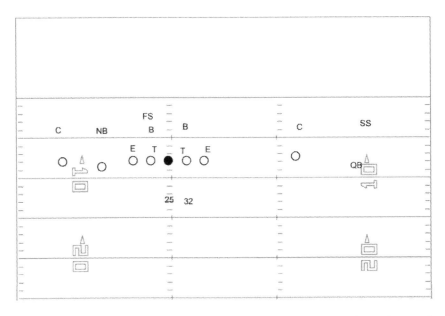

Mixon takes the snap and meets his fellow running back at the mesh point, with Perine aiming for the left edge. Mixon scans the defense and decides to keep the football, aiming for the interior:

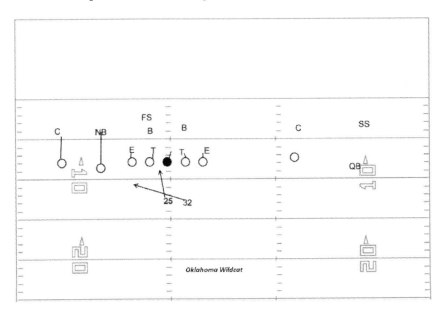

Oklahoma Wildcat

The ballcarrier is met immediately at the line of scrimmage by a trio of tacklers, and Mixon is held to no gain. The clock continues to run, approaching 2 minutes remaining.

Oklahoma wastes no time, hustling to the line for a critical third down play with the same personnel and formation. Mixon waits to take the shotgun snap in the Wildcat formation with Perine standing to his right. The Volunteers stay with their defense, showing Cover 1 in the secondary:

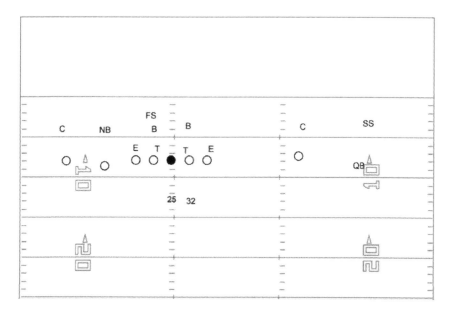

This time, Mixon hands the ball off to Perine, who is aiming for the left edge:

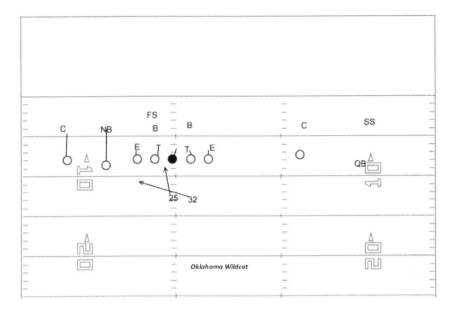

Oklahoma Wildcat

The running back secures the outside edge and cuts upfield inside the block from his slot receiver, Westbrook. Perine is able to get to the outside because Barnett reads the play and slides down inside, anticipating Mixon will keep the football. Perine plunges forward for a 5-yard gain. Tennessee coach Butch Jones is irate on the sidelines. Not at his defense, but at the officials. Replays show a false start before the snap, but the right guard was not flagged and the play stands.

For the third consecutive play, the Sooners line up in the Wildcat with Mixon ready to take the snap, while the defense stays in the same alignment, a Cover 1 look with 4-2-5 personnel:

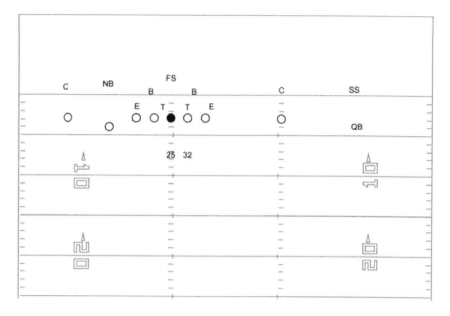

Mixon takes the snap and the offensive line again leaves Barnett unblocked so that Mixon can read the DE before making his decision:

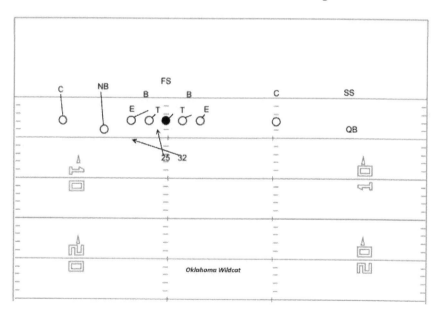

Oklahoma Wildcat

The defenders slide to the inside, expecting Mixon to keep the football, so the running back hands the ball to Perine, who is aiming for the left side, behind the block of Westbrook in the slot. The cornerback Foreman tries to twist around the blocking wide receiver to prevent Perine from turning the corner, but is stymied by Westbrook. Perine skips inside the pylon for the apparent game-tying score:

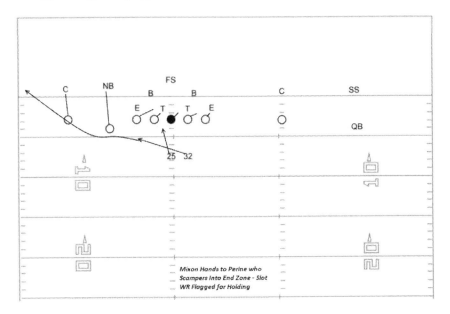

Mixon Hands to Perine who
Scampers Into End Zone - Slot
WR Flagged for Holding

Cue the flag.

Replays show Westbrook holding onto Foreman's jersey while twisting him to the ground. The holding penalty backs the Sooners up to the 12-yard line to repeat first down.

After the penalty, the Sooners line up with a more traditional offensive formation. Mayfield stands in the pistol formation with Perine behind him, and the offense has two running backs, two wide receivers and a tight end in the game. Running back Dimitri Flowers (#36) checks in, setting up in a wing alignment left, with both Westbrook and Neal outside of him. Shepard stands alone split wide to the right. The Volunteers stay with their 4-2-5 personnel, and bring safety Kelly down into the box. Mayfield makes an adjustment before the snap, moving Flowers to the right. When the ball is snapped Kelly has dropped back and Randolph is starting to move forward:

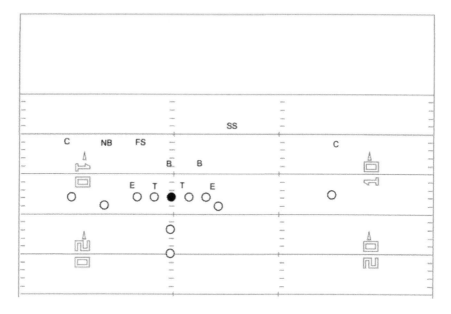

The offense uses a split zone design, with the offensive line flowing to the right and, again, leaving Barnett unblocked. Flowers is responsible for delivering a crack back block to the uncovered defensive end:

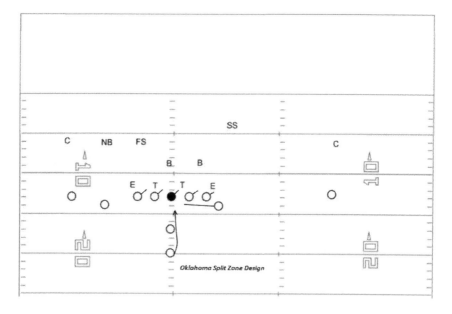

Oklahoma Split Zone Design

However, Williams explodes off the snap inside, using a quick rip move to get upfield past left guard Jonathan Alvarez (#68). Flowers quickly decides to take a detour in response to the interior pressure, helping contain the penetrating defender:

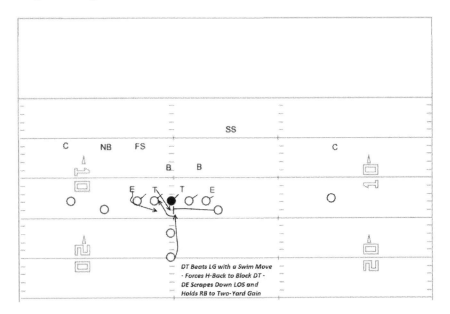

This leaves Perine one-on-one with Barnett, who is scraping down the line of scrimmage. The ball carrier tries to avoid him, but the defensive end goes low and secures Perine's ankles. The running back falls forward for just a 2-yard gain.

With the clock ticking away and less than a minute remaining, the Sooners adjust their personnel and bring in Mixon and Baxter, and line up for the next play with Mayfield in the shotgun. They split Perine out in a 3x2 alignment, with trips right and a slot formation to the left. The defense stays with its 4-2-5, but in response to the empty backfield both linebackers slide outside the tackle box:

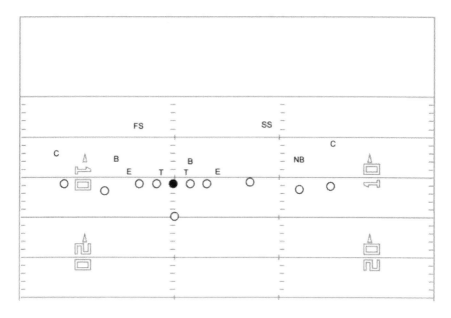

With the interior of the defense cleared out, the Sooners have the perfect play called – a QB draw:

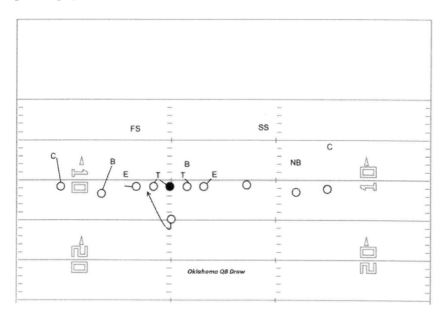

Mayfield takes the snap and uses a one-step drop in order to sell a pass play. Tennessee sends only four rushers, dropping seven defenders into coverage, including both linebackers from the edges. The QB tucks the football away and heads for the left B gap, where a hole has been created:

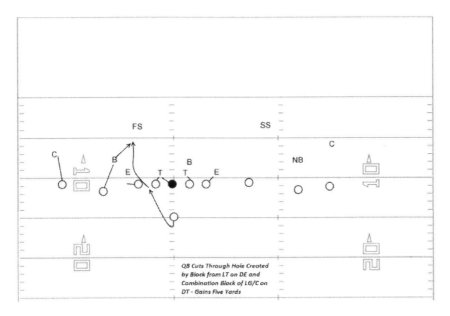

QB Cuts Through Hole Created
by Block from LT on DE and
Combination Block of LG/C on
DT - Gains Five Yards

Mayfield cuts through the line and stays inside of a block from Baxter in the slot. The QB lunges forward for a quick 5-yard gain, down to the Tennessee 5. The Sooners take their first timeout, with 45 seconds remaining in the game, to prepare for their play call on 3rd-and-goal.

Following the timeout, Mayfield is in the shotgun with a pair of running backs and three wide receivers against Tennessee's 4-2-5 defense, which is showing Cover 1. The offense puts two receivers in a slot formation on the left, and splits Shepard out wide right. The cornerback over Shepard lines up with inside leverage over the receiver, trying to take away any slant route. If the receiver wants to cut inside, he'll need to fight through Moseley to get to any pass thrown his way:

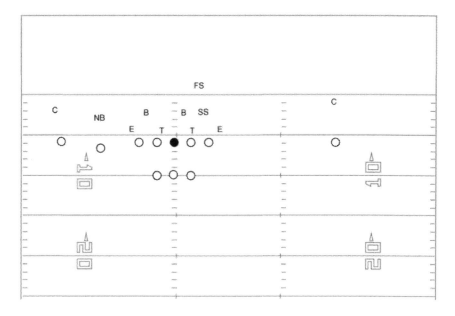

But if Shepard runs a route to the outside or a fade route, Moseley has the benefit of the sideline and end line as extra "help" defenders. Plus, with the football on the left hashmark any pass has to cover a bit of distance as well:

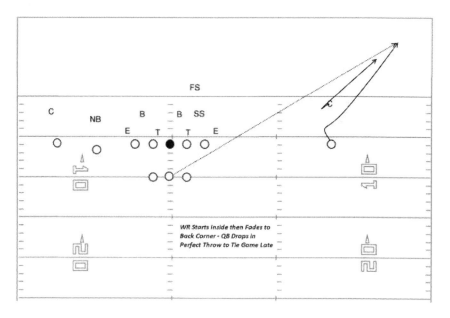

Moseley opens his hips toward the sideline at the snap, cementing his inside leverage – and giving Shepard the outside. The receiver runs the fade route, toward the back corner, and Mayfield drops the throw in perfectly. Moseley's pre-snap alignment and initial movements force the quarterback and wide receiver to execute this play to perfection – and they do.

The teams went to overtime where the Volunteers scored a touchdown on their first possession. But the Sooners scored the next two touchdowns, and left Knoxville with a 31-24 double-overtime victory that wouldn't have been possible without this 13-play, 60-yard drive to tie the game in the dying moments of regulation.

CHAPTER THREE

CLEMSON'S TRICKERY GIVES THE TIGERS A CUSHION

During Week 3 of the 2015 college football season, Clemson traveled to Louisville to take on the Cardinals in a nationally televised Thursday night game. More than 55,000 were in attendance, including the Greatest of All Time, Muhammad Ali. With the game tied 10-10 late in the third quarter, the Tigers forced a Cardinals punt, and took over possession on their own 38-yard line.

On the first play of this drive, the Tigers line up with three wide receivers, a tight end and a running back in a 2x2 alignment. Wide receiver Artavis Scott (#3) is in a slot to quarterback Deshaun Watson's (#4) left, while running back Wayne Gallman (#9) stands alongside the signal caller. The defense has its 3-4 personnel on the field, showing Cover 4:

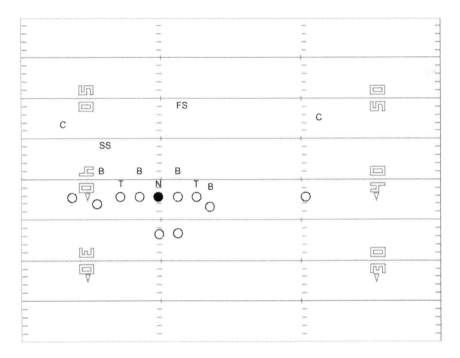

Prior to the snap, Scott comes in jet motion toward the quarterback. At the snap, he cuts in front of Watson, who shovel passes the ball to the receiver on the jet sweep. Gallman leads Scott to the right edge:

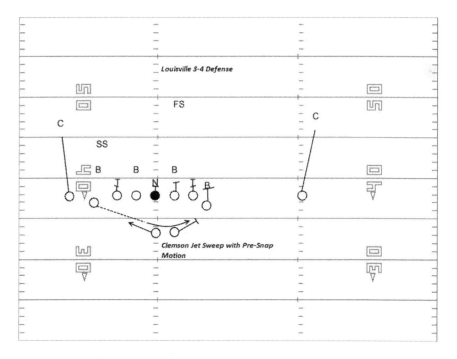

Strongside linebacker Keith Brown (#1) leads a trio of defenders toward the ball-carrier, but Gallman executes a perfect cut block in space, chopping the linebacker down to the turf. This crucial block gives Scott the edge:

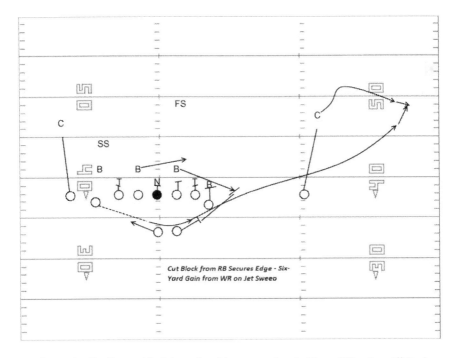

Cut Block from RB Secures Edge - Six-Yard Gain from WR on Jet Sweep

Scott is finally tackled by playside cornerback Shaq Wiggins (#6), but not until a 6-yard gain out to the Clemson 44-yard line.

On second down, the Tigers keep their same 11 personnel group on the field and again use a 2x2 alignment, with an inverted slot formation left and slot formation right, with tight end Jordan Leggett (#16) on the inside. Watson sets up in the pistol formation with Gallman behind him. Louisville stays with its 3-4 defense, and puts outside linebacker Trevon Young (#91) over the right tackle in a three-point stance. The Cardinals also slide Brown to the outside, over the slot receiver on the left, and show Cover 4 in the secondary:

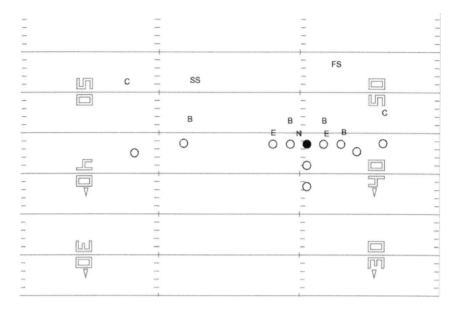

Prior to the snap, Leggett shifts into the backfield where he sets, standing to the left of the quarterback. Clemson uses a split zone running play – the five linemen flowing in unison to the left while Leggett takes a step to his left before crossing the formation to block the backside defender:

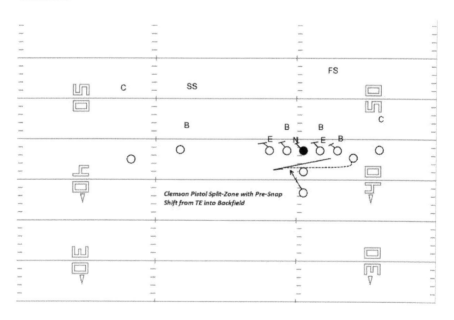

Clemson Pistol Split-Zone with Pre-Snap Shift from TE into Backfield

But defensive end Drew Bailey (#14) has other ideas, splitting the right tackle and right guard and slicing into the backfield just as Gallman accepts the handoff. Leggett tries to get a block on the defender, but the penetration forces the back to make a quick cut in the backfield, slowing the development of the play:

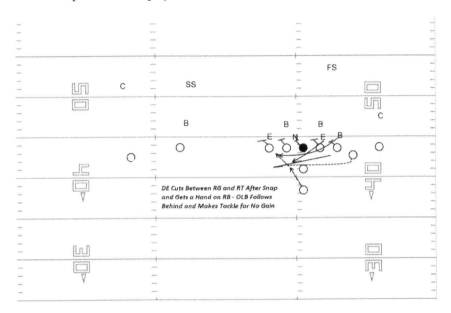

From there, Young finishes the job. Right tackle Joe Gore (#73) tries his best to contain the linebacker, but Young scrapes down the line of scrimmage and tracks down Gallman in the backfield. The Tigers running back manages to fight back to the line of scrimmage for no gain, setting up a critical 3rd and 4.

Watson stands in the shotgun on 3rd down, once again with three receivers, a tight end and Gallman as his running back as Clemson uses a 2x2 alignment with dual slot formations. Meanwhile, the Cardinals keep their base 3-4 in the game, but show a Cover 3 look and a potential blitz before the snap, putting seven defenders on the line of scrimmage:

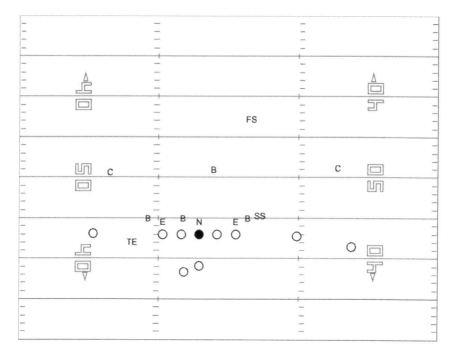

Safety Chucky Williams (#22) lines up outside the right tackle, while linebacker Keith Kelsey (#55) aligns several yards off the line of scrimmage, almost in Robber technique to disrupt a crossing or slant route.

The Tigers run a quick sail (or Indy 5) concept on the left with the outside receiver Trevion Thompson (#1) releasing vertically while Leggett runs a quick out route:

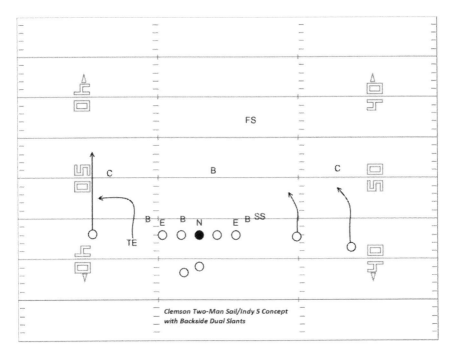

Clemson Two-Man Sail/Indy 5 Concept with Backside Dual Slants

The play is perfectly called against this defensive scheme and alignment. The linebacker responsible for the flat zone in this coverage – inside linebacker James Burgess (#13) – begins the play on the line, threatening to blitz. He has to try to rotate outside to pick up the tight end's out route – not an easy assignment. The vertical release from Thompson holds the playside corner, Jaire Alexander (#10), deep for just long enough to open space for Leggett:

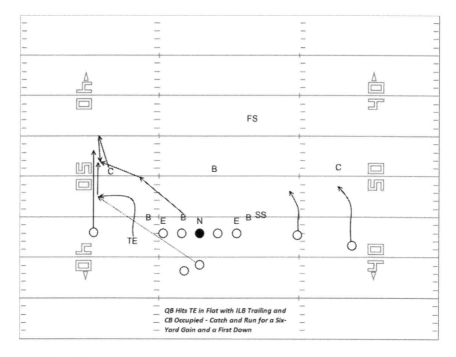

QB Hits TE in Flat with ILB Trailing and
CB Occupied - Catch and Run for a Six-
Yard Gain and a First Down

Alexander reads the play and breaks forward but cannot prevent the completion. Leggett secures the throw from Watson and spins into Louisville territory, picking up 9 yards and a fresh set of downs for Clemson.

The Tigers line up for this first-down play on the Cardinals' 47 with the same personnel on the field, now using a bunch alignment on the left and a single receiver split wide right. Louisville stays with its base 3-4, and shows Cover 3 with Williams near the box. The Cardinals also walk Burgess over toward the bunch alignment:

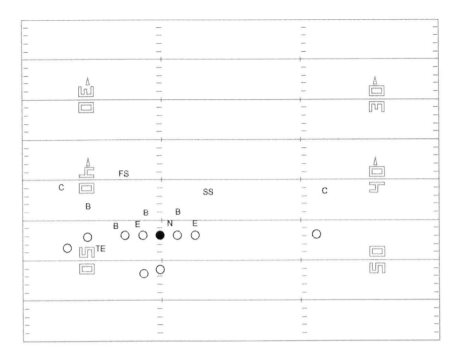

Clemson runs a quick screen to Scott, the outside receiver of the bunch, with both Leggett and WR Germone Hopper (#5) blocking:

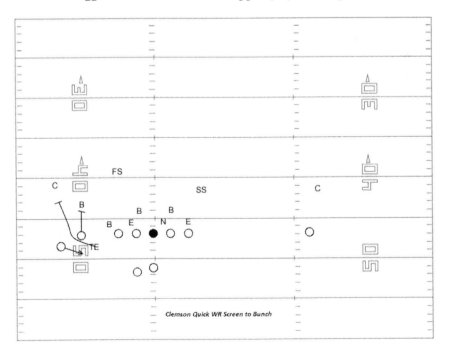

Clemson Quick WR Screen to Bunch

Hopper attempts to get a block on the linebacker, but Burgess shoves him backward 2 yards as the two players meet. Thankfully for the offense, Scott cuts to the inside, around this collision:

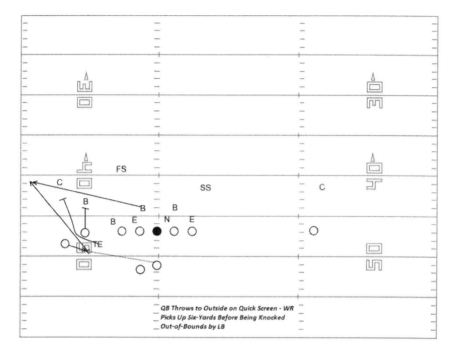

Leggett helps Hopper on the linebacker for a moment before cutting upfield to block the corner, Alexander. Scott follows behind and picks up 5 yards, before he is dragged down from behind by Kelsey.

On this second-down play the Tigers give Leggett a rest, and bring in reserve TE Stanton Seckinger (#81). They line up with Watson in the pistol formation and RB Zac Brooks (#24) behind him, while the tight end sets as an upback behind the right tackle. The Tigers have two receivers in an inverted slot to the right, and a single receiver split left.

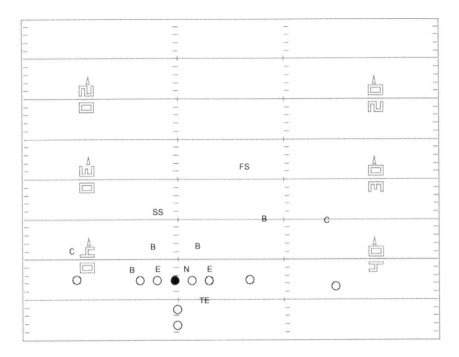

Louisville stays with its 3-4, putting a linebacker on the line of scrimmage over the left tackle, and moving Brown outside over the slot receiver.

The Tigers show the same split zone run design used previously on this drive, with the line flowing right at the snap while Seckinger blocks toward the left edge. However, Watson takes the ball and turns to his left, faking an inside zone running play to Brown, and then quickly throws to the tight end cutting away from the flow of the play:

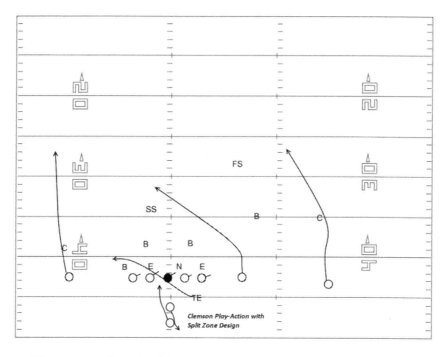

Clemson Play-Action with Split Zone Design

Thompson, the playside receiver, runs a vertical route to occupy Alexander. This frees up the outside for the tight end's flat route:

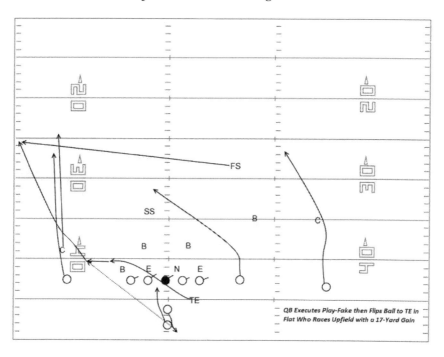

QB Executes Play-Fake then Flips Ball to TE in Flat Who Races Upfield with a 17-Yard Gain

The reserve tight end races up the sideline before he is knocked out of bounds at the Cardinals' 25-yard line, after a 17-yard gain.

On the next play the Tigers try to finish the drive using a bit of deception. They break the huddle with 22 personnel: two running backs, two tight ends and just one wide receiver. Initially, they line up with Watson in the shotgun and a very tight formation. Seckinger is in the backfield while Gallman is lined up as a tight end on the left, with reserve receiver Ray-Ray McCloud (#34) set up as a flanker outside:

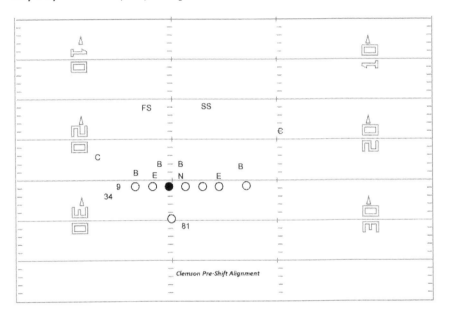

Clemson Pre-Shift Alignment

The Cardinals have their base 3-4 defense in the game showing Cover 4 in the secondary.

Prior to the snap, the Tigers shift to an empty backfield. They slide running back Thompson and tight end Seckinger out to the right, forming a trips look with offensive tackle Mitch Hyatt (#75), who stands on the line of scrimmage out wide. On the left side of the formation, McCloud and Gallman both slide to the outside, with McCloud standing on the line of scrimmage. This leaves five players in the interior to block, and seven total players on the line – which is the legal minimum.

However, the player on the left edge of the offensive line is an eligible receiver – tight end Leggett. His alignment is crucial – and deceptive. Splitting Hyatt, the actual tackle, out wide without declaring him eligible, and lining up Leggett in his place is designed to confuse the defense:

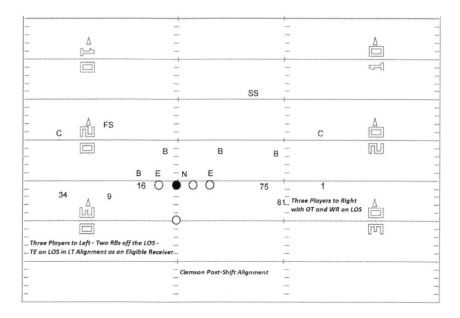

Clemson Post-Shift Alignment

The Cardinals scramble to re-align their defense in response to the shift, while still dropping the secondary into Cover 4 at the snap. As the play develops the five eligible receivers run vertical routes, while Hyatt backpedals into the backfield because he is not eligible:

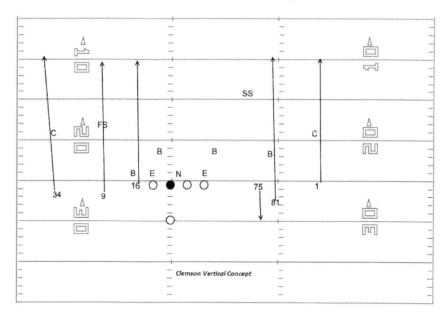

Clemson Vertical Concept

Four of the receivers are covered. One is not. As you might have guessed, it is Leggett:

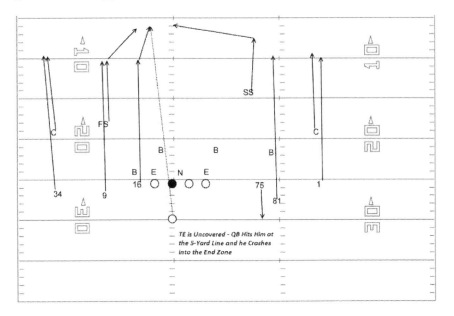

Watson drops in a touch pass that the tight end hauls in at the 2-yard line. Leggett spins into the end zone as both Alexander and Williams arrive a step too late to prevent the score.

The touchdown gave the Tigers a 17-10 lead with just over a quarter to play, and a late interception sealed the victory. The win kept Clemson undefeated and gave the Tigers an early road victory in a tough environment, building their confidence as they began their Atlantic Coast Conference schedule.

CHAPTER FOUR

PAXTON LYNCH LEADS A GAME-WINNER

Kicking off Week 4 of the 2015 college football season on Thursday night, the Memphis Tigers and quarterback Paxton Lynch hosted the Cincinnati Bearcats. Cincinnati starting quarterback Gunner Kiel was knocked out of the game early because of a concussion, bringing backup Hayden Moore off the bench. The reliever came in and threw four touchdowns, the last coming with just under 6 minutes remaining to tie the game at 46. After the teams traded possessions, the Tigers took over at their own 20 with less than 3 minutes remaining.

Memphis begins the drive with Lynch in the shotgun and 11 personnel (three wide receivers, one tight end, one running back) on the field. The Tigers deploy a slot formation on the right, with wide receivers Roderick Proctor (#18) inside and Anthony Miller (#3) outside. To the left, tight end Alan Cross (#40) and receiver Phil Mayhue (#89) line up in a stack-slot formation, with the tight end on the line of scrimmage and Mayhue stacked just behind him. Running back Sam Craft (#11) stands to the right of the quarterback.

The Bearcats have their base 4-3 defense in for this play. They take outside linebacker/defensive back Leviticus Payne (#9) and walk him outside over Cross, showing Cover 2 man underneath:

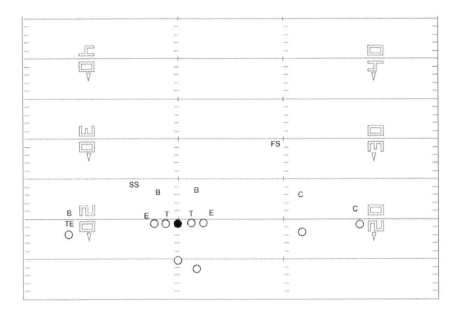

Before the play, Lynch sends the running back in motion out to the left, behind the stack-slot alignment. The Bearcats respond by shifting the two linebackers to the outside: Eric Wilson (#23) rolls outside, over the stack-slot, while Bryce Jenkinson (#45) trails Craft's motion:

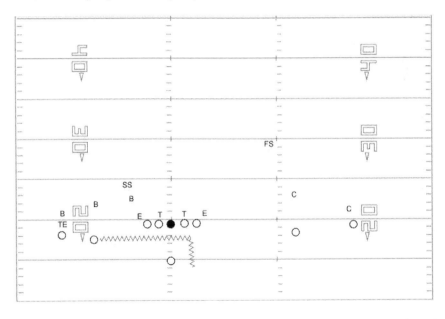

The Tigers show a screen to the trips side of the field, with Craft and

Cross set up to block for Mayhue. On the backside, Proctor and Miller run matching slant routes.

Lynch throws the inside slant route to the slot receiver, and Proctor secures the football at the 25-yard line:

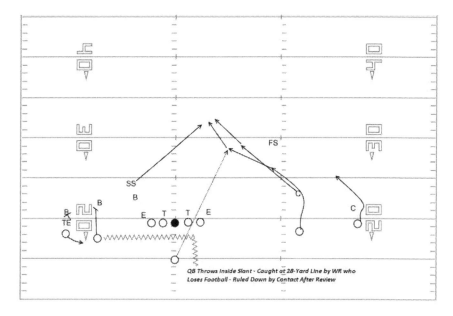

QB Throws Inside Slant - Caught at 28-Yard Line by WR who Loses Football - Ruled Down by Contact After Review

As the receiver gains additional yardage, safety Mike Tyson (#5) chases him down from behind, tackling the WR, with the help of safety Zach Edwards (#4). However, as he goes to ground, the ball comes out and Tyson recovers.

Go get another beer, fans, because it is time for an official replay. Some minutes later, the officials emerge to announce the decision: Upon further review, it is determined that Proctor's knee was down *just* before the ball pops free. Memphis retains possession.

Breathing a sigh of relief, the Tigers line up for 1st and 10 at their own 33-yard line with the same personnel and Lynch in the shotgun. They use the same formation and motion as the previous play, with Craft moving to the outside where Cross and Mayhue are in a stack slot. The Bearcats have adjusted their personnel, deploying a 4-2-5 nickel, and again showing Cover 2 in the secondary. A Bearcat defender slides to the outside, over the stack-slot:

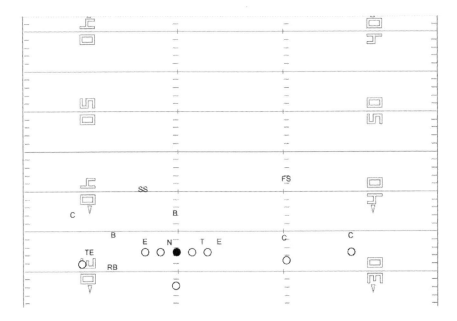

Memphis wants to attack vertically, setting up the screen look to the three-receiver side to Mayhue, but sending the tight end on a crossing route and the running back continuing on a wheel route down the sideline. On the opposite side, Proctor runs a quick out while Miller releases on a go route:

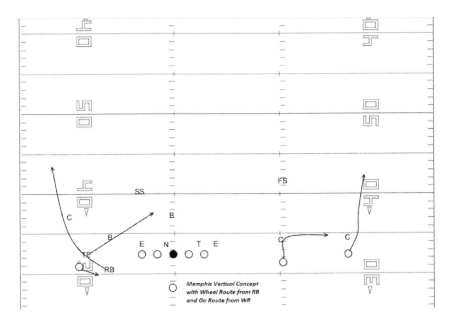

Memphis Vertical Concept with Wheel Route from RB and Go Route from WR

Cornerback Linden Stephens (#32) is in press alignment over Miller, and at the snap the receiver uses a quick hesitation move before releasing to the outside. He gets separation on Stephens and Lynch takes his shot:

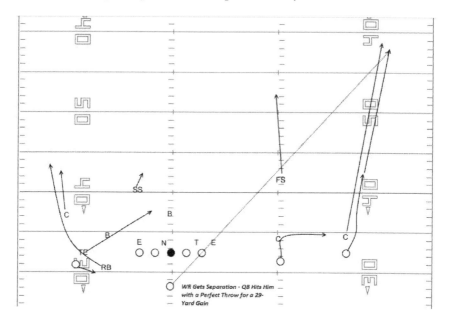

WR Gets Separation - QB Hits Him with a Perfect Throw for a 29-Yard Gain

The quarterback drops in a perfect throw to Miller along the sideline, with the receiver hauling in the football at the Cincinnati 40-yard line and sliding out of bounds at the 38. The long pitch-and-catch puts the offense on the cusp of field goal range for kicker Jake Elliott, but with more than two minutes remaining, Memphis can start to think about milking the clock a little bit.

Once again the Tigers line up with the same personnel and Lynch in the shotgun, this time alone in the backfield. Memphis sends out a trips look to the left this time, with Miller on the outside, Cross in the middle, and Proctor as the inside receiver. To the other side of the field, Craft stands in the slot while Mayhue aligns outside. The Bearcats stay with their 4-2-5 personnel, this time showing pressure with both linebackers on the edge in blitz posture:

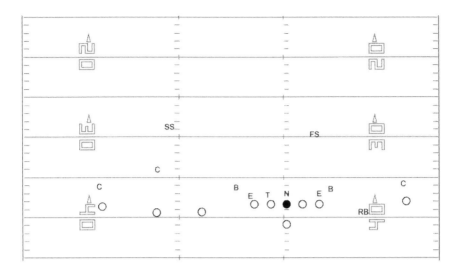

Memphis uses all curl routes for this play:

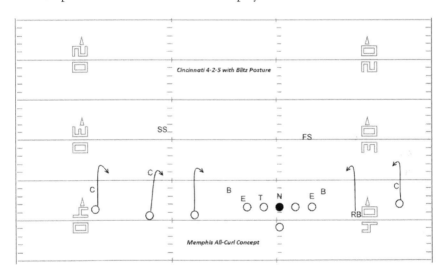

With the football on the right hash mark, Lynch reads this play to the short side of the field, finding Mayhue along the right sideline:

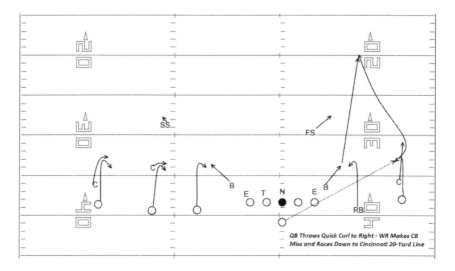

QB Throws Quick Curl to Right - WR Makes CB Miss and Races Down to Cincinnati 20-Yard Line

The receiver is matched up against Grant Coleman (#13), and when Mayhue stops to turn back on the curl cut, he gains separation from the cornerback. Lynch delivers a strong, accurate throw and when Coleman scrambles back to make the tackle, the receiver avoids him and race up the sideline. Mayhue is finally chased down from behind by a host of tacklers, but not until after his 18-yard gain earns Memphis another first down, this time at the Cincinnati 20-yard line.

The Tigers are now in a very good position, with the football and in no hurry, despite the clock ticking. They line up for the next play with Lynch in the shotgun, this time with one running back, two tight ends and two receivers in the game. Reserve tight end Daniel Montiel (#80) lines up on the right with Cross just behind him in a wing alignment, while Miller and Mayhue set up a slot formation to the left. Craft stands just to the right of the quarterback. The Bearcats go with their base 4-3, and bring Tyson over into the slot while showing Cover 3:

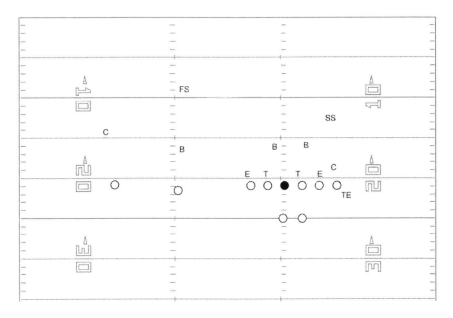

Memphis uses a power scheme, with Craft taking the handoff and aiming for the left edge. Cross leads for the RB, as does right guard Micah Simmons (#70), who pulls on the play:

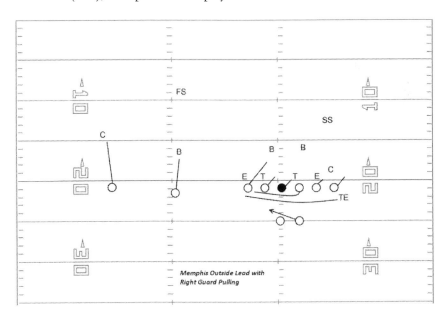

Memphis Outside Lead with
Right Guard Pulling

Simmons and Cross are able to set the edge – with an assist from Miller, who blocks to the inside from his slot alignment:

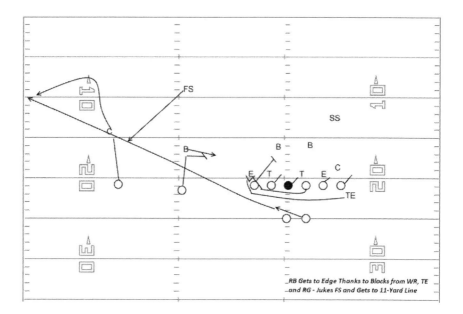

_RB Gets to Edge Thanks to Blocks from WR, TE
_and RG - Jukes FS and Gets to 11-Yard Line

The running back gets outside and picks up 9 yards, but is driven out of bounds, stopping the clock with less than 1:30 remaining. This causes head coach Justin Fuente to implore his offense to stay in bounds on the next play.

Facing 2nd and 1 at the Cincinnati 11-yard line, the Tigers align the same way, only putting the slot formation on the right side this time, with the two tight end wing set left. The Bearcats stay with their base defense, showing Cover 1 before the play:

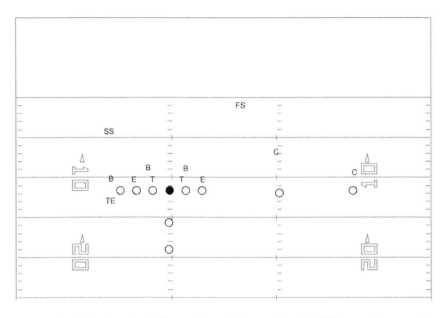

Lynch is in the pistol formation with Craft behind him, and Memphis runs an inside zone running play:

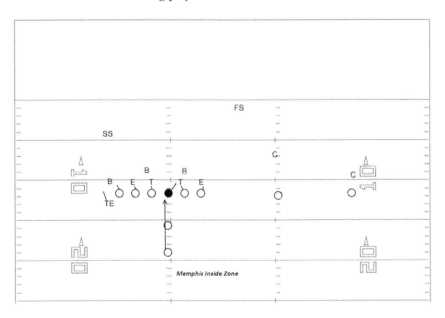

Memphis Inside Zone

The quarterback takes the snap and turns left, giving the football to Craft who aims for the back of the center. As he nears the line of scrimmage he makes a sharp cut to his right, slicing into the B gap:

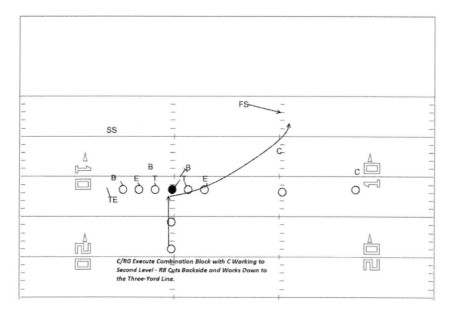

The running back finds enough of a crease that he barrels down to the Cincinnati 3, giving the offense a 1st and goal with a little more than a minute to play.

Memphis wastes no time, lining up with Lynch, Cross, Miller and Craft in the backfield:

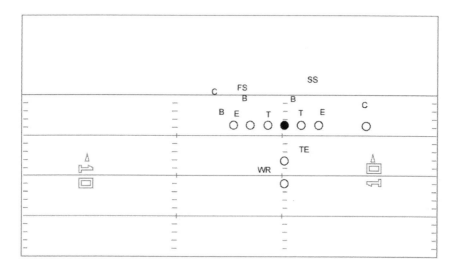

The Tigers run Craft to the left here, with the tight end leading the way:

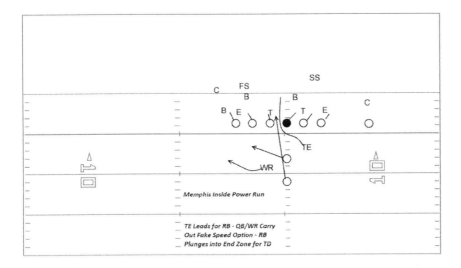

Memphis Inside Power Run

TE Leads for RB - QB/WR Carry
Out Fake Speed Option - RB
Plunges into End Zone for TD

The running back crashes into the end zone easily with the eventual game-winning score.

Cincinnati took possession after the kickoff but its last-ditch effort ended with an interception. The victory moved Memphis to 4-0 on the season, keeping the Tigers very much in the hunt for the American Athletic Conference West title.

From a player evaluation perspective, this performance opened the eyes of scouts and evaluators, who began to take serious stock of Lynch. As the season wore on, his continued high level of execution had him rocketing up draft boards. This night, and game-winning drive, were a crucial first step to becoming a top NFL draft prospect.

CHAPTER FIVE

BAYLOR STRIKES QUICKLY TO REGAIN THE LEAD

Week 5 of the 2015 college football season featured a key Big 12 conference matchup between then-fifth ranked Baylor and Texas Tech. The Red Raiders were coming off a three-point loss to TCU in the waning seconds of the game, but had proved they could score points on anyone by putting up 52 on the Horned Frogs. And when they scored a quick touchdown to tie the game at 7-7 early in the first quarter, the crowd at AT&T STadium in Dallas thought the Bears might be in for a long day.

But the following possession demonstrated just how capable Baylor's offense was and how quickly they could score.

Following a touchback on the kickoff, Baylor sets up on its 25-yard line with three wide receivers, one tight end and one running back on the field, using a stack slot alignment on the left and a single receiver split wide right. Quarterback Seth Russell (#17) stands in the shotgun with running back Shock Linwood (#32) to his left. Massive tight end LaQuan McGowan (#80) aligns as an upback, in B gap between the right guard and tackle:

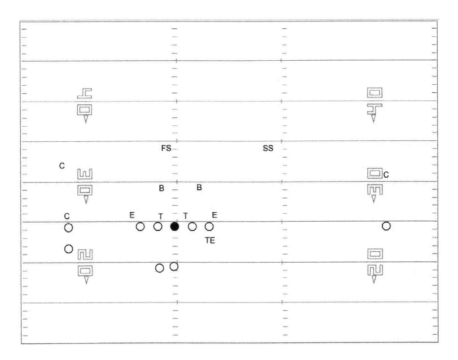

Texas Tech has its 4-2-5 package on the field, and put a press cornerback to the outside over the stack slot formation.

Baylor runs a packaged play on this snap. The run action is a power play to the right side, with left guard Blake Muir (#73) pulling into the B gap while McGowan executes an out block on the defensive end. If Russell keeps the football, then the offense could set up a quick bubble screen to the stack slot, with KD Cannon (#9) setting up to block for Corey Coleman (#1):

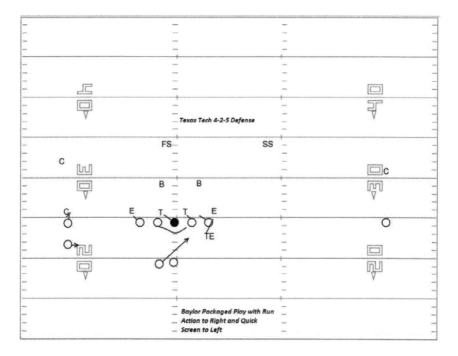

Russell instead hands the football off, as Muir turns the corner on his pulling action. Linebacker Micah Awe (#18) recognizes the run and crashes forward, but Muir folds him to the turf. McGowan is able to get the defensive end turned to the outside, opening up a big hole for Linwood:

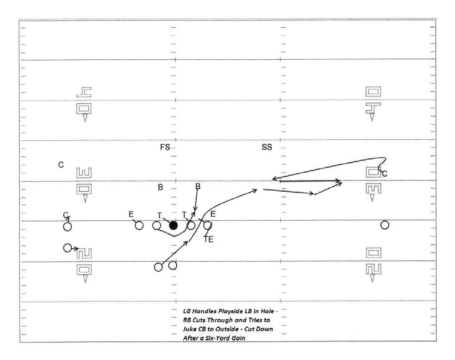

LG Handles Playside LB in Hole -
RB Cuts Through and Tries to
Juke CB to Outside - Cut Down
After a Six-Yard Gain

The RB cuts through the hole and then angles toward the sideline, where he is finally cut down by cornerback Thierry Nguema (#17) after a gain of 6 yards.

Using their quick tempo, the Bears quickly line up for the next play. They again use the same personnel group, this time using an unbalanced look by putting McGowan at left tackle and moving left tackle Spencer Drango (#58) to the right side into a tight end's alignment. Russell stands in the pistol formation with Coleman behind him, with running back Johnny Jefferson (#5) standing to the QB's right:

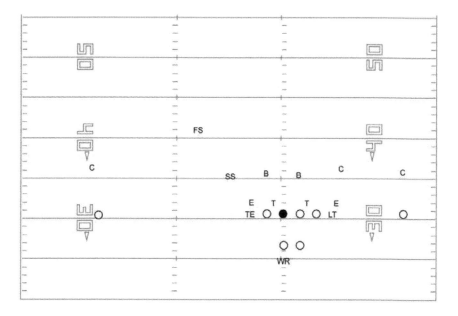

Texas Tech stays with its 4-2-5 personnel, but put both the slot cornerback and a safety down into the box. The Bears try to run Coleman to the right side on an outside zone, but the defensive line has other ideas:

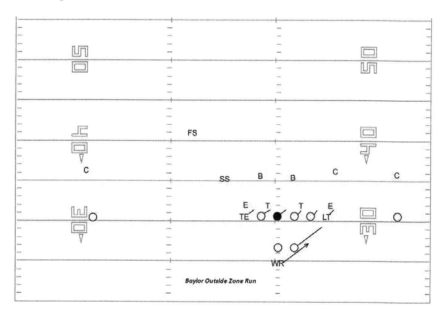

Defensive tackle Keland McElrath (#90) gets immediate pressure off the snap, splitting the gap between right tackle Pat Colbert (#69) and right guard Jarell Broxton (#61). His burst upfield forces Coleman to try and cut back. However, flowing to the ball is defensive tackle Demetrius Alston (#43):

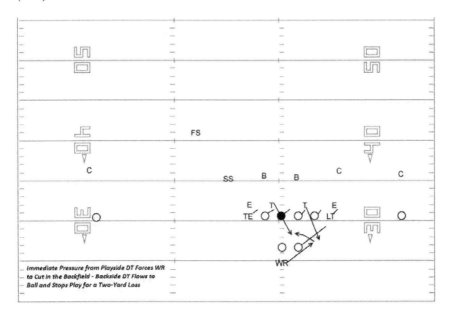

Immediate Pressure from Playside DT Forces WR to Cut in the Backfield - Backside DT Flows to Ball and Stops Play for a Two-Yard Loss

Alston wraps up the shifty wideout for a loss of 2 yards.

Now facing 3rd and 6, Baylor empties the backfield with one back and four receivers, deployed in a 3x2 alignment with trips to the left and slot formation to the right. The Red Raiders stay with their nickel defense, and show straight man coverage across the board:

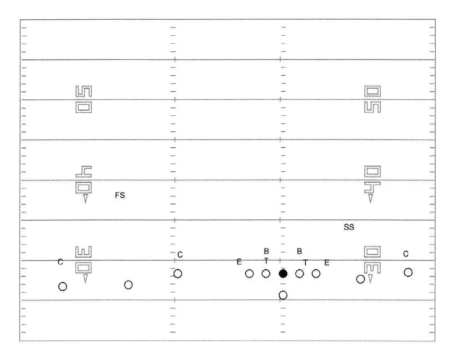

The Bears run a three vertical concept:

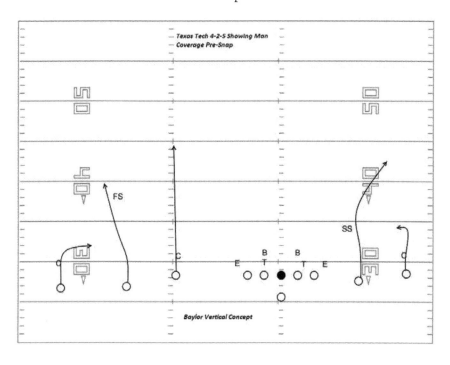

To the slot side, the outside receiver runs a quick hitch while the inside receiver runs a vertical route, bending toward the sideline. To the trips side, the outside WR also runs a quick in, while the other two receivers run vertical routes. Lynx Hawthorne (#7), the middle trips receiver, bends his route to the sideline while Coleman aims to go straight up the field.

Coleman is matched up against slot cornerback J.J. Gaines (#3), and the defensive back is in press alignment. At the snap the receiver uses a quick stutter-step, and when Gaines tries to get his hands on him, Coleman uses a swim move and gets free to the outside. Russell spots the WR gaining separation, and uncorks a throw:

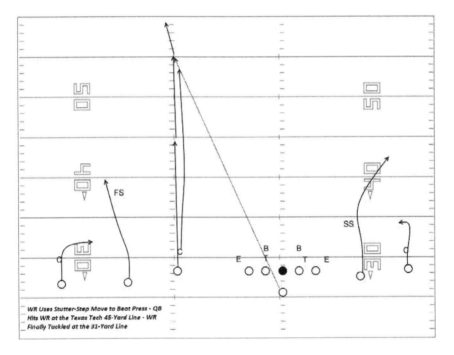

WR Uses Stutter-Step Move to Beat Press - QB Hits WR at the Texas Tech 45-Yard Line - WR Finally Tuckled at the 31-Yard Line

Coleman pulls in the pass at the 45-yard line, and when Gaines finally chases him down from behind, the 40 yard pitch-and-catch sets the Bears up just outside the red zone.

Wasting no time, Baylor heads right to the line of scrimmage and again Russell stands alone in the backfield with a 3x2 alignment, this time with trips formation to the right. Without time to substitute, the Red Raiders stay with their 4-2-5 package and show Cover 3 in the secondary:

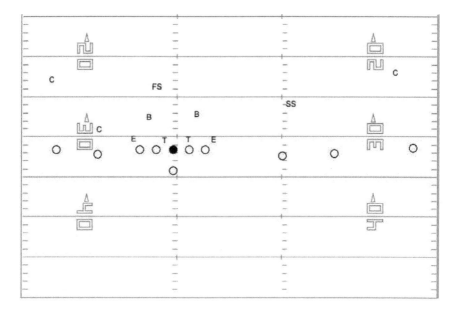

The offense looks to attack vertically again. On the left side of the formation, they utilize a switch vertical concept form the slot. On the trips side both the inside and outside receivers release vertically, running slow routes - basically taking the play off. The intended target is Cannon, the middle trips receiver, who dashes to the goal line:

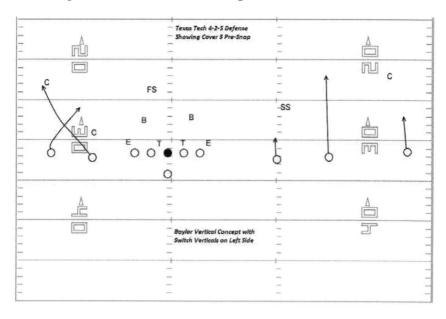

This play is designed to exploit a Cover 3 scheme: the two vertical routes from the inside and outside trips receivers are decoys. By running slow routes, these players are working to hold the free safety and the playside cornerback in place while Cannon tries to split them:

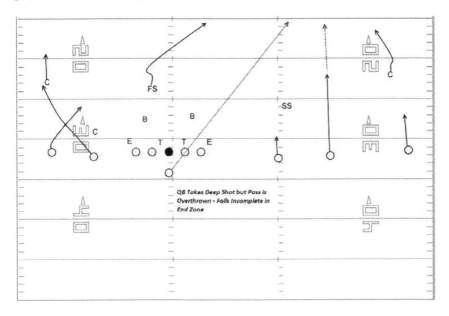

Cannon, and the play design, succeeds and the wideout is open near the 10-yard line when Russell releases the football. Unfortunately for the Bears, the throw just leads the WR too much. As Nguema and safety Keenon Ward (#15) scramble to catch Cannon, the pass falls just past his outstretched fingertips, falling into the end zone for an incompletion.

On second down, the Bears adjust personnel, returning to the package they began the drive with: one back, one tight end, three receivers. Russell sets in the shotgun with Jefferson to his right, and the right end McGowan aligned behind the right guard. They also deploy a slot formation to the right and have a single receiver split left. The Red Raiders stay with their nickel defense, and show Cover 2:

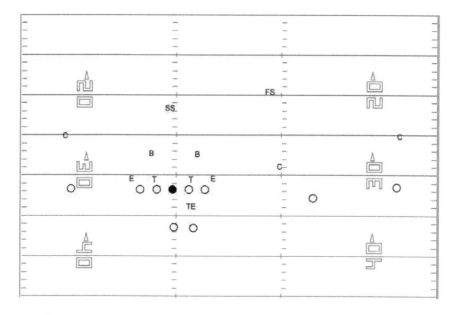

The Bears again use a packaged play look, showing a bubble screen to the right. But this play is a designed power run from the start, with all three receivers going through the motions on this snap. The massive tight end leads Jefferson to the left:

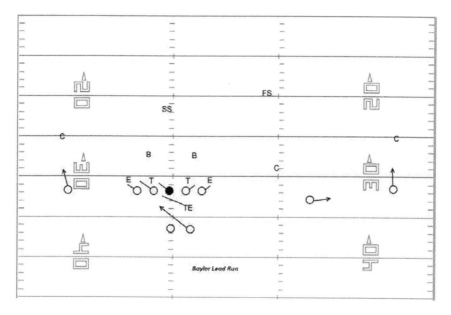

Jefferson takes the handoff and follows the blockers to the left, plunging forward for a short 3-yard gain:

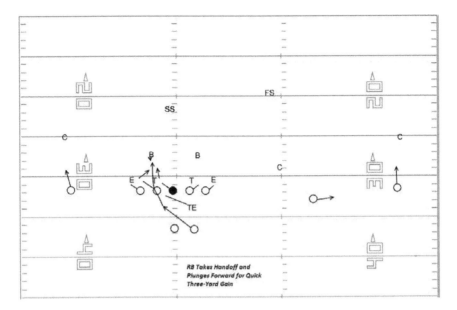

RB Takes Handoff and
Plunges Forward for Quick
Three-Yard Gain

Facing a critical third down early in the game, the Bears stay with the same personnel and put their QB in the shotgun. McGowan and Jefferson again align in their weak side i-formation, to the left of Russell, with slot formation on the right, and a single receiver wide left. The Red Raiders show Cover 1 before the play, with all three cornerbacks in press alignment. Both safeties shade the left side of the offense, with Ward down in a robber alignment and fellow safety Jah'Shawn Johnson (#7) deeper:

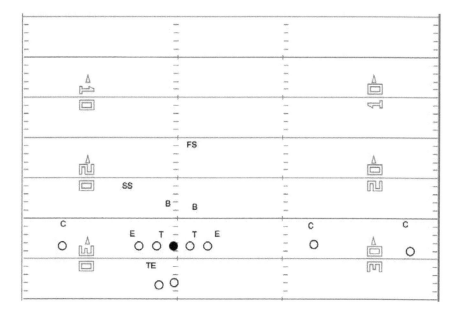

Jefferson and Russell meet at the mesh point and show the potential for a run or pass, but this is play action for a designed pass, with all three receivers releasing vertically:

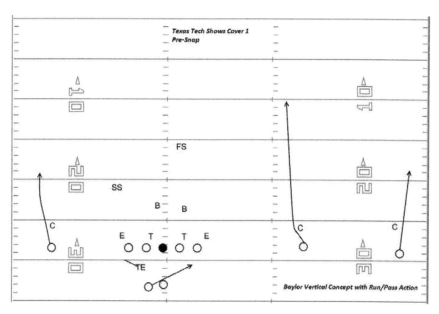

Cannon is the intended receiver once again on a seam route, and this time, he and Russell connect:

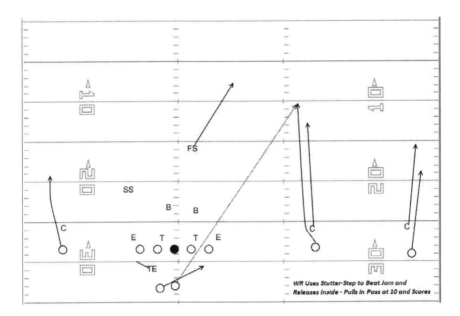

WR Uses Stutter-Step to Beat Jam and Releases Inside - Pulls in Pass at 10 and Scores

The receiver gets a step on Gaines, the slot cornerback, using a stutter-step at the line of scrimmage and then releasing to the inside. Russell makes a quick decision and throw here, and while the pass is slightly high, Cannon is able to get his fingertips to it, tipping it in the air and then securing the bobbling football at the 10-yard line with no defenders anywhere near him. From there he simply races into the end zone with the score.

The quick score erased the tie, and Baylor was never in danger again. After taking the 14-7 lead, the Bears roared to a 63-35 victory. While the game was lopsided, this drive showed just how explosive this offense was during 2015, and put every potential opponent on notice of its ability to strike quickly, using both the run and pass and a number of different personnel packages. Any future defense would know full well that against this team, there are no easy plays, nor plays off.

CHAPTER SIX

CONNOR COOK LEADS A GAME-WINNER ON THE ROAD

Week 6 of the 2015 college football season featured the Michigan State Spartans traveling east to take on the Rutgers Scarlet Knights in a Big Ten clash. While the visitors entered the game as the No. 7 team in the College Football Playoff poll, their hosts were proving less than hospitable, having tied the game at 24 on a field goal from Kyle Federico with just more than 4 minutes remaining. The ensuing drive would determine whether the Spartans would keep their undefeated record, or lose to an underwhelming team on the road and end their national championship hopes.

The MSU offense lines up at its own 24-yard line with Connor Cook in the shotgun and a personnel grouping of a running back, two tight ends, and two wide receivers on the field. Running back LJ Scott (#3) stands to the right of the quarterback, while the Spartans feature a tight trips to the left with two tight ends. Rutgers puts strongside linebacker Quentin Gause (#50) across from the tight trips formation, and show Cover 1:

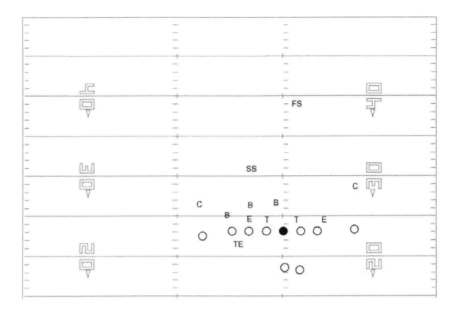

Michigan State tries a counter run to the right side: Left guard Brian Allen (#65) pulls to the right edge, kicking out the playside defensive end, while reserve tight end Paul Lang (#83) leads Scott to the right B gap. The RB takes a few steps to his left at the snap, then gathers the football and cuts toward the right. To add a misdirection element, wide receiver Macgarrett Kings Jr. (#85) fakes an end around:

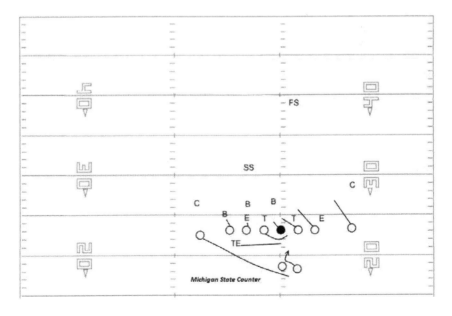

Even with Kings Jr. running the fake the defense is ready. At the snap both the playside defensive end Quanzell Lambert (#22) and defensive tackle Julian Pinnix-Odrick (#53) twist. As the right guard and tackle block to the inside, Lambert twists right into the intended hole:

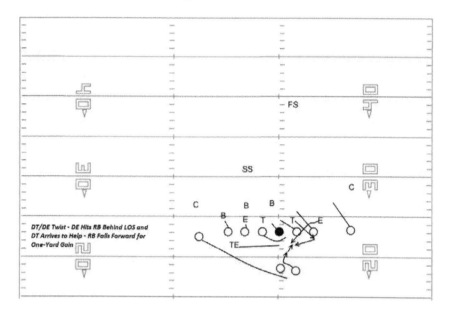

Allen pulls to the edge and blocks the defensive tackle but Lang runs right by the looping DT, who gets a hand on Scott two yards behind the line. As the ball carrier tries to disengage from the tackle by Pinnix-Odrick, Lambert comes off the block and finishes off the tackle.

Facing 2nd and 9, Michigan State lines up in dual slot formations with an 11 package consisting of a running back, a tight end, and three wide receivers. Rutgers adjusts its personnel as well, bringing on a nickel defense and showing Cover 2 man underneath:

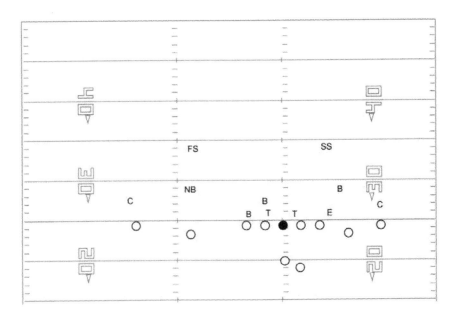

The Spartans employ a mirrored passing concept on this play, running a slant/flat combination to both sides of the field:

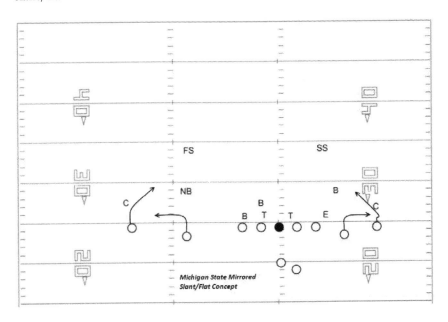

Pressure forces a very early throw on this play. Pinnix-Odrick follows up the previous play with another solid effort, beating right guard Benny McGowan (#75) with a vicious spin move to the inside. Once the defender angles through the A gap, he has a free shot at the quarterback:

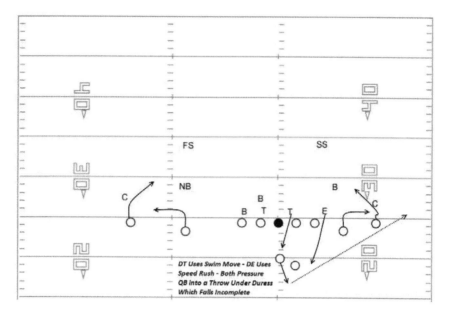

Cook tries to retreat to buy time, but he is forced to get rid of the ball quickly, and the pass falls well short of the flat route to the right.

For this critical third-down play Michigan State again employs three receivers, one tight end and a running back, with slot formation left and pro alignment to the right. Cook stands in the shotgun with Scott on his right. Rutgers brings on a 3-2-6 sub package, puts both linebackers on the edge and walks safety Kiy Hester (#2) up the second level where he aligns as a middle linebacker:

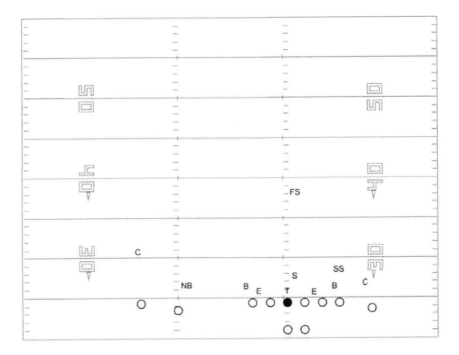

Michigan State turns to one of its favorite passing schemes, a switch vertical concept from the slot receivers. Aaron Burbridge (#16) is the outside receiver, and he runs a go route that drifts inside. R.J. Shelton (#12) lines up in the slot, running a wheel route against slot cornerback Andre Hunt (#30):

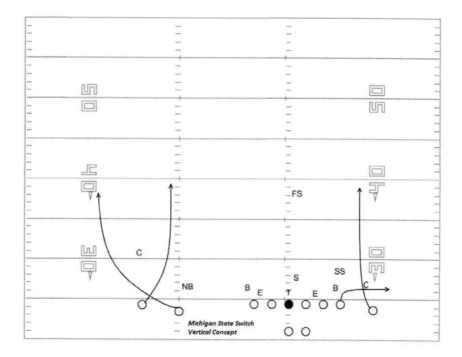

Michigan State Switch
Vertical Concept

Hester and linebacker Gause both blitz, and while Scott does a good job of picking up the safety on his inside rushing threat, Gause has a free shot at Cook coming off the edge. But the quarterback has enough time to find the matchup he likes: Shelton on the wheel route against the slot cornerback:

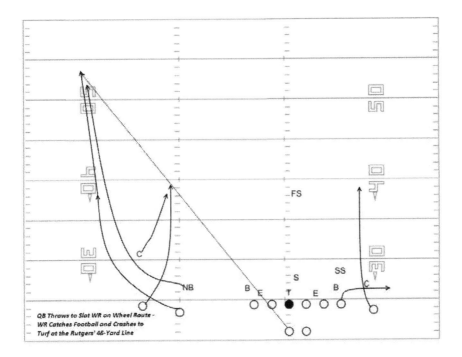

QB Throws to Slot WR on Wheel Route -
WR Catches Football and Crashes to
Turf at the Rutgers' 46-Yard Line

The aggressive decision pays off. Shelton high-points the throw from Cook and crashes to the turf at the Rutgers 46-yard line, picking up a huge first down for the visitors.

When the clock starts running again, 3:10 remains in the contest. That moment also finds Cook under center for the Spartans with two receivers, two tight ends and a running back in the game. They send a single receiver split wide to the left and a tight trips right, with the two tight ends to that side of the field. The defense returns to its base 4-3 look, showing Cover 2 and a linebacker aligned over the bunch formation:

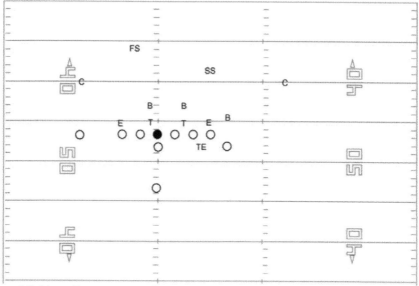

Michigan State runs a split zone running play to the right. Scott takes the handoff and heads to the right edge, with the offensive line firing out in unison to the right at the snap. Lang, in the game again and lined up as a wing to the right, blocks across the formation on the backside defensive end:

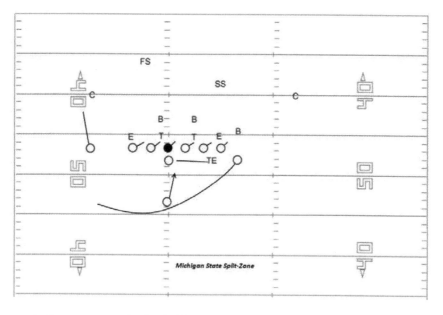

Michigan State Split-Zone

As Lang cuts to the backside, fellow tight end Jamal Lyles (#11) gets a good block on the right edge against Gause. Allen delivers a solid block on defensive tackle Eric Wiafe (#92) at the point of attack, and Scott cuts in right behind the block from his right guard:

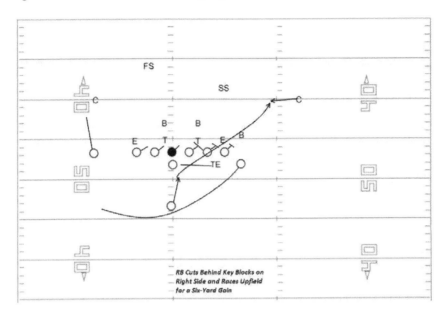

RB Cuts Behind Key Blocks on Right Side and Races Upfield for a Six-Yard Gain

The RB splits through traffic at the line of scrimmage and gets into the secondary quickly. Cornerback Blessuan Austin (#10) crashes down quickly and holds this play to only a 6-yard gain, but it could have been much worse for the Scarlet Knights.

On second down, the Spartans adjust their personnel once more and line up with a two backs, two tight ends and one receiver set, with Scott the deep back in an offset i-formation with fullback Trevon Pendleton (#37) staggered to the left, behind the B gap. Lang motions into the backfield as well, giving the offense a full-house look behind the quarterback:

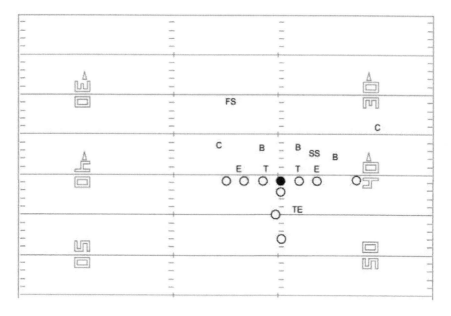

Rutgers stays with its base 4-3 defense, and brings nine defenders into the box in this Cover 1 look. The offense tries a power run to the left, with Allen pulling in front of the play, while Lang and Pendleton serve as lead blockers for Scott:

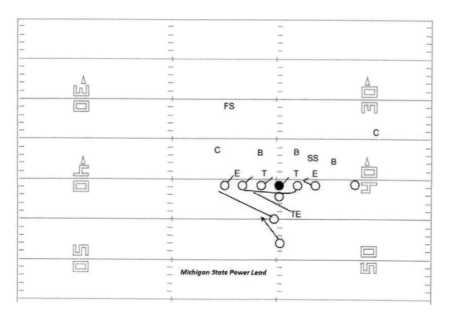

Michigan State Power Lead

The RB finds a tiny crease on the left side and follows Lang into the hole, but Gause does a good job of getting off an initial block and chops down the running back after a 2-yard gain, setting up another third down.

Facing 3rd and 2 at the Rutgers 38, Michigan State lines up with the clock running and the same 22 offensive personnel from the previous play in the game. The Spartans use an unbalanced line, shifting left tackle Kodi Kieler (#79) to the right between tackle Donavon Clark (#76) and Lang, who sets on the line of scrimmage. Cook is in the shotgun with Scott to his right, and Pendleton aligns on the right edge in a wing alignment. Burbridge is the flanker to the left, and with tight end Lyles on the line of scrimmage in a left tackle position, the flanker comes in jet motion before the play:

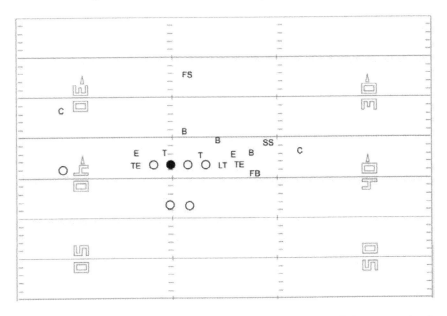

As the play begins, the WR races in front of Cook and the quarterback flips the ball to Burbridge, who aims for the right edge. The linemen all attempt to cut their defenders to the turf, except for Clark, who immediately gets to the second level to block middle linebacker Kaiwan Lewis (#14), and center Jack Allen (#66) who seals off the weakside linebacker:

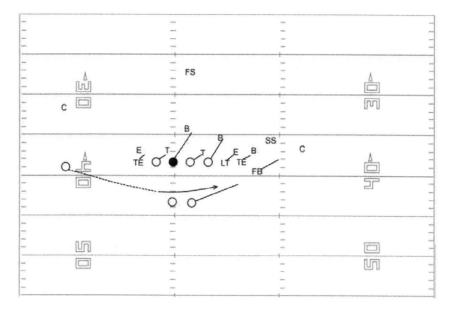

Clark's block is crucial to the play's success. As Burbridge heads for the right side, Rutgers flows to the outside well and sets the edge. The receiver is forced to try and cut upfield rather than bounce to the outside. As he stops on a dime - nearly touching his knee to the turf in the process - he cuts right behind the block from Clark on the middle linebacker:

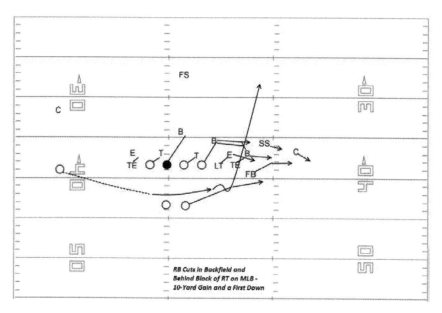

This block opens a hole, and Burbridge races down to the Rutgers 28-yard line for a gain of 10 yards - and another set of downs for the Spartans. Having surrendered the first down, the Scarlet Knights are forced to burn their second timeout.

On the next play, the Spartans line up with Cook under center and again the same 22 package on the field, in a tight i-formation with the flanker left. Rutgers shows Cover 6 in the secondary, with both a linebacker and the weakside cornerback on the line of scrimmage:

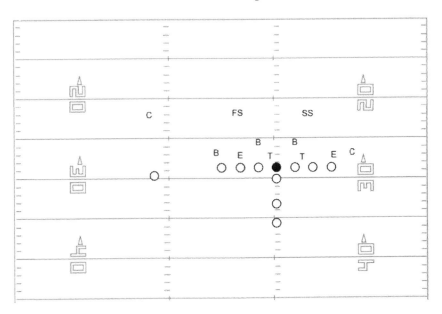

MSU uses another split zone concept. The offensive line all blocks to the right at the snap, while Pendleton crosses to pick up the backside defensive end. Scott takes the handoff aiming for the right A gap:

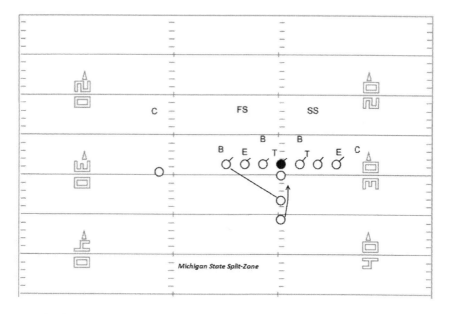

Michigan State Split-Zone

The key blocks on this play come from Jack Allen and McGowan, the right guard. At the snap, the center is able to control the nose tackle using simply his left arm, pinning him away from the right A gap. McGowan is able to turn the playside defensive tackle toward the sideline, and this opens a hole for Scott to race through:

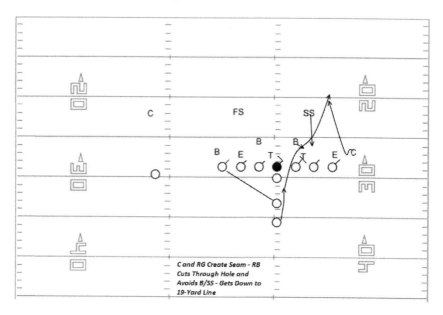

C and RG Create Seam - RB Cuts Through Hole and Avoids B/SS - Gets Down to 19-Yard Line

As the RB cuts through the gap he breaks tackle attempts from both the middle linebacker and the strong safety. Cornerback Isaiah Wharton (#11) is able to drag down the RB from behind, but the 9-yard gain gets the Spartans to the 19, and inside field goal range. Rutgers burns its final timeout.

On the next play, Michigan State lines up with 23 personnel - three tight ends and two backs - on the field, using Lang as a fullback:

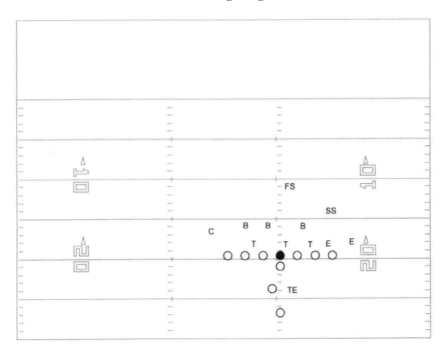

The defense adjusts to a 5-3, stacking the box with 10 defenders anticipating a short power running play from the offense. The Spartans are happy to oblige:

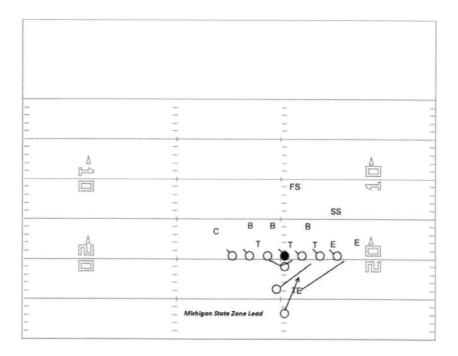

While the majority of the line blocks down to the left, Brian Allen pulls in front of this play to the right side, with Pendleton and Lang leading Scott to the right B gap. They look to have this play blocked well, with Lang sealing off the outside edge defender toward the sideline while his fellow tight end Lyles collapses down on the defensive end, Lambert:

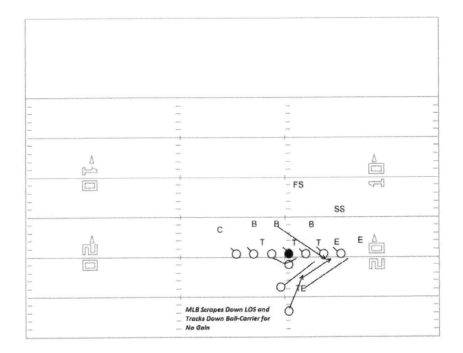

MLB Scrapes Down LOS and
Tracks Down Ball-Carrier for
No Gain

But as Scott nears the hole, he is tracked down by middle linebacker Lewis, who does a tremendous job of scraping down the line and tracking the ball carrier. He holds Scott to no gain, forcing another third down attempt for the offense. However, Rutgers cannot stop the clock.

But the Spartans are forced to take a timeout, when center Jack Allen suffers an injury on the play.

When play resumes, the Spartans line up for third down with 23 personnel still in the game. Their starting center is still on the sideline, so Brian Allen slides over the football and is replaced at left guard by David Beedle (#59). Scott is the deep back in the offset i-formation with Pendleton staggered to the left side as an up back. The offense puts all three tight ends on the left side, with Lyles and Dylan Chmura (#80) on the line of scrimmage and Lang in a wing alignment just outside. The Scarlet Knights flood 10 defenders into the box once more using their 5-3 personnel:

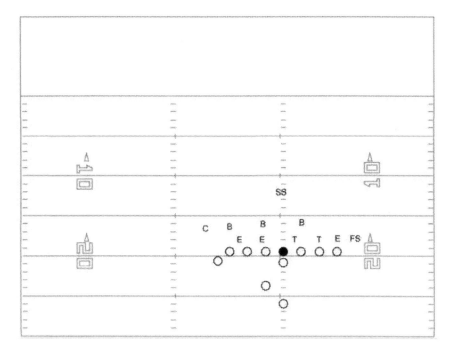

The Spartans run an outside zone play to the left side. As the linemen come out of their stance and flow to the left, Pendleton aims for the edge defender:

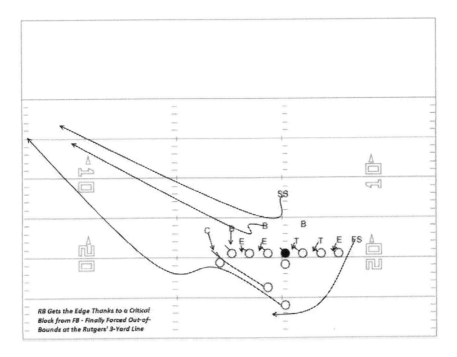

RB Gets the Edge Thanks to a Critical Block from FB - Finally Forced Out-of-Bounds at the Rutgers' 3-Yard Line

The fullback gets enough of a block on the cornerback that Scott is able to bounce around the block and cut to the sideline, before finally being run out of bounds at the Rutgers 3 yard line. This stops the clock, but with the Scarlet Knights out of timeouts, the visitors are in good position to play for a field goal try or end the game with a touchdown.

On the ensuing play, the Spartans use the same personnel grouping. They also use an unbalanced line, moving all three tight ends to the right side, with Pendleton shaded to the right side as an upback in the offset i-formation. Rutgers uses its jumbo defensive personnel here, once more putting 10 defenders on the line of scrimmage:

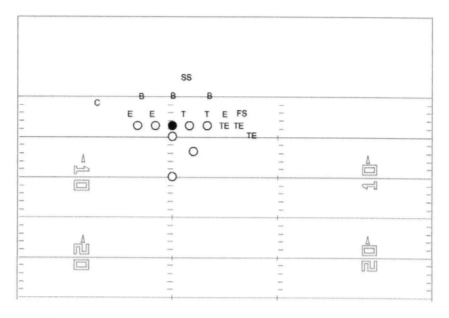

Michigan State gives Scott another carry, this time aiming the running back to the right side with Brian Allen, still in the game at center, pulling to the right in front of the ball carrier while Clark pulls around the edge:

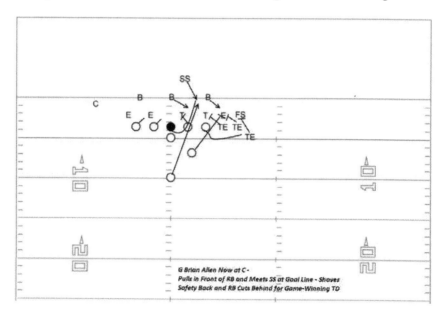

As the offensive linemen pulls into the hole, Hester is involved in a crucial moment. The safety meets Brian Allen at the goal line and the lineman overpowers the defender. Scott plunges into the endzone behind him with the go-ahead score.

Rutgers did have a chance to pull off the late miracle win, and got the football to midfield on its ensuing possession. But a pass attempt on 4th and 20 fell incomplete, and the Spartans were able to simply kneel on the football and run out the clock.

It was an ugly win for the Spartans, but over the course of a season teams that hope to win a championship teams need to find a way to win games like this one. Connor Cook and the rest of the Spartans' offense did just that on this critical, game-winning drive. And it would not be the last time Michigan State did something like this.

CHAPTER SEVEN

LES MILES'S BAG OF TRICKS

A huge week 7 matchup took place in Death Valley between Florida and LSU. Both teams were ranked in the top 10 entering the contest, with Florida at #6, and LSU checking in at #8. Following the suspension of starting quarterback Will Grier, the Gators turned to Treon Harris under center, and in the wake of Antonio Callaway's 72-yard punt return for a touchdown, the visitors pulled even as Death Valley fell into a mix of concern, despair, and fear.

What better way to calm a restless crowd than by feeding the football to your talented running back and using the staples of your offense?

Starting at their own 25-yard line after the touchback, Brandon Harris lines up under center and 21 offensive personnel on the field in an i-formation, with pro alignment on the right. Heisman candidate Leonard Fournette (#7) aligns behind fullback Bry'Kieiethon Mouton (#47). The Gators are showing Cover 2 in the secondary:

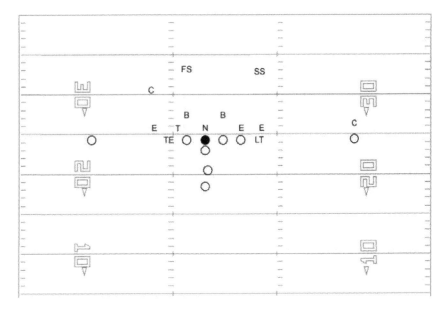

X receiver John Diarse (#9) is completely uncovered before the snap, but Harris has no intention of calling an audible here: It's time for the lead toss play. LSU employs an unbalanced line, moving left tackle Jerald Hawkins (#65) to the right, giving the Tigers a guard and two tackles to the right. Tight end Colin Jeter (#81) lines up in Hawkins's usual spot of left tackle:

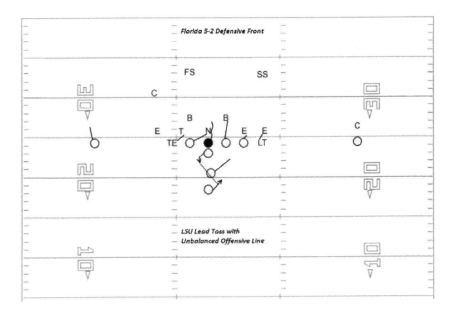

On the backside, both Jeter and left guard Maea Teuhema (#75) need to cut off the nose tackle and the defensive tackle from pursuing the ball carrier. The tight end gets inside the defensive tackle, while Teuhema uses a cut block on nose tackle Caleb Brantley (#57). Playside, the linemen flow to the right, with Hawkins blocking the edge defender. Meanwhile, right tackle Vadal Alexander (#74) is handling the other defensive end, and right guard William Clapp (#64) is flowing to the second level to take on the middle linebacker. Center Ethan Pocic (#77) makes sure that Teuhema has handled Brantley before he works to the second level to seal off the backside linebacker:

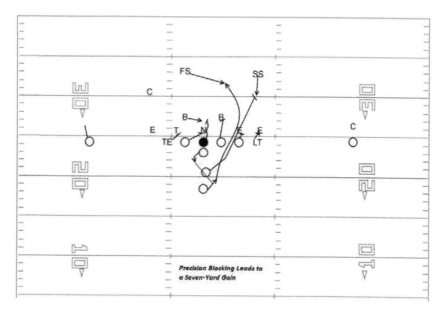

Precision Blocking Leads to a Seven-Yard Gain

One player poses a problem for LSU on this snap: Florida strong safety Marcus Maye (#20). As the play begins, the safety explodes into the box and into the designed hole. However, fullback Bry'Keithon Mouton (#47) leads Fournette into the hole and turns the blitzing safety toward the sideline with an effective block. The back cuts inside off the block and rips off an easy seven-yard gain on first down.

On the next play the Tigers turn to another pillar of their offense, the HB lead play. LSU lines up with Harris under center with two running backs, a tight end, and two receivers on the field, and a standard alignment up front with the TE on the right side of the offense in pro formation. Florida adjusts to their base 4-3 defense, showing Cover 3 in the secondary with free safety Keanu Neal (#42) down in the box. At the snap Neal drops with the rest of the defensive backs into a Cover 4 scheme.

The Tigers run their lead play to the weak side of the formation with Mouton in front of Fournette as the two players head for the B Gap:

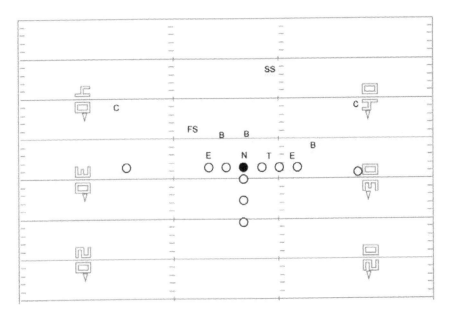

Where the previous play worked because of execution up front, this run works because of the footwork from the big RB. Off the snap Brantley gets a good initial push on Pocic, driving the center into the backfield. This forces Fournette to make a quick cut behind the line of scrimmage. The RB looks to bounce outside after cutting, but defensive end Bryan Cox Jr. (#94) has established outside leverage on the left tackle, forcing Fournette to make another cut before even leaving the backfield:

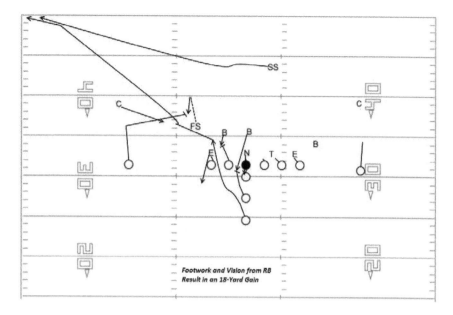

Footwork and Vision from RB
Result in an 18-Yard Gain

After these first two moves, Fournette is in the secondary, where he puts a quick juke move on cornerback Jalen Tabor (#31). Maye finally pushes the back out of bounds, right at midfield after a 14-yard gain.

First down, time for more Fournette. The Tigers line up with Harris under center and the same personnel grouping in the game, using a stack-slot formation on the right. The big running back dots the i in the LSU i-formation, behind Mouton. Florida stays in their 4-3 defense and shows Cover 2:

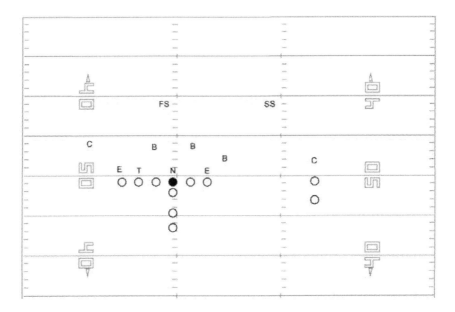

The Tigers run Fournette to the right side, with the fullback leading the way, using a similar design as the previous snap:

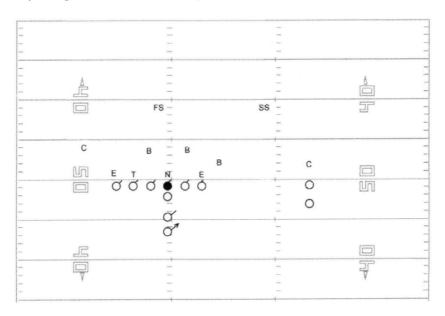

This time, the Gators are ready. Brantley gets good push yet again off the snap, driving Pocic into the backfield once more. This forces Fournette to angle outside while still behind the line of scrimmage. But Powell has burst into the backfield off the edge, and as the ball carrier cuts to his left, the linebacker hurdles two bodies in front of him, and with the help of DE CeCe Jefferson (#96) and Davis, holds Fournette to no gain:

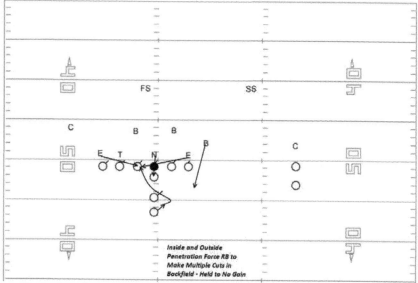

Inside and Outside Penetration Force RB to Make Multiple Cuts In Backfield - Held to No Gain

On 2nd and 10 the Tigers spread the offense out a little, putting Harris in the shotgun with trips right, the tight end on the edge of the offensive line, and split a single receiver out to the left. Florida counters with a 4-2-5 nickel package, sliding nickelback Brian Poole (#24) outside the right tackle in a linebacker's alignment. Up front they use three defensive ends, putting senior Jonathan Bullard (#90) inside over the left guard. The secondary displays Cover 2 before the play, with both cornerbacks in press alignment:

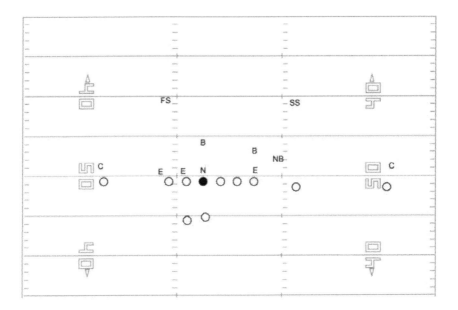

LSU runs the zone read to the left on this play:

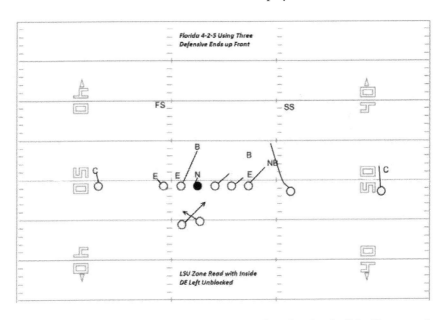

Harris takes the snap and turns left, putting the football in Fournette's belly. With the running back aimed for the right side, the QB reads the defensive end. Four of the offensive linemen, plus the tight end, block to the right side. But the left tackle, Jerald Hawkins (#65), blocks Cox on the edge, and the line leaves the inside DE, Bullard, unblocked. He slides into Fournette's path and, seeing the edge sealed, Harris tucks the football away and darts toward the left side:

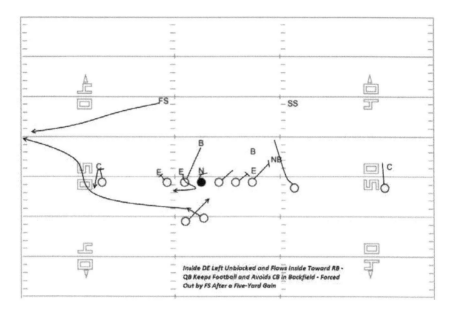

Inside DE Left Unblocked and Flows Inside Toward RB -
QB Keeps Football and Avoids CB in Backfield - Forced
Out by FS After a Five-Yard Gain

After he turns the corner, the QB encounters receiver Tyron Johnson (#3) struggling on the outside to block cornerback Jalen Tabor (#31). Harris bounces to the outside, but the CB is able to disengage and make a diving tackle attempt. However, his lunge misses the quarterback's ankles, and Harris turns upfield before being forced out of bounds by Cox. The five-yard gain gives the Tigers a more manageable situation for the next play.

The Tigers burn a timeout before third down with the ball at the Florida 45-yard line. They send out the QB in the shotgun and a single back and four receiver set featuring a trips formation on the right. The Gators display Cover 1 in the secondary. One linebacker shows an A Gap blitz while the defensive backs to the the trips side of the formation show off man coverage:

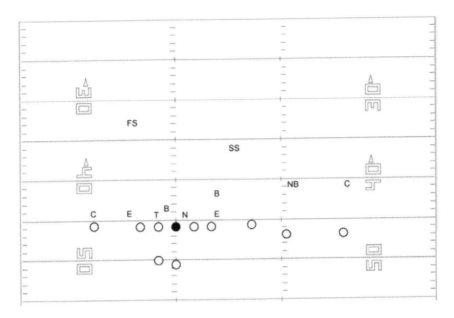

At the snap, the defense rolls into Cover 2 while the Tigers set up three in routes from the trips receivers:

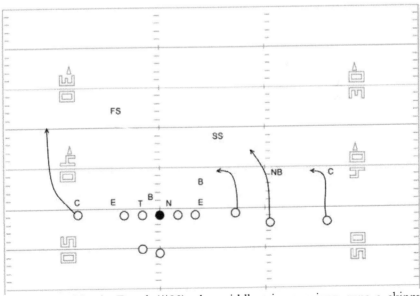

Receiver Travin Dural (#83), the middle trips receiver, runs a skinny post route. He is able to get inside leverage on nickelback Brian Poole (#24) thanks to the deep alignment from the defensive back before the play:

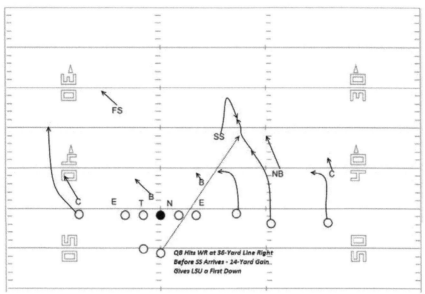

QB Hits WR at 36-Yard Line Right
Before SS Arrives - 14-Yard Gain
Gives LSU a First Down

Harris takes advantage of the big throwing window, delivering the football before Mays is able to break down on the route. The 14-yard gain gives the Tigers another set of downs and keeps the drive alive.

On the next play, the Tigers return to the ground and Fournette. They line up with Harris under center and come back to a 21 offensive personnel package, with their running back deep in the i-formation. Again they use an unbalanced line, moving Hawkins over to the right side in a tight end's alignment, and putting the tight end on the left edge where Hawkins would usually set up. The Gators adjust their defense, lining up with their base 4-3 and putting Powell down near the line over Jeter. Right before the snap safety Marcus Mays (#20) starts walking down near the right edge:

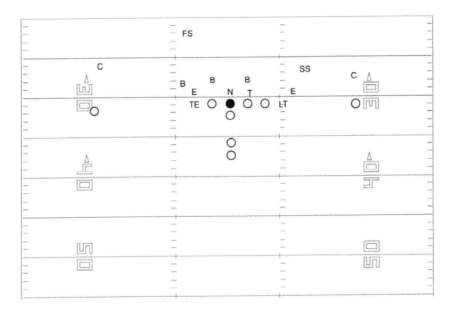

This time the Gators run their lead toss play to the right, and the safety reads and reacts perfectly:

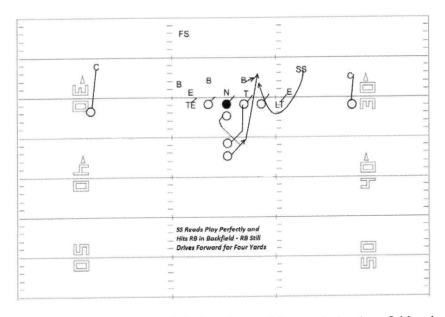

As Fournette takes the pitch from Harris, Mays explodes downfield and around Hawkins. Mouton cuts to the inside and Fournette tries to follow, but the SS bends around the edge and hits the running back in the backfield. Despite the early contact, Fournette is able to stay upright and manages to fall forward for a four-yard gain, with Mays draped over his chest the entire time.

Now facing 2nd and 6 at the Florida 27-yard line the offense sets up with another i-formation using the same personnel, but this time has the tight end on the left side of the field to the slot formation, covered by the X receiver. Florida has a 4-3 defense in the game, using three defensive ends up front:

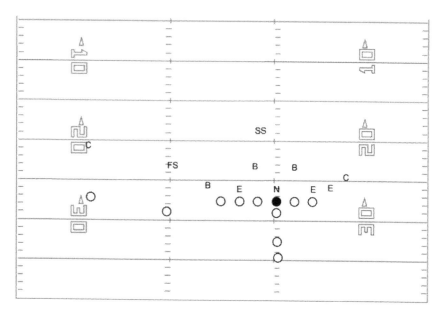

LSU runs a split zone play with the offensive line moving to the left at the snap, leaving the backside edge defender unblocked. While Fournette heads left, Mouton cuts right to seal off the defender's pursuit angle:

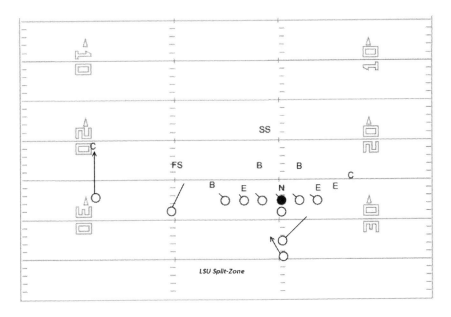

LSU Split-Zone

As with any zone play, Fournette has some options. But Hawkins and Jeter make it easy for him:

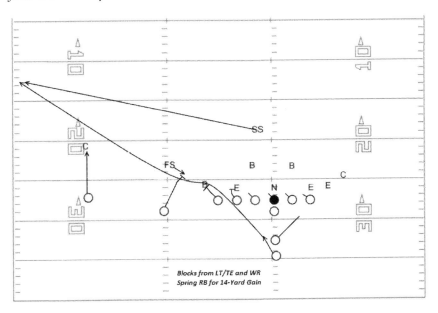

Blocks from LT/TE and WR
Spring RB for 14-Yard Gain

At the snap, the left tackle executes a perfect reach block, firing out his left foot wide toward the sideline before turning upfield and driving his upper body into the defensive end. From there, Hawkins remains engaged with the upper body while using his legs to drive the defender upfield, away from the play.

The tight end has an easier angle, with outside linebacker Jeremi Powell (#23) lined up outside of him before the play. Jeter simply uses his alignment and positioning against the linebacker, sealing him off from the hole. Fournette makes his bang read and splits the gap between Jeter and Hawkins. From there, the first player he faces is DB Keanu Neal (#42). But remember, the Tigers still have two receivers to the outside with this unbalanced look. Slot receiver Trey Quinn (#8) is in position to make a block on Neal, freeing up Fournette for his second 14-yard gain of the drive.

Armed with a fresh set of downs, the Tigers keep the football on the ground. Harris lines up under center again with 21 offensive personnel on the field, a pro alignment to the right and an i-formation in the backfield. The Gators respond with their base personnel on the field, with Powell down near the line of scrimmage over the tight end, with strong safety Mays close behind. Once more they employ three defensive ends along the front:

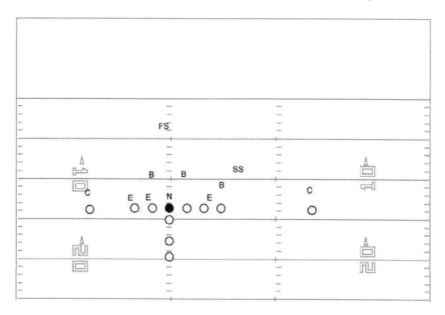

Once more the offense runs the lead toss play to the right:

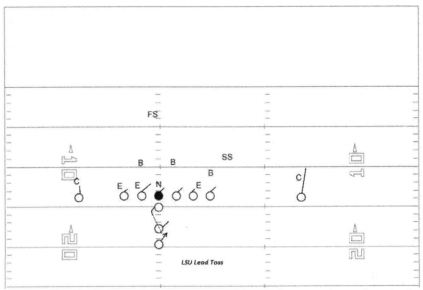

LSU Lead Toss

Powell and Mays combine to prevent this run from getting going. At the snap the outside linebacker slides to the outside a bit, to set the edge. Jeter comes out of his stance to block Powell, but the linebacker holds his ground. Edge defender Alex McCalister (#14) angles inside at the start of the play, and occupies the right tackle. With Powell setting the edge and the DE occupying the interior, there is one hole for both the offense and Mays;

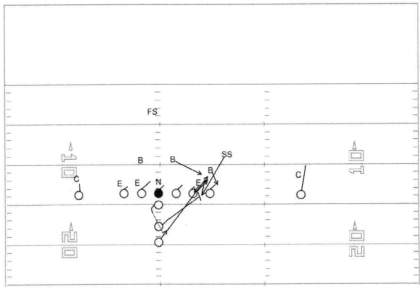

The safety fills the hole perfectly, meeting Mouton at the line of scrimmage. He drives the fullback into the ball-carrier, slowing Fournette just past the line of scrimmage. Mays then works off the block, and with the help of Davis and McCalister, the trio of defenders drag Fournette to the turf for just a two-yard gain.

On second down, both teams adjust personnel and bring on a heavier package. The Tigers line up with two backs, two tight ends and a receiver in a tight i-formation to the left. Florida lines up with 5-3 personnel, putting McCalister in a linebacker's alignment on the right side of the offense:

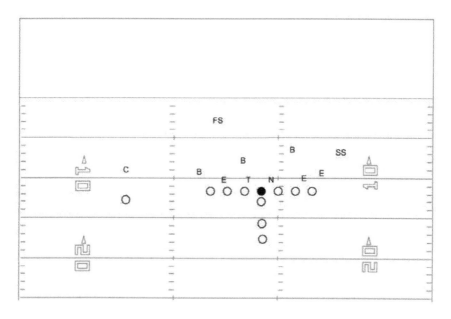

Harris tries to hit Dupre on a fade route in the end zone, and the pass falls incomplete:

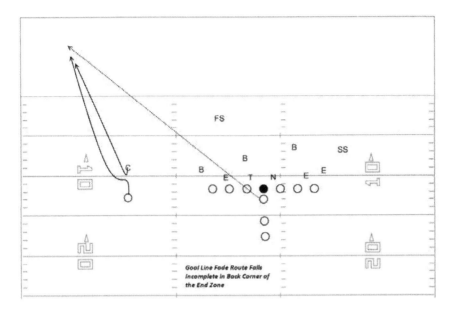

Goal Line Fade Route Fails
Incomplete in Back Corner of
the End Zone

This brings up third down, with under twelve minutes remaining. LSU lines up with Harris in the shotgun, three receivers, one tight end and a running back on the field. Dural and Jeter are on the right, both off the line of scrimmage, with the tight end in a wing alignment just outside the right tackle. The other two wide receivers set up on the left in a slot, with both players on the line of scrimmage:

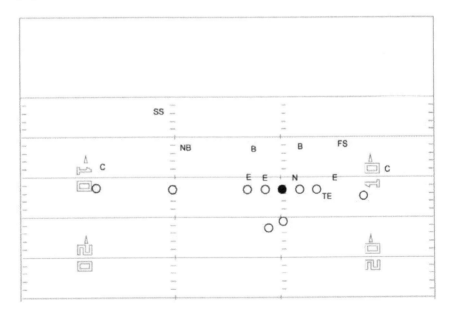

Dural comes in jet motion toward the football. Defensively, the Gators have their 4-2-5 nickel in the game using three defensive ends up front. They show Cover 0 in the secondary, with cornerback Vernon Hargreaves III trailing Dural as the receiver comes in motion:

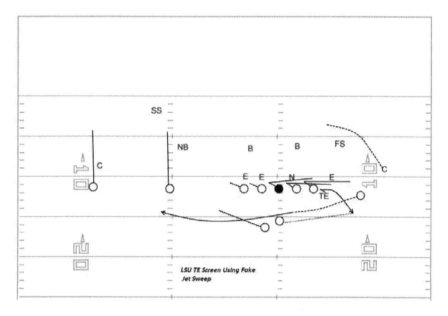

The design is to get the entire defense flowing to their right. Harris fakes the jet sweep before dropping back to pass. The offensive line flows to the left as well to sell the fake sweep. Jeter blocks the defensive end before releasing to the outside and remaining behind the line of scrimmage. The delay allows the right side of the line to release from their initial blocks and try and get in front of the TE before Harris dumps the ball off to Jeter.

But Neal is having none of that:

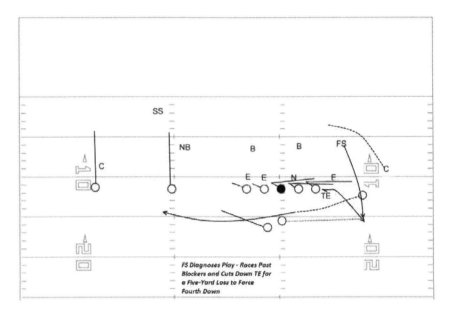

FS Diagnoses Play - Races Past Blockers and Cuts Down TE for a Five-Yard Loss to Force Fourth Down

The defensive back reads this play perfectly, and races forward like a cannonball. Neal chops Jeter down for a five-yard loss, setting up the Tigers with a 4th and 13 on the Florida 16-yard line.

Drive over, send out the kicking team*.

The Tigers line up to kick from the right hash. Trent Domingue (#14) steps off his normal approach, stares down the center of the uprights, and nods at his holder. The long-snapper fires the ball back with Domingue... taking off to his left?

Yes. While kickers may not be the strongest or biggest players on the field, LSU nevertheless turned to the most unlikely of players on this fake. Holder Brad Kragthorpe delivers a perfect toss to Domingue, who bobbles the ball for nearly five yards before sprinting into the end zone for the eventual game-winning score:

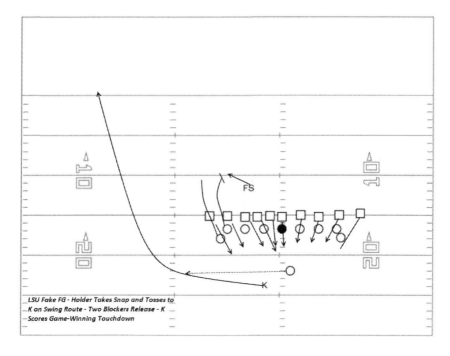

LSU Fake FG - Holder Takes Snap and Tosses to K on Swing Route - Two Blockers Release - K Scores Game-Winning Touchdown

And he drilled the extra-point right down the middle for good measure. Tigers win, 35-28.

The victory gave LSU a huge win in the SEC, and although they would falter down the stretch and even contemplated firing Les Miles, that decision was reversed in the wake of the season's final game. But the drive also illustrated that even when an offense runs one or two plays at a high ratio, a defense might not be able to stop those plays - especially when the ball carrier is Leonard Fournette.

*The last play of this drive was written by Inside the Pylon special teams guru, Chuck Zodda.

CHAPTER EIGHT

ALABAMA EDGES TENNESSEE

The eighth week of the 2015 college football season saw a marquee matchup in Tuscaloosa, Ala., where the Crimson Tide looked to keep their national championship aspirations alive against a Tennessee Volunteers squad itching to spoil Alabama's title hopes. With favorite son Peyton Manning watching from the sideline, the visitors took a 14-13 lead on a Jalen Hurd touchdown run with 5:49 left in the game. Would the Crimson Tide see their hopes erased in the upset? The next drive would answer that question.

Following the kickoff, Alabama lines up with quarterback Jake Coker (#14) in the shotgun and 12 offensive personnel, with a pro alignment to each side of the field. Running back Derrick Henry (#2) stands to the left of his quarterback. The Volunteers have a 4-2-5 nickel defense in the game, and they slide nickelback Malik Foreman (#13) down into the box in a linebacker's alignment, while showing Cover 2 in the secondary:

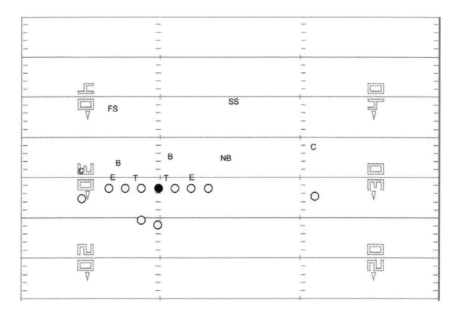

The offense attempts a four verticals concept, with all four receivers running seam or go routes:

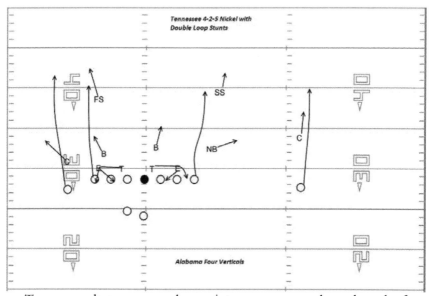

Tennessee drops seven players into coverage and sends only four rushers after the quarterback, but uses a double cross-stunt up front, which pays dividends. Both defensive ends crash to the inside off the snap, while the defensive tackles loop around to the outside. Left defensive end Corey

Vereen (#50) is the first to generate pressure, as he drives left tackle Cam Robinson (#74) back into Coker's face. But while Robinson starts to hold his ground, right DE Derek Barnett (#9) breaks free from right guard Alphonse Taylor (#50) and flushes the QB to his right:

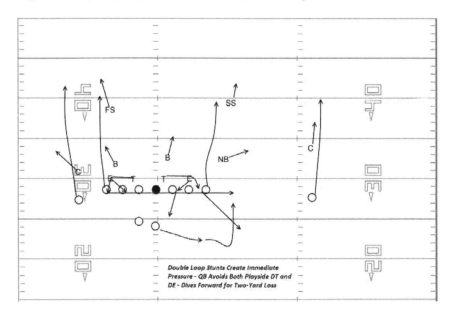

As Coker rolls to his right, he manages to escape Taylor but nearly runs into the waiting arms of the nose tackle. Having looped to the outside, Kendal Vickers (#39) is in perfect position to finish the sack for a huge loss, but Coker manages to wriggle away from him at the Alabama 12-yard line. Now in complete flight mode, the quarterback tries to race back toward the line of scrimmage, and is finally chased down at the 27-yard line.

The play goes in the scorebook as a 2-yard loss, but it could have been much, much worse for the Crimson Tide.

Now facing 2nd and 12, Alabama adjusts its offense by bringing on a third wide receiver, joining him with a running back and tight end (11 personnel). They have an inverted slot to the left, with receivers Calvin Ridley (#3) to the outside and Richard Mullaney (#16) inside and on the line of scrimmage. Tight end O.J. Howard (#88) is in a pro formation on the right with receiver ArDarius Stewart (#13) lined up as a flanker. The Volunteers keep their 4-2-5 nickel formation in the game, with Foreman lined up across from Mullaney in the slot, and show Cover 1 with safety Todd Kelly Jr. (#6) near the box in a robber technique:

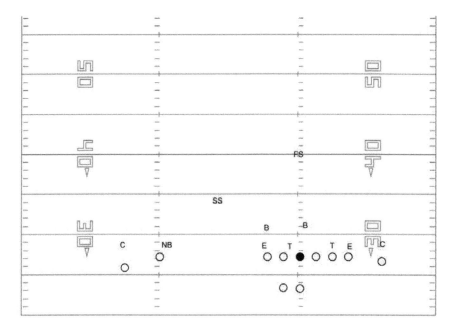

Alabama tries the four verticals concept again, but this time Kelly and linebacker Darrin Kirkland Jr. (#34) blitz off the edge. Tennessee also drops a defensive end in coverage over the tight end:

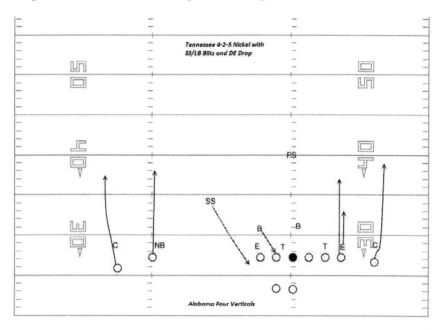

On this snap, the protection holds. Henry does a very good job sliding to the left and picking up the blitzing safety while center Ryan Kelly (#70) handles the blitzing linebacker, giving Coker enough time to make a throw. He takes a shot downfield to Stewart:

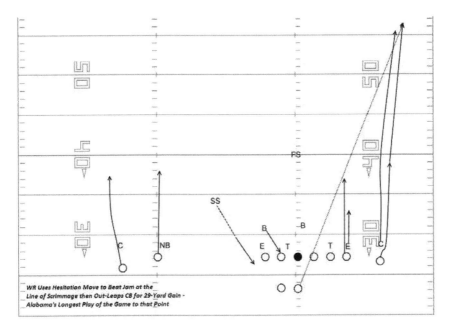

The receiver uses a hesitation move off the snap to beat the press coverage from Justin Martin (#8). Stewart then wins the battle at the catch point, out-leaping the cornerback for the football and pulling in the pass from Coker. Stewart crashes to the turf with the football in his hands for a gain of 29 yards – the longest play of the game for Alabama.

Now in Tennessee territory, Alabama lines up for the 1st and 10 with Coker under center and 11 personnel again, with a bunch formation on the right and Ridley alone on the left and split out very wide. The Volunteers stay with their nickel defense and show Cover 1, with Foreman down near the line of scrimmage over the bunch formation:

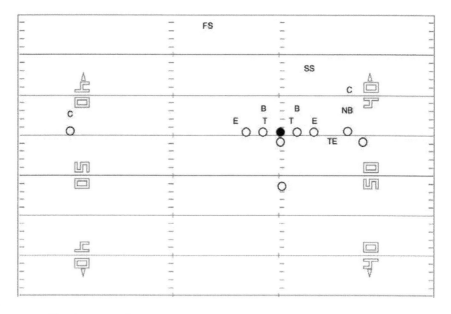

Offensive coordinator Lane Kiffin calls for an inside zone run, with Coker turning to his left and handing off to Henry. An inside zone run is an interior running play where the line blocks in unison to one side of the field and the running back aims for the interior, between the tackles, and reads the development of the play.

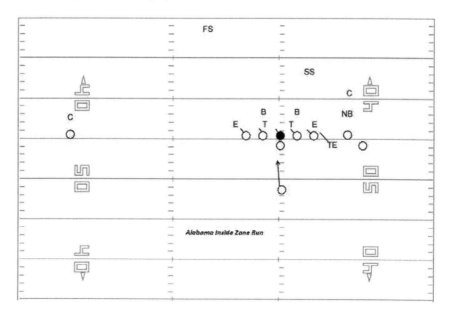

Initially, the blocking holds and Henry has a crease. But when he hits the line of scrimmage and tries to race north-south, he runs into Barnett:

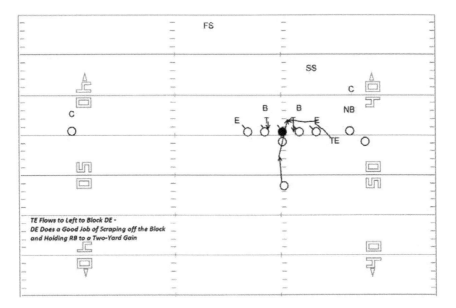

Howard was tasked with blocking the defensive end on this play, and Barnett does a good job of scraping off the tight end to the inside, where he stops Henry after a short 2-yard gain.

Facing 2nd and 8, the offense lines up with Coker in the pistol formation and Henry a few yards behind him. Alabama stays with the same personnel, in a tight slot to the right with Howard in a wing alignment, and an inverted slot look on the left with Mullaney inside of Ridley. Tennessee stays with its nickel defense and this time uses Cover 2 in the secondary:

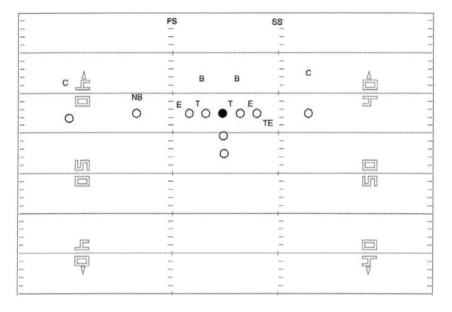

With the inside zone having been stopped on the previous play, the Crimson Tide try an outside zone run (running back aims outside the tackles):

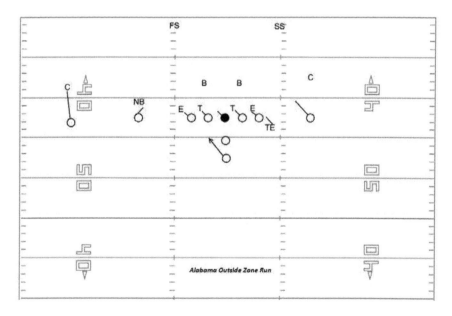

Alabama Outside Zone Run

Henry takes the handoff from Coker heading to the left side, as the offensive line fires out in unison blocking to its left. Once more, Vereen shows himself to be a disruptive force. Using a speed move, he bursts around the left tackle and into the backfield, forcing Henry to make a cut shortly after taking the handoff. But he doesn't get too far on his cut, as Vereen lunges and grabs the running back around his waist:

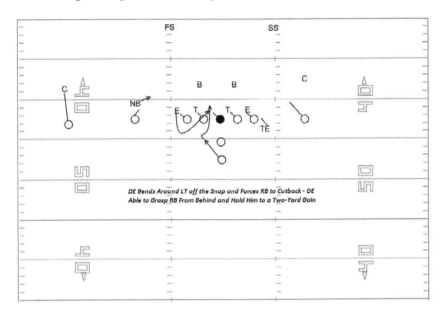

DE Bends Around LT off the Snap and Forces RB to Cutback - DE
Able to Grasp RB From Behind and Hold Him to a Two-Yard Gain

The defensive end wrestles Henry to the turf, but the running back manages to fall forward for another 2-yard gain, setting up a critical 3rd and 6 with less than 4 minutes remaining.

With the crowd at Bryant-Denny Stadium looking on nervously, Alabama lines up for the third down play with Coker in the shotgun and keeping the same 11 personnel group on the field, with trips formation to the right and Ridley a single receiver split to the left. Tennessee stays with its 4-2-5 nickel, but lines up in a 3-3-5 alignment with Vereen in a linebacker's position:

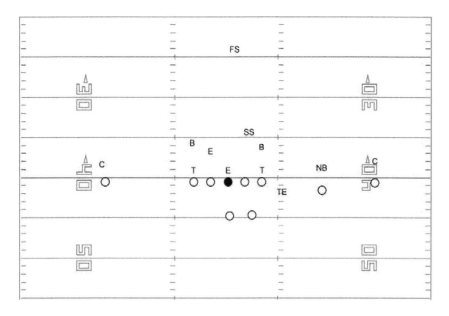

The defense shows Cover 1 in the secondary, and again brings pressure:

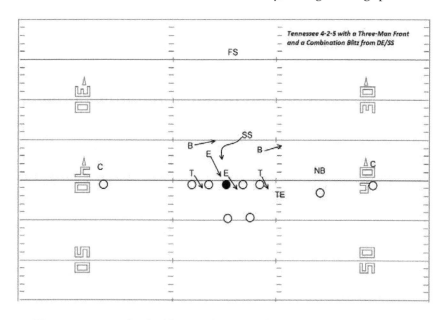

Vereen cuts to the inside on his blitz, where he is followed by safety LaDarrell McNeil (#33), while the rest of the defense sets up in Cover 1. The Crimson Tide use vertical routes on the outside from Stewart and Ridley, and use a trail concept with Mullaney and Howard to the right. The tight end runs to the flat, while the wide receiver cuts under him and releases vertically, but then bends back toward the sideline behind Howard:

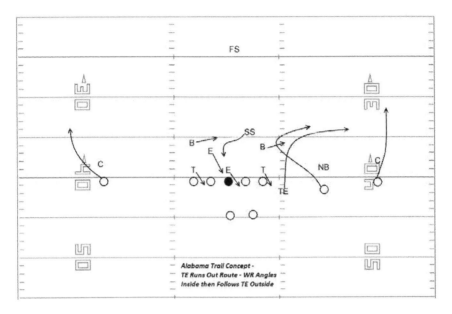

Alabama Trail Concept -
TE Runs Out Route - WR Angles
Inside then Follows TE Outside

Despite the beautiful play design to the trips side of the field, Coker ignores all this, and instead throws a jump ball to Ridley. The receiver is matched up with cornerback Cameron Sutton (#7) in press technique. At the snap Ridley uses a stutter-step move, then plants his right foot to the inside of the field and drives to the outside and gains leverage along the sideline. Sutton fails in his attempt to get a jam, giving the receiver just enough separation for Coker to take his shot:

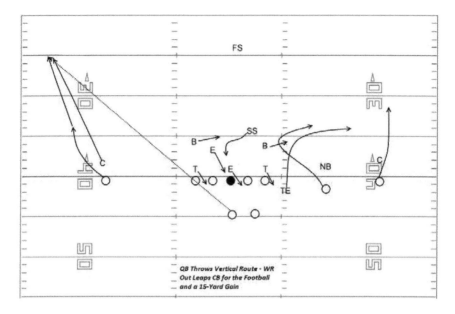

QB Throws Vertical Route - WR
Out Leaps CB for the Football
and a 15-Yard Gain

The throw is high, but Ridley beats the cornerback at the catch point and pulls down the pass, for a gain of 15 yards and another first down.

Now just outside the red zone, the Crimson Tide turn back to their talented running back. They line up with Coker under center and 11 offensive personnel in the game, with a TE trips formation to the right and Ridley using a tight split on the left. Tennessee stays with its nickel personnel, and shows Cover 1 in the secondary with the cornerbacks to the trips side of the field using off man alignment before the play:

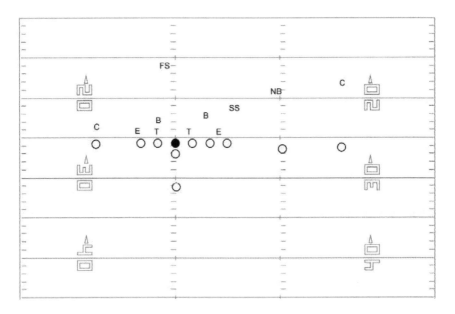

Alabama runs another zone play here, with Henry taking the ball and heading to the left side while the offensive line slides to the left at the snap:

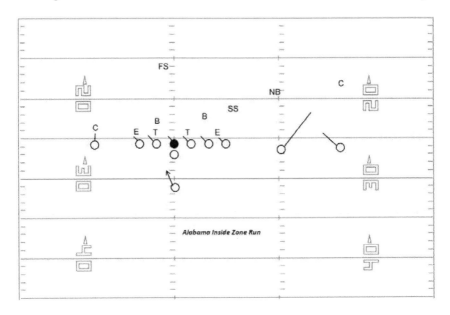

Alabama Inside Zone Run

The critical block on this play is thrown by Howard on Barnett. At the snap, the defensive end angles to the inside, in the direction the tight end is heading. Howard drives him to the inside, and as Henry takes the handoff penetration in the interior forces him to bend this rush to the backside, right behind the crushing block from his tight end:

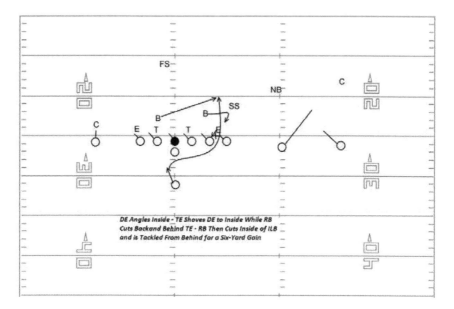

DE Angles Inside - TE Shoves DE to Inside While RB Cuts Backand Behind TE - RB Then Cuts Inside of ILB and is Tackled From Behind for a Six-Yard Gain

Henry does a tremendous job of sticking his left foot in the grass and knifing to the backside, then darts vertically once he bends around the block from Howard. He avoids an initial tackle attempt around his ankles, before he is brought down after a 6-yard gain.

With less than three minutes remaining, the Crimson Tide line up for second down with Coker under center and the same personnel grouping on the field; however, wide receiver Chris Back (#1) checks into the game.. Henry is the deep back, and Black sets up as an upback shaded to the left side. The Volunteers stay with their 4-2-5 defense, and walk Foreman down on the line of scrimmage over the bunch look on the left side of the offense:

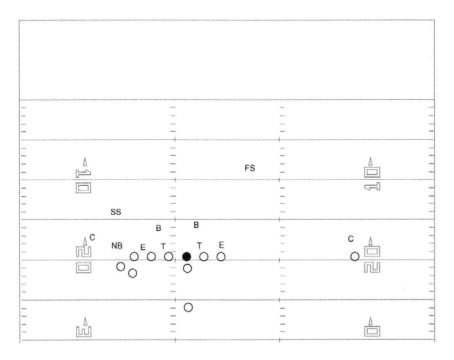

Alabama uses a split zone running play here. The linemen zone block to their left, while Black blocks across the formation on the backside defensive end. Henry takes the handoff aiming for the left interior of the line:

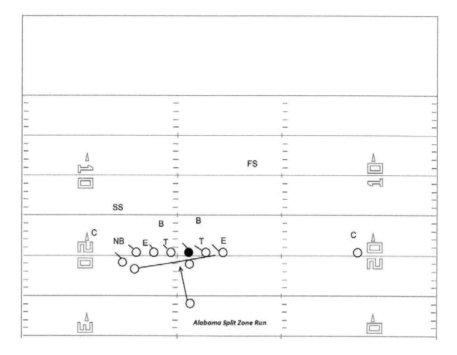

Alabama Split Zone Run

As he takes the handoff, Henry sees a slight crease open up on the right side, just behind the blocks of Black and right tackle Dominick Jackson (#76). The running back angles through this narrow lane, past the line of scrimmage and into the second level:

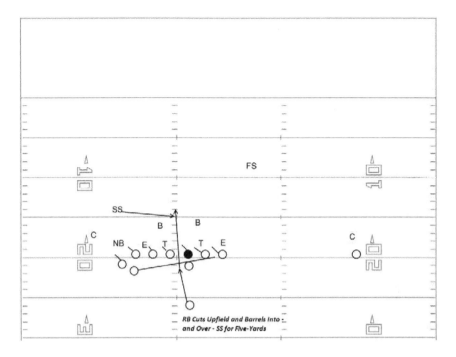

Kelly Jr. slides down into the hole, and Henry barrels into – and over – the safety. The tackle is made, but not before Henry picks up another 5 yards and a fresh set of downs for Alabama.

Having done the hard work, it is time for the bruising running back to cash in. The Crimson Tide switch to a personnel grouping that includes Henry as the sole running back with two tight ends and two wide receivers, with Howard aligned as a wing on the right and a slot formation to the left. Coker stands in the shotgun with Henry on his right. The Volunteers have their nickel package in the game, and they show Cover 2 in the secondary:

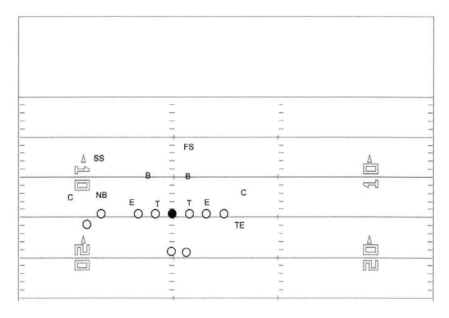

Prior to the snap, Ridley comes in jet motion toward the quarterback. As the play begins, Coker fakes a jet sweep to the receiver, then hands the football to Henry, who is aiming for the left edge on a lead zone design that calls for both Howard and Jackson to lead Henry to the outside:

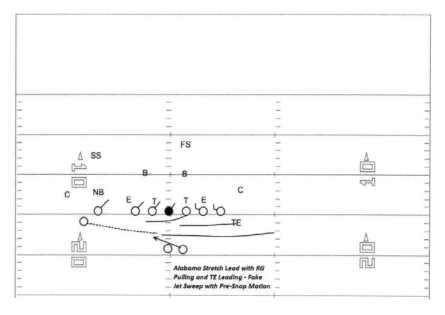

As these blocks unfold, the rest of the offensive line steps to the right at the snap, hoping to seal off backside pursuit angles.

The play works to perfection:

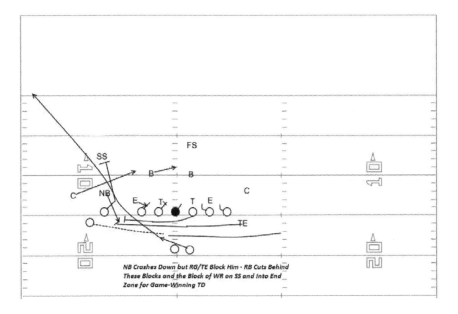

NB Crashes Down but RG/TE Block Him - RB Cuts Behind
These Blocks and the Block of WR on SS and Into End
Zone for Game-Winning TD

Foreman is the only defender who has a chance to stop this play, as the pre-snap motion from Ridley draws the attention of the defense. But the slot cornerback finds himself in the unenviable position of having both Jackson and Howard bearing down on him as he tries to disrupt the play. He is quickly erased to the turf, giving Henry the edge. Once the running back cuts upfield, he bounces to the outside and outruns the defense to the end zone.

The touchdown gave Alabama a 19-14 lead, and although the Crimson Tide failed the two-point conversion attempt, their defense held during the final drive to preserve the narrow victory. While the game was not pretty from an Alabama fan's perspective, when the offense needed to put together a championship drive, it responded. Sometimes the difference between winning and losing is simply execution.

CHAPTER NINE

NOTRE DAME STEALS A WIN IN PHILLY

History was made on Halloween night in 2015, when for the first time in school history, the Temple Owls played a football game in which both teams were nationally ranked. The Owls were 7-0 for the first time, and welcomed Notre Dame to Philadelphia in a primetime game. The hosts took a three-point lead with just less than 5 minutes remaining, and all that stood between them and the biggest victory in program history were quarterback DeShone Kizer and the Fighting Irish offense.

On first down, the Irish line up with Kizer (#14) in the shotgun and a personnel grouping that includes a running back, tight end, and three wide receivers on the field, set in a trips alignment on the right and a single receiver split to the left. The Owls set their 3-3-5 defense in a Cover 6 look, with all three linebackers stacked in the middle of the formation and the secondary showing a press cornerback over the single receiver aligned to the left:

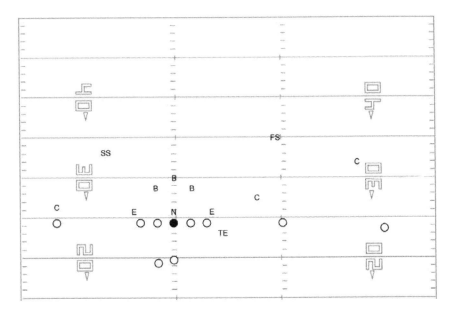

At the snap all three receivers on the right release vertically while Amir Carlisle (#3), the single receiver split to the left, runs a comeback route. The Owls rotate into a Tampa 2 scheme, with middle linebacker Michael Felton (#31) dropping into the intermediate middle zone, sending only three rushers after the quarterback:

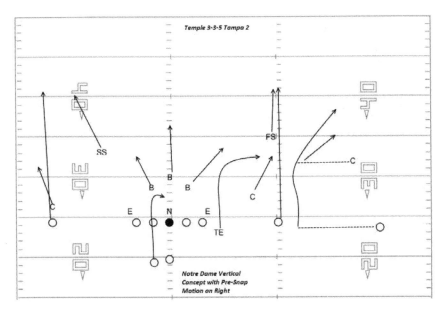

Kizer drops and scans the field, but with eight defenders in coverage there are no available options. He glides to his left attempting to buy time, before cutting upfield and sliding to the turf at the Notre Dame 31-yard line, for a gain of 6 yards.

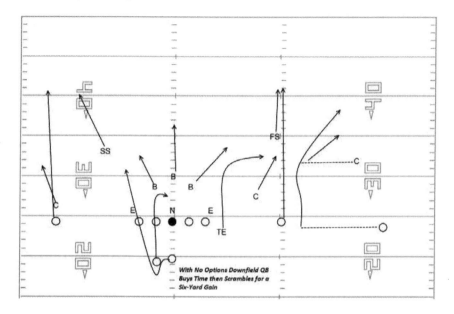

With No Options Downfield QB Buys Time then Scrambles for a Six-Yard Gain

On second down, both the Irish and the Owls keep the same personnel groups on the field. Notre Dame puts the quarterback in the shotgun with trips to the right and Carlisle again split to the left. Temple shows a slightly different look before the play with its 3-3-5 defense. The Owls put linebacker Jarred Alwan (#41) just outside the right defensive end, and they show Cover 1 in the secondary:

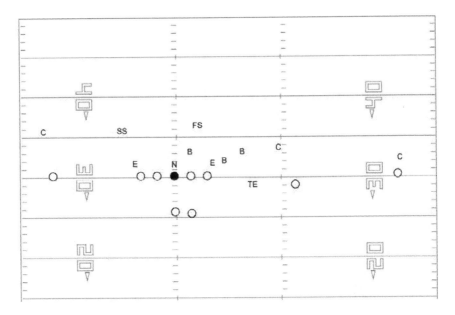

The defense drops into Cover 1 at the snap, but runs a cross stunt between Alwan and middle linebacker Tyler Matakevich (#8). The outside linebacker angles to the inside along with defensive end Nate D. Smith (#35) while the All-American linebacker, Matakevich, loops from the middle around the right tackle. While the Owls bring pressure, the Irish have a perfect play call, a running back screen:

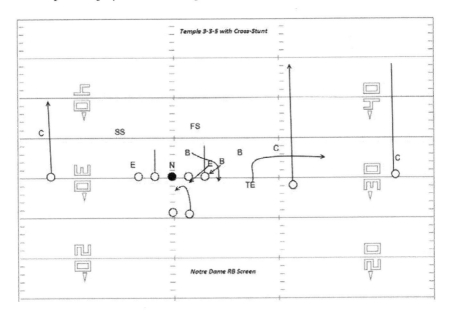

Both the left guard and right tackle are able to release into the secondary after the initial rush. The other blocker who tries to get downfield is right guard Steve Elmer (#79). At the snap he helps pass the nose tackle to the center, then tries to release. But he runs right into Smith, and the defensive end knocks the guard to the turf, directly in front of running back C.J. Prosise (#20). The running back has just hauled in the short toss from Kizer, but with Elmer crashing to the ground in front of him, Prosise is forced to try to loop around his fallen teammate. He can't, and Smith finishes off the impressive individual effort by grabbing onto Prosise and twisting the running back to the turf:

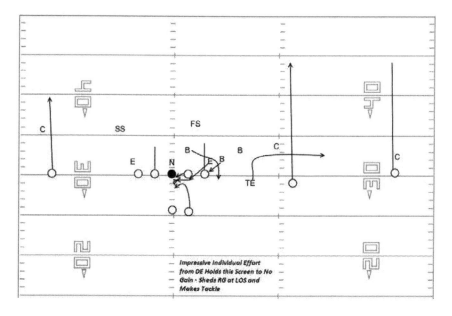

Impressive Individual Effort from DE Holds this Screen to No Gain · Sheds RB at LOS and Makes Tackle

The stop by the defensive end sets up a critical 3rd and 4 with less than four minutes remaining.

Needing a first down to keep the drive alive, Notre Dame puts Kizer in the shotgun with the same offensive personnel grouping on the field, again using trips to the right and a single receiver split to the left. Temple changes its defense, going with a 4-1-6 dime package, and showing Cover 2 man underneath in the secondary:

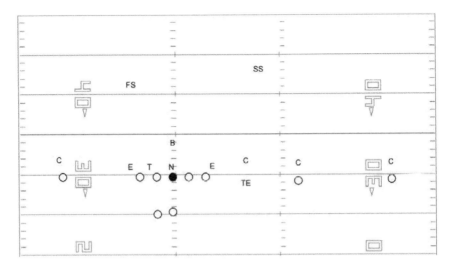

The Owls stay with Cover 2 man underneath, while the Irish use three routes that start to the inside from the trips side of the formation. Tight end Alizé Jones (#10) is the inside receiver and runs a deep slant route, while WR Torii Hunter Jr. (#16) runs a pivot route from the middle alignment and fellow receiver Will Fuller (#7) runs another slant from the outside:

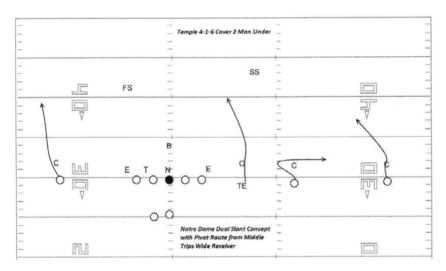

At the snap, the protection holds but the coverage on the three receivers is tight, with each defender establishing inside leverage to take away the in cuts from the trio of receivers. In an effort to buy time, Kizer slides back and to his right in the pocket, looking for a receiver to break open while scrambling. Finally, Fuller creates some daylight, with the wide receiver working back toward the sideline:

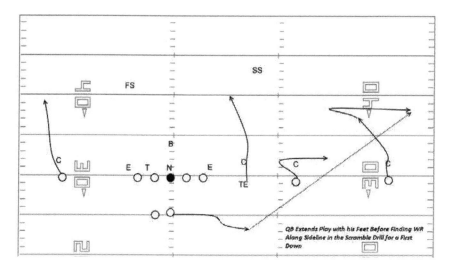

Kizer gets him the football angling to the outside, for a gain of 7 and a crucial conversion for the Irish.

Armed with a fresh set of downs, Notre Dame looks to push the football vertically on the next play from scrimmage. The Irish stay with the same 11 offensive personnel grouping, with Kizer remaining in the shotgun, now using trips to the left side of the formation. Temple lines up with its base 4-3, and shows Cover 1 before the snap:

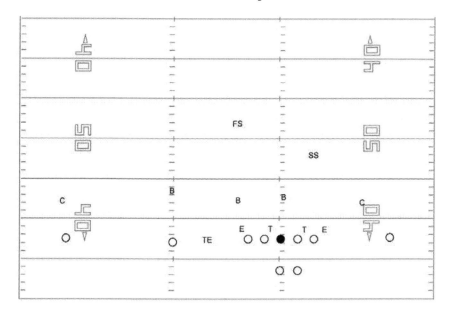

The Irish use a double-in design from the trips side, with both Fuller and Hunter Jr. running shallow dig routes while the tight end runs a deep corner route. The Owls blitz and roll their coverage to a Cover 3 matching concept:

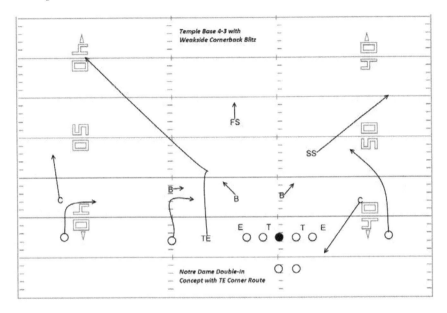

On the weak side, the cornerback blitzes while the strong safety rotates toward the sideline to cover the deep outside third. Over the trips formation, cornerback Tavon Young (#1) drops into the deep outside zone while linebacker Stephaun Marshall (#6), who begins this play lined up over the middle receiver, starts to cover that receiver in man coverage. But as the middle receiver moves to the inside, Marshall appears to try to pass him off to the inside linebacker and stick on Jones' corner route:

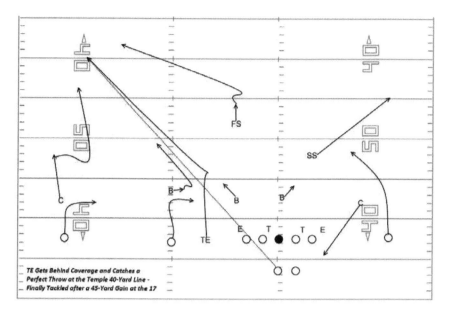

TE Gets Behind Coverage and Catches a
Perfect Throw at the Temple 40-Yard Line -
Finally Tackled after a 45-Yard Gain at the 17

However, Marshall sticks on the dig route a moment too long (as does Young along the outside), which opens up the deep outside area for Jones on the corner route. Kizer reads this play perfectly and with his tight end breaking free on the deep corner route, he drops in a perfect throw. Only free safety Nate L. Smith (#13) stands between Jones and a touchdown. The free safety makes the tackle, but not before a 45-yard gain. Smith drags the tight end to the ground at the Temple 17.

The Irish are now within field goal range, but they would rather not settle for a tie. They line up for this 1st and 10 play keeping the same personnel grouping, sending trips to the right and a single receiver split to the left. The Owls have their 4-3 defense in the game and show Cover 3 before the play, with the free safety shaded over the trips side of the offense:

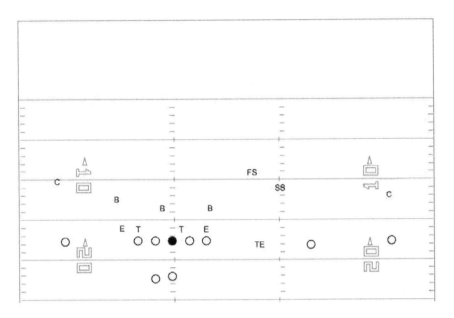

Notre Dame sends Kizer on a QB power draw to the right side:

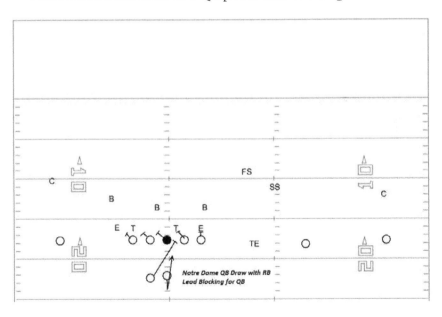

The only problem is, the middle linebacker is ready:

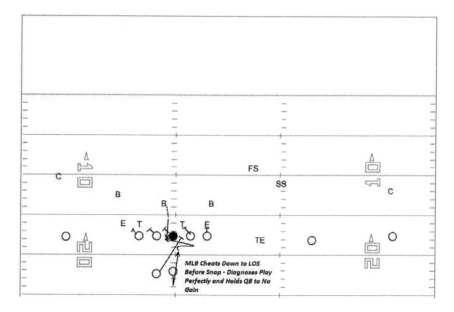

Matakevich reads this play beautifully, and as he sees the running back flow to the right to lead for Kizer, he scrapes down the line of scrimmage, keeping his eyes trained on the quarterback. When Kizer stops and tries to cut back against the grain, the LB mirrors him precisely and makes a solid open-field tackle, holding Kizer to no gain and setting the Irish up with second and long.

Despite the down and distance, Notre Dame cashes in. The offense lines up once more with a personnel grouping of one running back, one tight end, and three wide receivers but this time with trips to the right and Jones on the line of scrimmage next to the right tackle. Temple keeps its base 4-3 in the game, and slides Marshall to the outside between the tight end and the middle trips receiver:

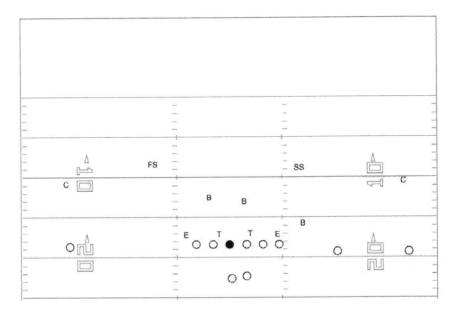

Before the snap the Owls show Cover 4, but as the play unfolds they rotate into Tampa 2, with Alwan opening his hips toward the trips and dropping into the intermediate middle zone:

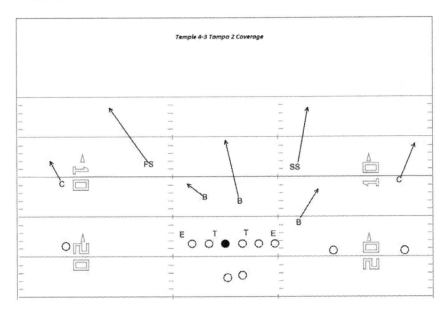

The Irish have the perfect play called to attack the coverage. They run Carlisle, the middle trips receiver, on a deep curl route. Meanwhile Chris

Brown (#2), the single receiver to the left, runs a vertical route, as does Fuller, the outside trips receiver:

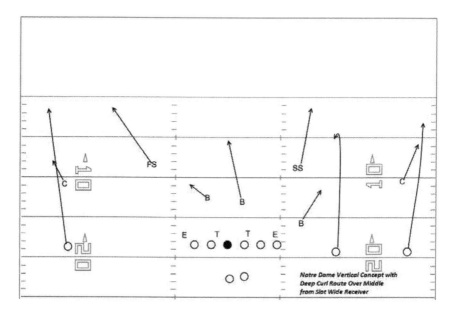

Notre Dame Vertical Concept with Deep Curl Route Over Middle from Slot Wide Receiver

This is a perfect design to attack Tampa 2. The linebacker drops into the middle zone, but the deep curl route from Carlisle is enough to put pressure on Will Hayes (#32), the playside safety, holding him in the middle of the field and preventing him from helping on the vertical route to the outside. Eventually the safety recognizes the threat to the sideline and tries to race over, but not before Kizer takes his shot:

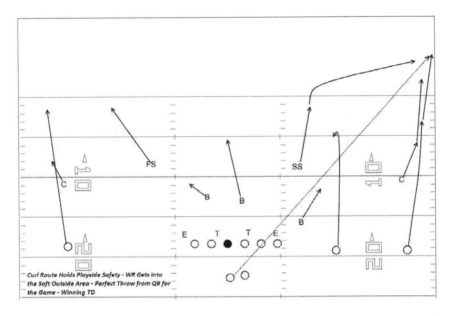

Curl Route Holds Playside Safety - WR Gets into the Soft Outside Area - Perfect Throw from QB for the Game - Winning TD

The quarterback throws a perfect strike to Fuller in the end zone, and the wide receiver hauls in the pass just as Hayes arrives. The safety cannot prevent the connection, and Fuller secures the catch and gets a foot down before falling out of bounds with the eventual game-winning score.

This play is an example of how an offense can attack Tampa 2 in the red zone, which is the primary zone concept that teams use in this area of the field. Using an inside vertical release to hold the playside safety, an offense can create an opportunity to attack that soft outside hole between the safety and cornerback. The timely play-call and precise execution added up to a big score – and win – for the Irish.

CHAPTER TEN

FLORIDA STATE AT CLEMSON FOR A DIVISION TITLE

When the calendar flipped to November, the Clemson Tigers found themselves the top-ranked team in the College Football Playoff poll, with a chance to secure a berth in the ACC Championship Game. Standing in the way of their Atlantic Division crown were the Florida State Seminoles, who entered the game in Death Valley ranked 16th in the nation and looking to improve their own standing in the national polls. While the Seminoles got off to a hot start, the hosts held a three-point lead in the fourth quarter when their defense stopped Florida State running back Dalvin Cook on a 4th and 1 play at the Clemson 40-yard line. This gave the Tigers the ball with just more than six minutes remaining, and a chance to clinch the division with their offense.

On first down, Clemson lines up with quarterback Deshaun Watson (#4) in the shotgun and a personnel group including a running back, tight end, and three wide receivers on the field, using slot formation to the right and with a single receiver split to the left. Running back Wayne Gallman (#9) is in the backfield to the staggered left and behind of the quarterback, while tight end Jordan Leggett (#16) lines up in front of the running back, behind the left B gap:

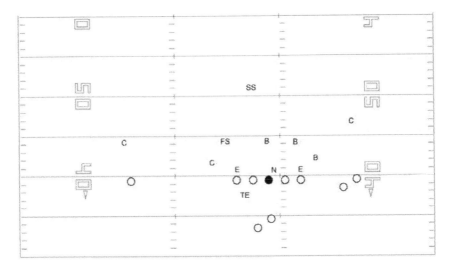

The Seminoles have a 3-3-5 defense in the game, and when slot receiver Artavis Scott (#3) starts in jet motion from the right, the defense slides two defensive backs, Javien Elliott (#14) and Derwin James (#3), down into the box in response:

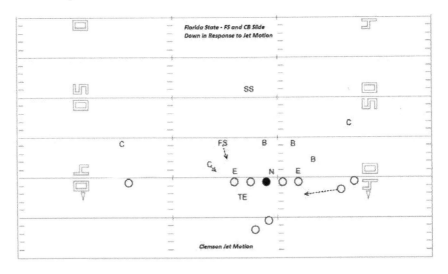

At the snap, Watson meets both Scott and Gallman at the mesh point, the point where the quarterback and running back meet with the ball. The quarterback fakes a handoff to the reciever on the jet sweep, then gives the ball to his running back on a power run aiming to the right side using this blocking scheme:

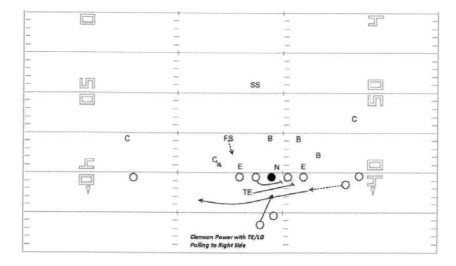

Clemson Power with TE/LG Pulling to Right Side

Left guard Eric Mac Lain (#78) pulls in front of Gallman, and the tight end leads as well, giving the running back two lead blockers. The running back follows right behind this two-man convoy, makes himself small through the hole and gets his shoulders turned upfield for a short 4-yard gain.

On second down, the Tigers stay with this personnel grouping and the same basic formation, this time setting up with slot alignment on the left side of the field. The Seminoles show a four-man front using 3-3-5 personnel, putting linebacker Jacob Pugh (#16) on the edge as a defensive end. They also place defensive back Lamarcus Brutus (#42) in a linebacker's alignment before the play:

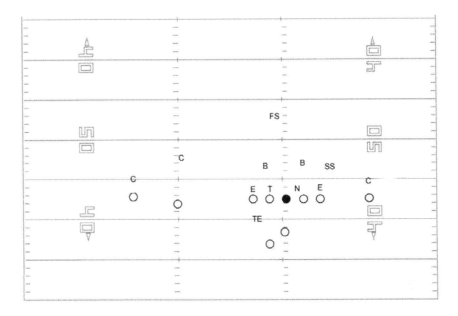

The offense uses a packaged play here, with Gallman and Watson meeting at the mesh point on a potential inside run. To the outside, slot receiver Hunter Renfrow (#13) shows a bubble screen look while Scott looks to block the cornerback:

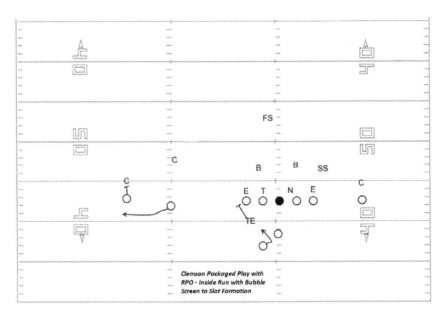

Clemson Packaged Play with RPO - Inside Run with Bubble Screen to Slot Formation

At the snap, Elliott, who begins the play over the slot receiver, breaks forward on the potential screen. Watson sees this and gives the ball to Gallman heading inside. There is just one problem for the offense: big defensive tackle Nile Lawrence-Stample (#99).

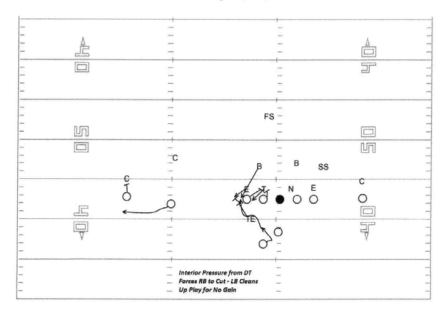

Left tackle Mitch Hyatt (#75) tries to block the big defensive tackle, but Lawrence-Stample does a tremendous job of standing up the left tackle at the point of attack, driving him back toward the ball-carrier. This forces Gallman to attempt to cut, giving linebacker Terrance Smith (#24) time to diagnose the play, flow to the football and stop the running back for no gain, setting up a huge third down play.

On this critical play, the Tigers set up with Watson in the shotgun with the same personnel grouping, but this time in dual slot formations. To the right Clemson has wide receiver Charone Peake (#19) on the outside, with Leggett in the slot. The Tigers have both Scott and Renfrow to the left in an inverted slot alignment, with Scott near the sideline. Backup running back Zac Brooks (#24) checks in for this snap and he starts to the right of Watson before shifting to the left of the quarterback. Florida State shows another four-man front on the defensive side of the ball with 3-3-5 personnel, and the secondary lines up in a Cover 2 scheme:

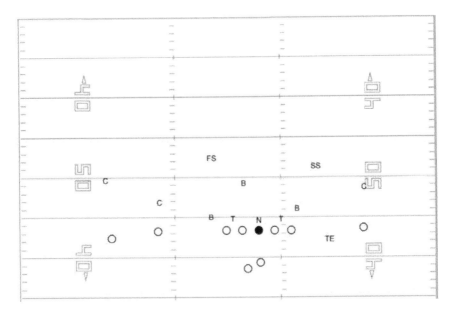

Clemson sets-up dual screens: A running back screen to the left, and a tunnel screen to Peake on the right:

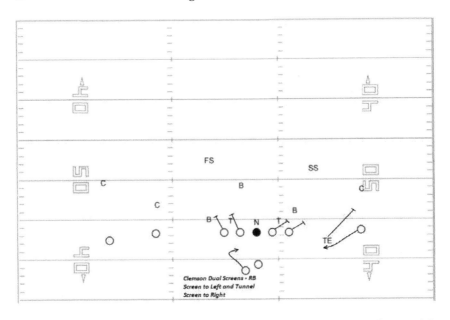

Watson throws to the right on the tunnel screen. Right guard Maverick Morris (#69) and center Jay Guillermo (#57) set up the convoy here, with both players leaving their positions quickly and racing downfield. Leggett flares out toward the sideline to block cornerback Jalen Ramsey (#8), who is lined up across from Peake at the snap. Pugh diagnoses the screen and flows to the football, but then meets a mountain of a man in the form of Morris. Peake takes the quick throw from Watson and cuts underneath these first two blocks, then follows Guillermo into the secondary:

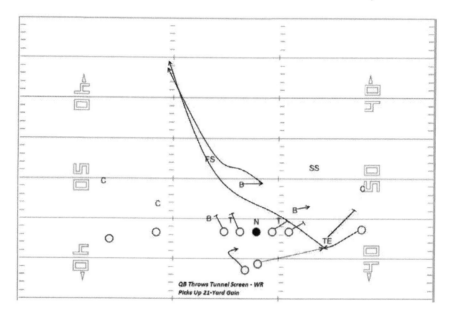

QB Throws Tunnel Screen - WR
Picks Up 21-Yard Gain

Smith finally chases this play down from behind, but not until Peake has earned a 21-yard gain. The running back is tackled at the Florida State 35-yard line, giving the Tigers not only a fresh set of downs, but a chance to perhaps ice the game with a score, or at least bleed the clock for another few minutes.

On the next play, the Tigers line up again with 11 offensive personnel on the field, this time in a trips look to the right with Leggett set as the inside receiver. Watson stands in the shotgun with Brooks to his right. The Seminoles stay with their 3-3-5 personnel, employing a four-man front and aligning in a Cover 2 look before the snap of the ball:

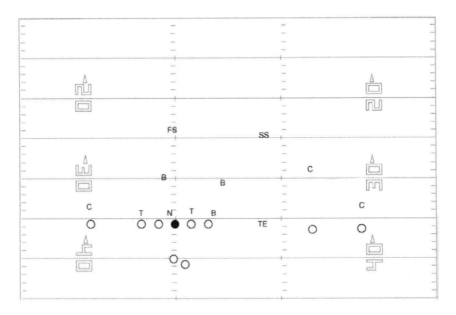

Clemson keeps it simple here, running a quarterback draw play with Brooks leading Watson through the right A gap:

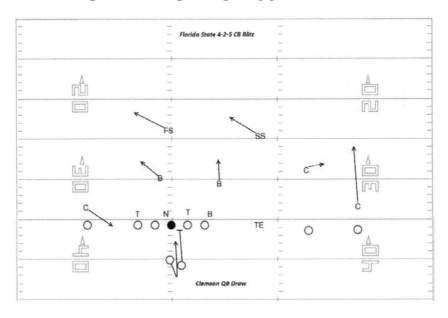

Watson sells this well, taking the snap and briefly dropping to pass while flashing a look toward the trips side of the field, before tucking the football and getting behind his lead blocker:

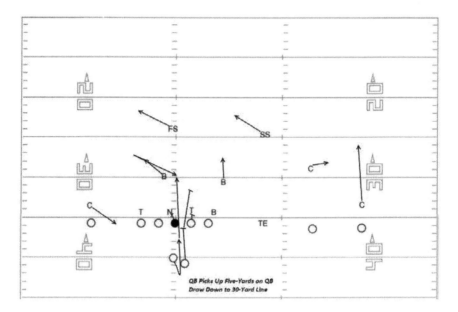

He picks up a quick 5 yards before he is tackled by Reggie Northrup (#5), putting the Tigers on the verge of field goal range while the seconds keep ticking away.

Facing a 2nd and 5, Clemson stays with its personnel grouping and puts Watson in the shotgun with Brooks to the right of the quarterback. Leggett lines up as an upback, right behind the B gap between the right tackle and the right guard. The Seminoles adjust to a 4-2-5 nickel, but now put Smith near the line of scrimmage just outside the left tackle:

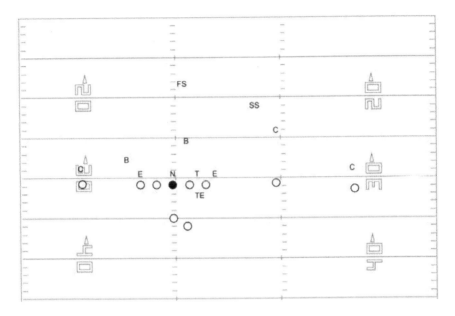

Clemson tries a sprint draw play here, with Watson taking the snap and rolling a few steps to his right to show the defense a potential rollout passing play. But Brooks stands his ground and waits for the quarterback to come to him, before taking the handoff and heading for the left edge:

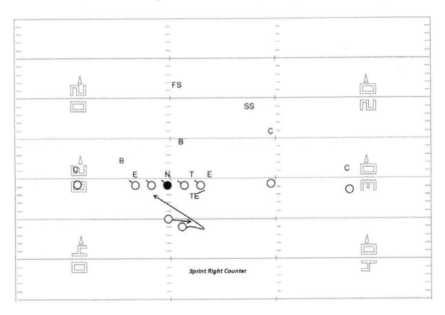

Sprint Right Counter

The entire line turns their hips toward the left sideline at the snap, with the left tackle and the left guard looking to block to the outside to create a crease behind them for Brooks. A hole is created, as Hyatt rides the blitzing Smith to the outside while Mac Lain handles the defensive tackle. But big nose tackle Derrick Nnadi (#91) is the disruptive force on this occasion. Off the snap he drives his arms into the chest of the center, shoving Guillermo back a few steps. Morris tries to come and help, but Nnadi splits between the center and right guard, and forces Brooks to make a cut 5 yards behind the line of scrimmage:

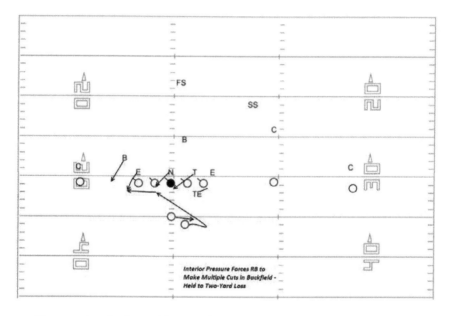

The running back avoids Nnadi, and then Lawrence-Stample, but not a third defender. Defensive end DeMarcus Walker (#44) cleans up the job, and drives Brooks to the turf for a loss of 2 yards. Not only does Clemson lose yardage here, but the Seminoles stop the clock with their first time out of the half.

Now the Tigers face a critical 3rd and 7, and with the clock stopped they need to make a play, otherwise Florida State might get the football with time and a chance to tie, or even take the lead. They set up for this huge play with Watson in the shotgun and a personnel group including a running back, tight end, and 3 wide receivers in a dual stack-slot formation. Renfrow is the receiver on the right side of the line of scrimmage, with Scott behind him, while Leggett is on the LOS on the left side, with Peake behind the tight end. Gallman has returned to the field, and stands to the right of the quarterback:

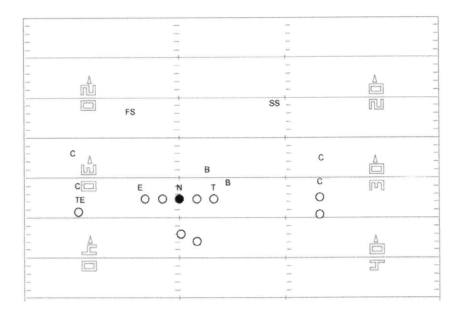

The Seminoles counter with a 3-2-6 sub package on the field, with Pugh on the line of scrimmage over the right tackle and Smith lurking behind the line. They have press cornerbacks over each outside receiver with a third cornerback using off-man technique on the two slot receivers.

Just prior to the snap, Gallman uses deep motion toward the right, causing Smith to slide to his left in response. As the play begins, Watson takes a few steps to his right, but then he snaps his head back toward Peake.

This is another screen:

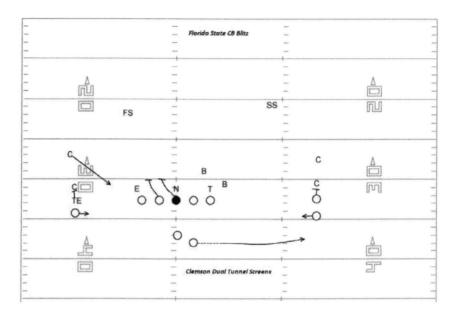

It is called at the perfect moment too. Ramsey, who begins the play over Leggett, executes a cornerback blitz off the edge, leaving only Nate Andrews (#29) in position over the stack-slot. The roll to the right by Watson gives him enough separation from the blitz, and he drops in the throw to Peake just over the leaping effort from the blitzing cornerback:

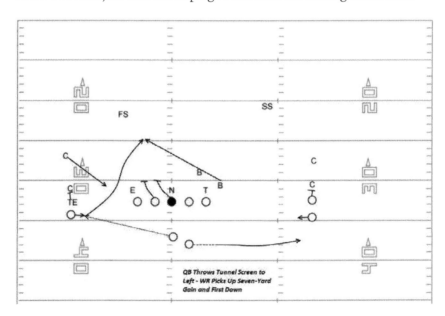

Peake hauls in the toss and cuts behind the block from Leggett on Andrews, as well as a convoy of Hyatt and Guillermo, and with Pugh draped around his back and shoulders, the receiver picks up just enough for the first down.

Armed with a fresh set of downs, the Tigers waste no time cashing in. They line up for the next play with a new personnel group of a running back, two tight ends, and two wide receivers, with Leggett on the left aligned next to the left tackle, and a tight end trips look on the right with reserve tight end Jay Jay McCullough (#89) next to the right tackle. The Seminoles adjust their defense, using a 3-3-5 grouping with Elliott down in the box over McCullough:

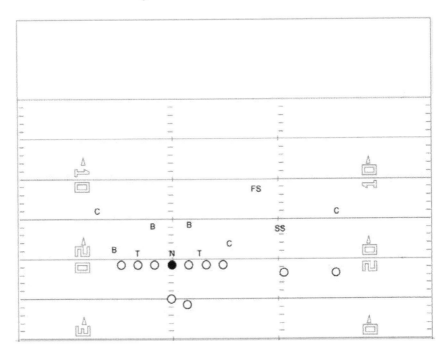

The Tigers run the outside zone play to the left, with Gallman taking the handoff and heading toward the outside:

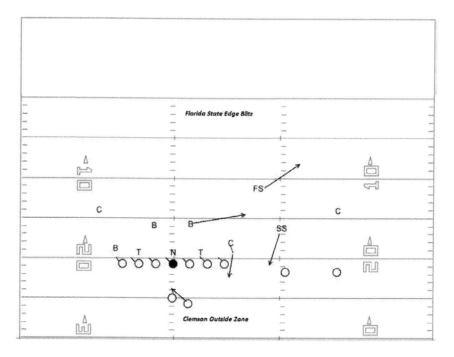

As he takes the handoff, Gallman notices that McCullough and company have created a huge hole backside. Coupled with the edge blitz from Elliott, this makes the running back choose to execute his bend read, cutting the run to the backside:

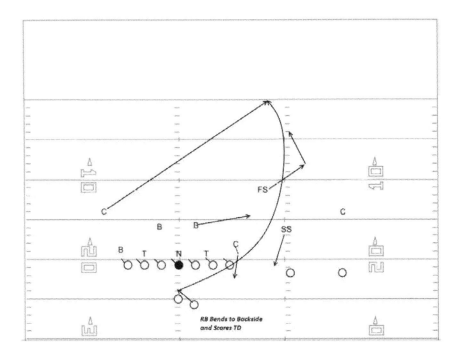

RB Bends to Backside
and Scores TD

Once Gallman gets to the second level, he faces two potential tacklers in the form of Smith, coming from his left, and James, angling toward him from the right. Using a burst of speed the running back charges ahead, and the two defenders are left colliding with each other in his wake. From there, Gallman puts a juke on Brutus in the open field, and then collides with Ramsey just before the goalline before crashing into the end zone with the game- and division-clinching, touchdown.

Championship teams make championship drives, and this is a perfect example of an offense doing just that. Twice during this drive the Tigers faced a make-or-break third down, and on each occasion their offense was able to convert, using a timely play-call, great blocking and execution, and tremendous effort from skill position players. Drives like this one, all season long, carried Clemson to its division title, the ACC Championship Game, and eventually the National Championship Game.

CHAPTER ELEVEN

OKLAHOMA SEALS IT LATE

In Week 11 of the 2015 college football season, the Oklahoma Sooners traveled to Waco, Texas, to take on the Baylor Bears, owners of the nation's longest home winning streak at 20 games. At this point in the season the Bears were the sixth-ranked team in the nation, and stood atop the Big 12 standings with a 5-0 conference record and an 8-0 record overall. The Sooners were nipping on their heels, entering the primetime contest with an 8-1 overall record, 5-1 in the Big 12.

In a physical contest described by ESPN's Kirk Herbstreit as a "battle of wills" the teams traded blows in the rain, leaving many players battered and bruised. The Baylor defense alone lost three starters to injury during the course of the game. But early in the fourth quarter the Bears capitalized on a short field. Backup quarterback Jarrett Stidham, starting in place of injured starter Seth Russell, connected with Jay Lee for a 17-yard touchdown pass to cut Oklahoma's lead to 37-34. The ensuing Sooners' possession changed the course of the Big 12 title race, and the national championship push.

After Alex Ross (#28) returned the kickoff to the 22-yard line, Oklahoma lines up with quarterback Baker Mayfield in the shotgun flanked by two running backs and with three wide receivers on the field. Joe Mixon (#25) stands to the right of Mayfield while Samaje Perine (#32) aligns to the left of the quarterback. The Sooners have their three receivers set in a slot to the left with wide receiver Sterling Shepard (#3) alone on the right. The Bears have their 4-2-5 package on the field and they show Cover 2 man underneath:

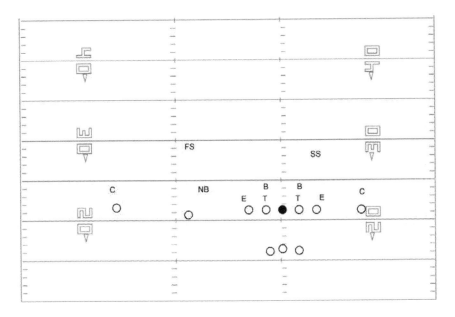

Oklahoma runs a lead outside zone play to the left, with the line flowing to that side of the field at the snap and Perine trying to escort Mixon around the left tackle to the outside:

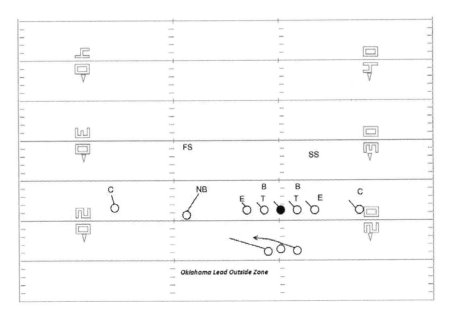

But the speed of the Bears' defense blows this play up before it gets going. At the snap defensive end Shawn Oakman (#2) beats left tackle

Orlando Brown (#78) and knifes into the backfield. The defensive end gets a hand on Mixon, but the running back escapes. Soon, though, the cavalry arrives:

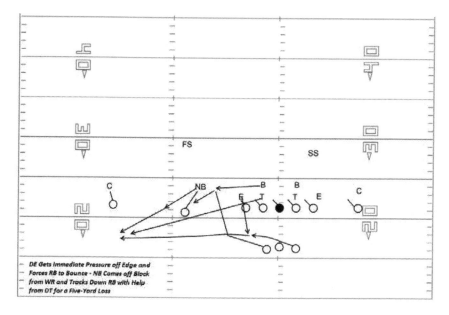

DE Gets Immediate Pressure off Edge and Forces RB to Bounce - NB Comes off Block from WR and Tracks Down RB with Help from DT for a Five-Yard Loss

Nickelback Travon Blanchard (#48) accelerates past the block attempt of slot receiver Durron Neal (#5) and is next to arrive, forcing Mixon to make another cut in the backfield. But his juke attempt fails, and Blanchard, along with defensive tackle Andrew Billings (#75) and linebacker Grant Campbell (#5) force the back to the ground for a 5-yard loss.

Facing 2nd and long, the Sooners set up in the same formation with the same personnel. Baylor keeps its 4-2-5 nickel in the game, and this time nickelback Blanchard aligns on the weak side of the formation, just off the line of scrimmage. Baylor stays with Cover 2 in the secondary:

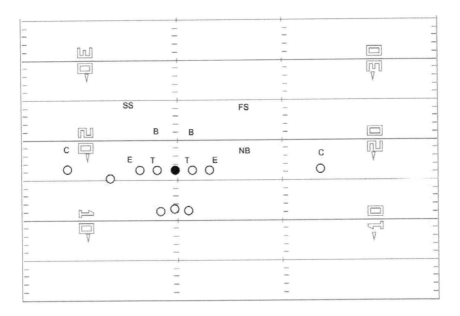

The Sooners use play-action, with Mayfield faking the handoff to Mixon aiming for the left edge. Perine crosses the formation to block, and after the fake the quarterback rolls to the right. Shepard runs a deep comeback route along the sideline while Neal runs a deep crossing route:

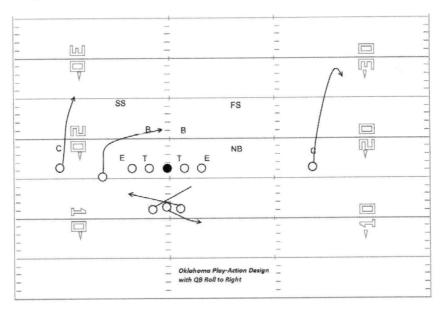

Oklahoma Play-Action Design
with QB Roll to Right

After the fake, Mayfield rolls to his right and scans the secondary. But there are no available options. He tries desperately to buy time and string this play out, hoping either Neal or Shepard can get separation from the coverage. Perine picks up a blitzing linebacker, but to the outside and coming off the edge is the nickleback. Blanchard explodes forward and tracks down the quarterback:

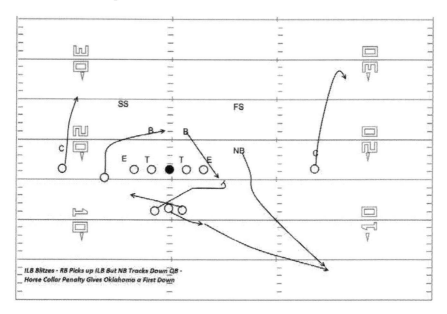

Mayfield waits as long as he can, but with the nickelback closing in on him he throws the ball away. Blanchard lunges forward for the attempted sack, grasps the back of Mayfield's jersey, and the two players crash down on the turf.

Cue the flag.

Blanchard is flagged for a personal foul (horse collar tackle). The 15-yard penalty advances the football to the Oklahoma 32-yard line, and gives the visitors a fresh set of downs.

On the ensuing play, the Sooners adjust personnel and bring on a fourth wide receiver in place of Perine. They line up with Mayfield in the shotgun with Mixon to his right and the receivers aligned in dual slot formations. Baylor adjusts in response, lining up with a 3-3-5 nickel defense but staying with Cover 2 man underneath in the secondary:

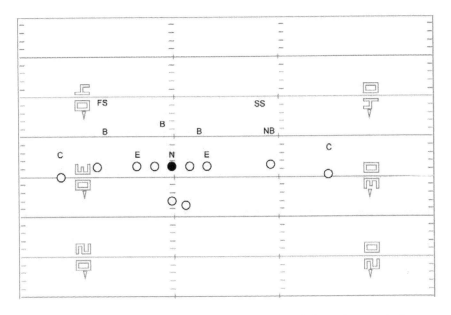

The offense runs two slant patterns from the left, and a vertical route from Neal on the outside to the right. Shepard runs a quick curl from the slot on the right, and Mixon releases from the backfield vertically down the seam:

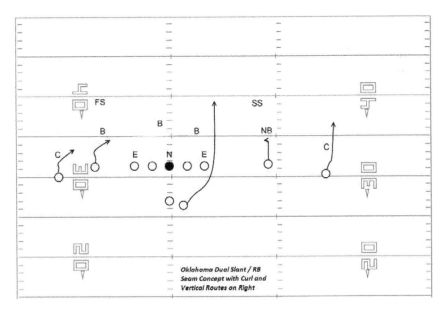

Oklahoma Dual Slant / RB
Seam Concept with Curl and
Vertical Routes on Right

As the play develops, Mayfield first looks to hit Dede Westbrook (#11) on the inside seam from the left. But with this option covered, he is forced to tuck the football and escape the pocket to his left:

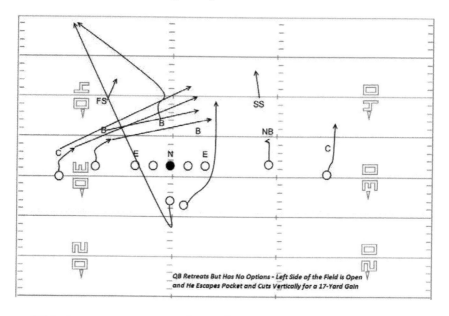

QB Retreats But Has No Options - Left Side of the Field is Open and He Escapes Pocket and Cuts Vertically for a 17-Yard Gain

With the man coverage, and two slant routes coming from the left, this side of the field is open for the QB to exploit. Mayfield picks up 17 yards before linebacker Taylor Young (#1) bangs him to the turf. The quarterback lands hard on his right arm and gets up in visible pain, but for his effort his offense has another first down.

Facing 1st and 10 on their own-49 yard line, the Sooners line up with the same personnel grouping again, with Perine standing in the backfield with the quarterback. Oklahoma lines up in a 2x2 formation once more, with slot formation on the left and an inverted slot alignment to the right. Baylor stays with its 3-3-5 personnel, walking Young down to the line of scrimmage just outside the left tackle:

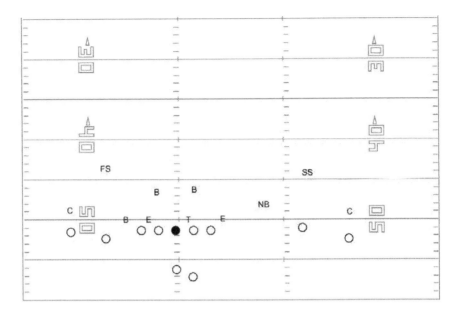

The Sooners run the ball, with both Brown and left guard Jonathan Alvarez (#68) pulling in front of Perine, who takes the handoff after meeting the quarterback at the mesh point. Mayfield reads the defensive end to decide whether to keep the football or give to his running back:

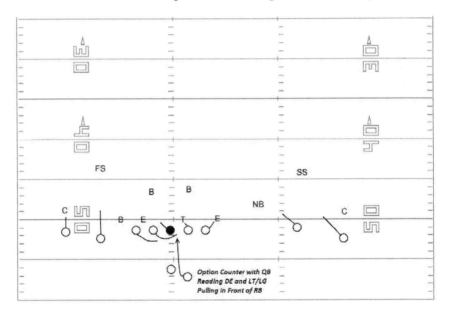

Two defenders excel on this snap. Defensive end Jamal Palmer (#92)

performs a well-timed and well-executed swim move on right tackle Dru Samia (#75) off the ball. This gets the defensive end into the backfield just as Perine takes the handoff. Campbell expertly diagnoses this play, and explodes forward into the hole. The LB meets Alvarez and drives the LG back a few steps, clogging Perine's intended lane. Palmer, after his swim move, scrapes down the line and lunges for the RB's ankles:

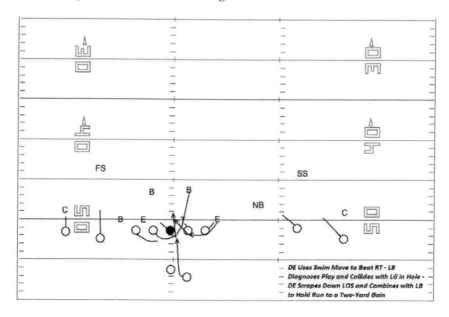

The defensive end grabs Perine's legs, and after contact with Alvarez, Campbell disengages and helps Palmer finish off the tackle, holding the running back to a 2-yard gain.

On second down the Sooners head right to the line of scrimmage, as the clock ticks under 9 minutes to play. They set up with Mayfield again in the shotgun and a personnel grouping of one running back and four wide receivers. Mixon checks into the game, stands to the left of the quarterback in the backfield as the receivers align in dual slot formations, using an inverted alignment on each side of the field. Baylor 3-3-5 defense remains on the field, showing Cover 2 once more:

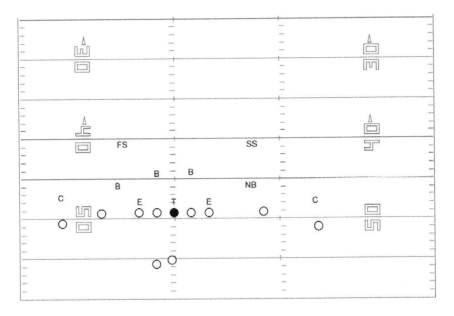

Oklahoma uses a three-curl concept working off play-action. Mayfield fakes a handoff to Mixon on another counter design, then drops to throw:

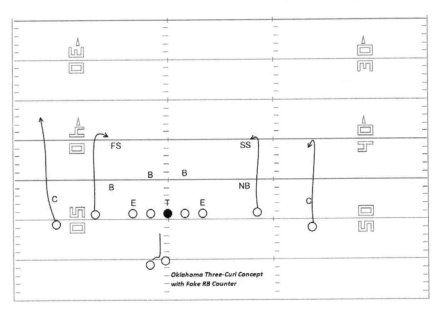

Oklahoma Three-Curl Concept with Fake RB Counter

As Mayfield retreats into the pocket the zone coverage brackets each receiving option. He tries to buy time with his feet vacating the pocket to his left, and spots Westbrook working back toward the sideline underneath:

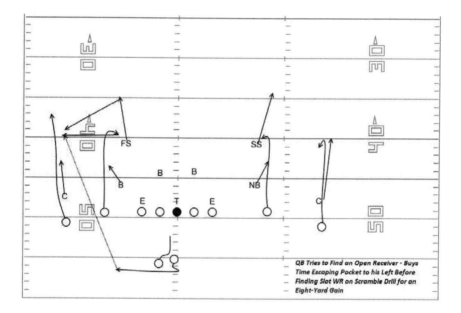

QB Tries to Find an Open Receiver - Buys Time Escaping Pocket to his Left Before Finding Slot WR on Scramble Drill for an Eight-Yard Gain

The receiver sees his quarterback trying to extend the play, so he breaks to the outside on the scramble drill. Mayfield makes a strong throw while moving to his left, and the football arrives just before the coverage. Westbrook cradles the throw while sliding to the turf, picking up 8 yards and a first down for his offense.

Oklahoma lines up for the next snap with a different look offensively. H-Back Dimitri Flowers (#36) comes onto the field and sets up in a tight end's alignment to the left, with Westbrook set as a flanker to that side. Shepard and Neal align in an inverted slot to the right, with Shepard on the inside. Mayfield stands in the shotgun with Perine just to his right. The Bears stay with their 3-3-5 alignment, walking Young down to the line of scrimmage across from Flowers:

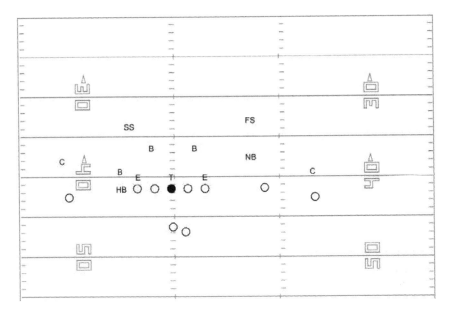

The Sooners return to the option / counter design used earlier in the drive, with Brown and Alvarez pulling in front of the running back. At the snap Perine shuffles a few steps to his left, then meets Mayfield at the mesh point and bursts forward, aiming for the right A gap:

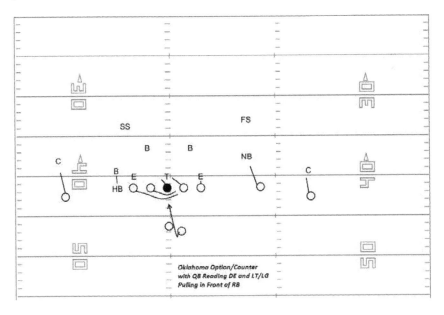

As the play begins, Samia executes a great block on the right end.

Working against backup defensive end K.J. Smith (#56), the freshman right tackle gets a good initial punch before the defensive end tries to bend to the outside, but Samia maintains contact with Smith and keeps him away from the ball carrier. The two inside linebackers, Campbell and Aiavion Edwards (#20), identify the play and push forward, but both Brown and Alvarez win their blocking assignments:

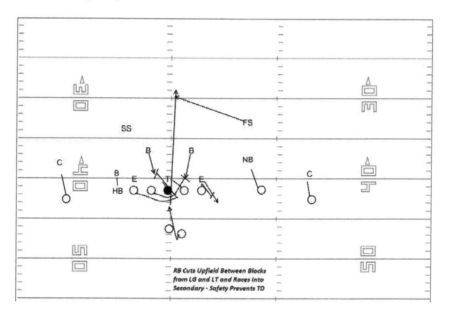

Perine cuts between these two pulling blockers and bursts into the Baylor secondary. Safety Terrence Singleton (#24) rushes forward to meet the threat, and grabs enough of the RB's legs to prevent a huge run. Perine drags the backup safety a few yards before falling to the turf with a 12-yard gain. This play was extremely close to finding the end zone for the offense, thanks to the perfect blocking execution.

On the next snap, Oklahoma tries another running play. The Sooners align with the same personnel and formation as on the previous play. Baylor stays with its 3-3-5 defense, but puts both Young and Blanchard at the line of scrimmage, with the linebacker over Flowers and the defensive back just outside the right tackle:

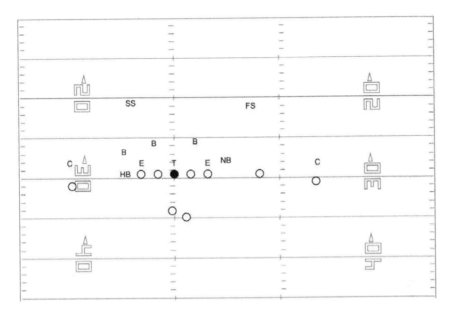

For the third time in the drive, the Sooners run their option counter with Brown and Alvarez pulling to the right in front of Perine:

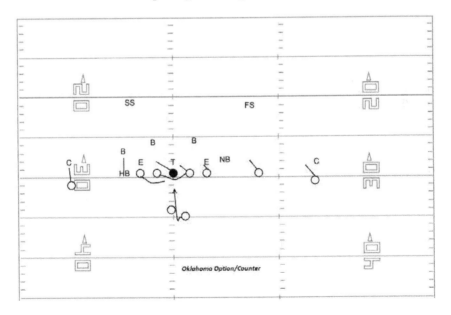

Oklahoma Option/Counter

The blocking scheme is a bit different on this play. While the left tackle and left guard pull to the right, the right tackle blocks down rather than to the outside. As Samia blocks to the inside, Blanchard explodes forward and his quick penetration forces Alvarez to block the defensive back. This leaves Brown to confront the two inside linebackers, Campbell and Edwards:

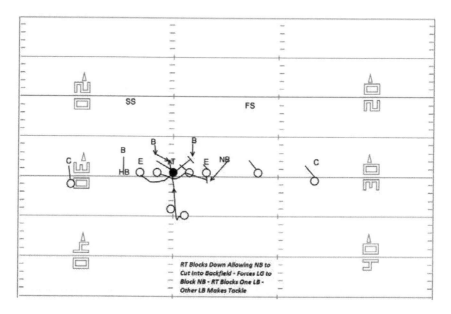

The left tackle chooses to block Campbell, leaving the other linebacker free to thump Perine down to the turf after just a 1-yard gain.

After successive running plays, Oklahoma returns to the air on second down. The Sooners line up with one running back and no tight end on the field, the four receivers set up in dual slot formations. On the right, Shepard is on the inside of the inverted slot with Neal on the outside. The Bears keep their 3-3-5 nickel defense on the field, and once more put both the nickelback and the third linebacker on the edge, giving Baylor a five-man front. The Bears show a Cover 2 look in the secondary, as they have throughout the drive:

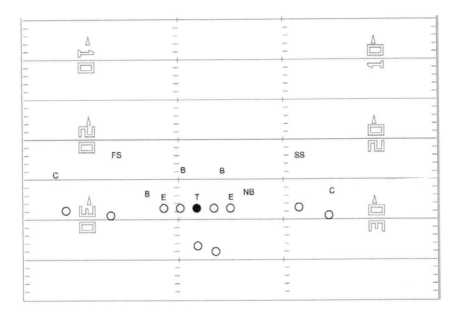

The Sooners run dual slant patterns on the left side of the field. To the right, they implement a variation of the smash concept. Neal runs a quick in route from the outside, while Shepard runs the corner route:

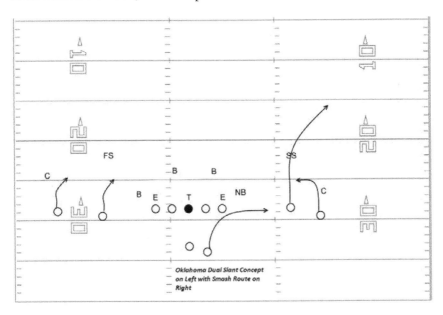

Oklahoma Dual Slant Concept on Left with Smash Route on Right

Standing across from the slot receiver, around 8 yards off the football, is Singleton, the safety. He was listed as the third-string safety on the depth chart, but was pressed into action because of injuries suffered during this physical game. This fact rears its head here, as Mayfield spots his favorite target isolated on a backup:

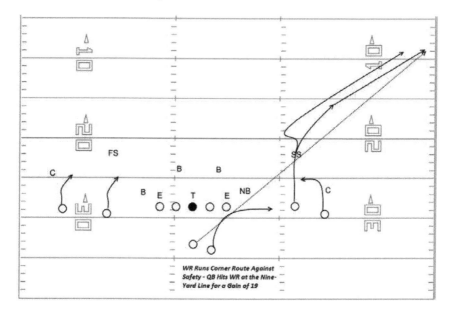

WR Runs Corner Route Against Safety - QB Hits WR at the Nine-Yard Line for a Gain of 19

Shepard releases vertically, and at the top of his stem he plants his inside foot hard to the middle of the field and then drives himself to the outside on his corner route. Singleton backpedals as the play begins, and when the receiver makes his cut the safety takes a single step inside. This allows Shepard to gain separation as he accelerates to the outside. Mayfield drops in a perfect throw, the wide receiver hauls in the pass and is banged out of bounds by the reserve safety at the Baylor 9.

The big gain gives Oklahoma the football inside the Baylor 10, but the Sooners don't stay there for long. The Sooners line up for the next play but Mayfield fails to notice the play clock winding down. Head coach Bob Stoops tries to call a timeout before the play clock falls to zero, but fails. This leaves Stoops visibly irate on the sideline, although it is unclear who is the focus of his ire: His quarterback, the officials or himself.

Now facing 1st and goal at the Baylor 14-yard line, the offense lines up with two running backs and three wide receivers in the game. Mayfield is flanked in the backfield by his two running backs, with Perine to his left and Mixon on the right. Neal and Westbrook align in a slot to the left and Shepard splits to the right by himself. The Bears stay with their 3-3-5 defense. They put the linebacker, Young, on the edge outside the right tackle, and Blanchard is on the line of scrimmage, splitting the difference between Neal and the left tackle:

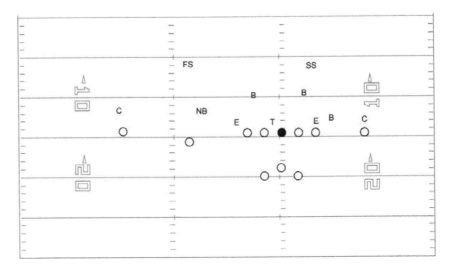

Prior to the play, Mayfield sends Mixon in deep motion to the left. At the snap Perine and Mayfield meet with the quarterback reading the defensive end, all while the offense sets up a swing screen to Mixon, with the receivers looking to clear a path. Westbrook releases vertically to run off the playside CB, while Neal looks to block Blanchard:

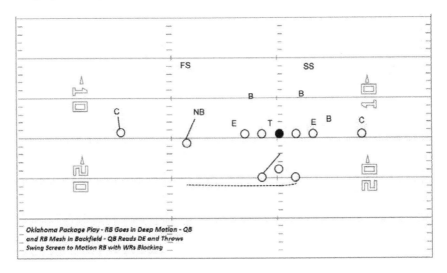

The nickelback does a tremendous job on this play, as he identifies the swing screen and works toward the sideline to set the edge, all while Neal is draped on his inside shoulder. Blanchard sets the edge, and forces Mixon to try make a move:

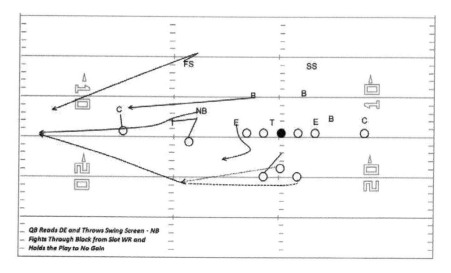

QB Reads DE and Throws Swing Screen - NB
Fights Through Block from Slot WR and
Holds the Play to No Gain

The back tries to fake to the inside before cutting back along the sideline, but even with Neal clinging to him Blanchard doesn't fall for the fake. He maintains his leverage and when Mixon angles to the outside, Blanchard knocks the running back out of bounds, holding him to no gain on the play.

As the Sooners lined up for the next play, Herbstreit observed from the booth that "the next two or three plays are vitally important." Oklahoma sends Perine to the sideline and brings on a fourth wide receiver, Jarvis Baxter (#1). The offense sets with a 2x2 formation, using an inverted slot to each side of the field. Mayfield stands in the gun with Mixon to his right. The Bears stay with their 3-3-5 defense, but soften a bit up front with both Young and Blanchard off the ball, while staying with their two-high safety look:

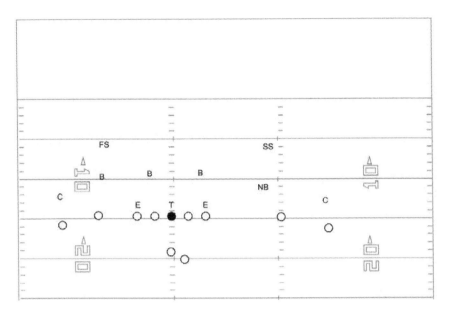

The Sooners look to throw the ball off of a play-action fake. Mayfield and Mixon mesh in the backfield with the running back aiming to the left, while the offensive line flows to the left as well simulating an outside zone run. After the fake, Mayfield rolls to the right, with Baxter and Westbrook running matching slant patterns from the left. To the other side Oklahoma uses a two-man sail concept, with Shepard running an out while Neal releases vertically:

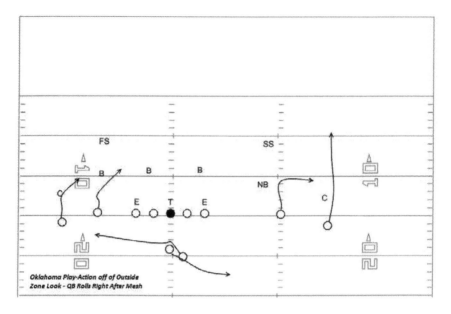

Oklahoma Play-Action off of Outside Zone Look - QB Rolls Right After Mesh

As Mayfield rolls, the coverage on Neal and Shepard is lock solid. He quickly makes the decision to tuck the football, and picks up blocks from both Shepard and Westbrook. The quarterback is knocked out of bounds after a gain of 7 yards down to the Baylor 7-yard line, setting up a pivotal 3rd and goal.

The Sooners line up for the next play, but once more Mayfield fails to notice the play clock running down. They are forced to burn their second timeout of the half, Stoops this time getting the call signaled to the officials just in time.

When play resumes, the Sooners line up with some personnel adjustments. Flowers returns to the game, and is in a wing on the right side with Shepard and Neal to the outside of him. Reserve tight end Mark Andrews (#81) is split to the left as the single receiver. Mayfield stands in the shotgun with Perine to his right. Baylor sticks with its 3-3-5 defense, with Young across from Shepard and Blanchard just off the line of scrimmage and outside the left tackle:

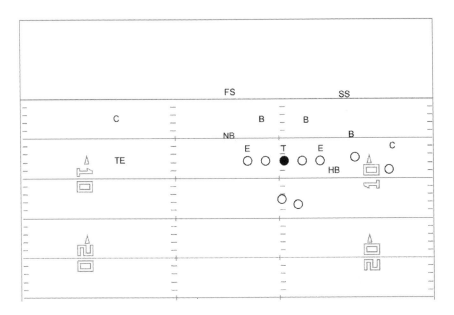

After the snap Mayfield and Perine mesh in the backfield, with the back continuing to the left while Mayfield keeps the football and looks to throw. Andrews runs a slant pattern from the left, Neal runs a quick in route from the right, and Shepard breaks to the corner on his pattern:

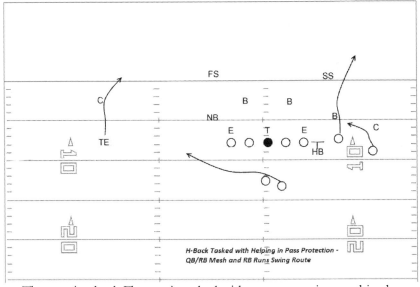

H-Back Tasked with Helping in Pass Protection - QB/RB Mesh and RB Runs Swing Route

The running back Flowers is tasked with pass protection on this play. As Mayfield drops, the coverage is stout in the secondary. Mayfield reads his progressions from right to left, and when the clock in his head goes off, he knows he has to buy time with his feet. He starts to climb the pocket, but then retreats and takes a few steps to his left. Seeing big defensive end Oakman start to come off a block, Mayfield reverses field and races toward the right sideline, with both Billings and Edwards chasing after him. Channeling his inner Joe Montana, the quarterback buys enough room for his throw by driving backward into the air as he makes his late throw. His target? Flowers.

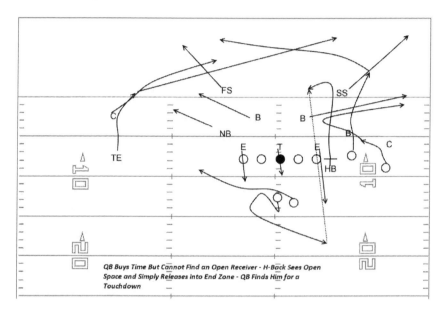

QB Buys Time But Cannot Find an Open Receiver - H-Back Sees Open Space and Simply Releases Into End Zone - QB Finds Him for a Touchdown

As the play goes on and receivers begin to fly around the end zone in the scramble drill, the blocking back finds himself alone in a small area of the end zone unoccupied. He has the presence of mind to release and sit down, where Mayfield spots him. The throw and catch give the Sooners a much-needed touchdown, with just under 5 minutes left in the game.

After kicking off with a 44-34 lead, Oklahoma sealed its huge road victory with an interception on the next play from scrimmage, allowing the Sooners to run the clock out with another long drive. The win not only ended Baylor's home winning streak, but vaulted the Sooners atop the Big 12 standings and well into the mix for the College Football Playoff discussion. As we have already highlighted, this was one more long, crucial drive that the Sooners executed in a key spot during 2015, and their ability to execute in key moments was a huge part of their success this season.

CHAPTER TWELVE

IOWA BUILDS THE LEAD OVER PURDUE

Iowa entered its home finale against Purdue with a chance to clinch the Big Ten West Division and ensure a berth in the Big Ten Championship Game. In front of a 62,920 fans the Hawkeyes rode an early outburst to a 40-20 victory over the Boilermakers. This five-play touchdown drive that began late in the first quarter established the tone for the afternoon.

After the Iowa defense forced and recovered a Purdue fumble, the offense takes over on its own 48-yard line with the football on the right hashmark. Quarterback C.J Beathard (#16) lines up in the shotgun and the Hawkeyes empty the backfield, with trips to the left and an inverted slot formation to the right. The Boilermakers have a 4-2-5 nickel package in the game, and they show zero, or all out, blitz before the snap, with both linebackers on the line of scrimmage in blitz posture and the secondary in man coverage across the formation:

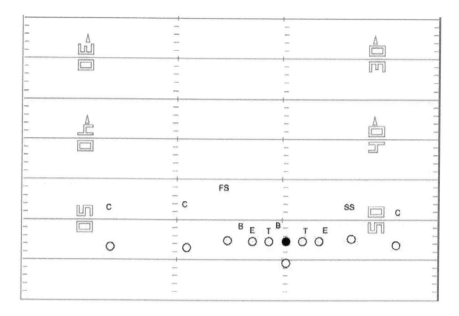

Iowa shows a bubble screen look to each side of the field:

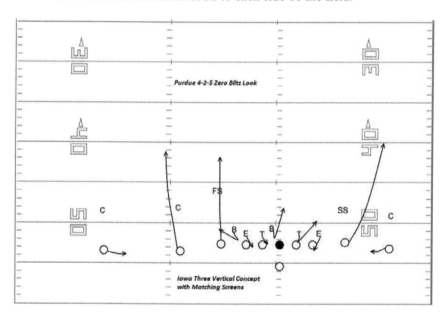

To the trips side of the formation, the outside receiver takes a few steps toward the quarterback on the bubble screen while the other two players release vertically. This action is utilized on the other side of the formation as well, where wide receiver Jacob Hillyer (#17) bends toward the middle of the field on the screen look, while fellow WR Tevaun Smith (#4) angles to the outside and then vertically on a wheel route from the slot. Purdue fakes the blitz, dropping three front defenders into underneath zones, but staying in man coverage in the secondary with safety Robert Gregory (#7) matched up on Smith in the slot. The receiver gets enough of a step on Gregory that Beathard takes a chance on the vertical route:

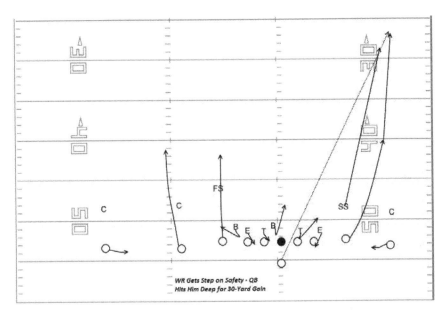

Smith twists his body back toward the sideline to reel in the pass for a 30-yard gain, giving the offense a fresh set of downs just outside the red zone.

On the second play of the drive, Iowa turns to its ground game – a staple of its offense in the 2015 season. Beathard lines up under center with two running backs, two tight ends, and a wide receiver on the field, with an i-formation behind the quarterback and a tight i-left formation. Purdue has its base 4-3 defense on the field, and the Boilermakers put strongside linebacker Andy James Garcia (#42) down on the line of scrimmage with strong safety Leroy Clark (#3) next to him, giving the defense eight defenders in the box:

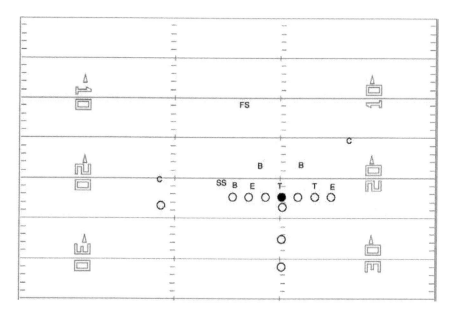

The Hawkeyes run an outside zone running play, with running back Jordan Canzeri (#33) heading for the right side led by fullback Adam Cox (#38). The offensive linemen all fire out to the right in unison:

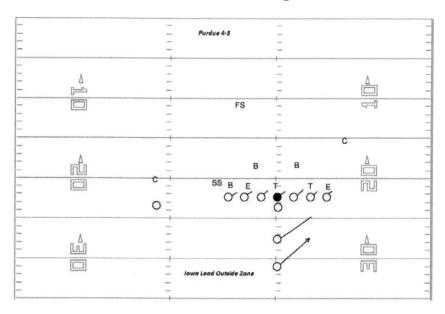

The play works to perfection. Tight end George Kittle (#46) starts the play with an excellent block on playside defensive end Gelen Robinson

(#13) while right tackle Cole Croston (#64) and right guard Jordan Walsh (#65) execute a combination block on the playside defensive tackle. This opens up a big running lane through the C gap, and Cox and Canzeri trail right through this alley:

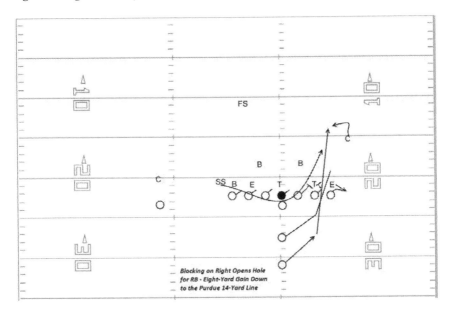

Clark chases this play down from the backside and gets a hold of Canzeri's ankles, and playside cornerback Anthony Brown (#9) wraps up the ballcarrier, but not until the running back rips off a quick 8-yard gain, giving Iowa a 2nd and 2 inside the red zone as the first quarter ends.

Run it until they stop it.

On the first play of the second quarter, Iowa lines up in the same formation as the previous play, with Beathard under center and Cox and Canzeri in an i-formation with the same personnel on the field. The Boilermakers adjust to a 4-4 defense, but this time bring a ninth defender into the box, anticipating run on this 2nd and 2 play:

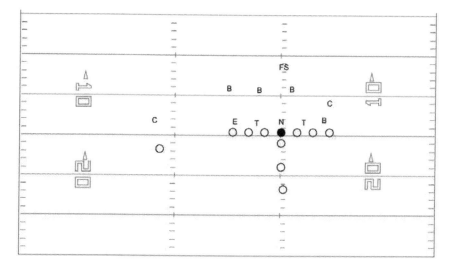

Iowa does run the ball, this time to the left on the outside zone:

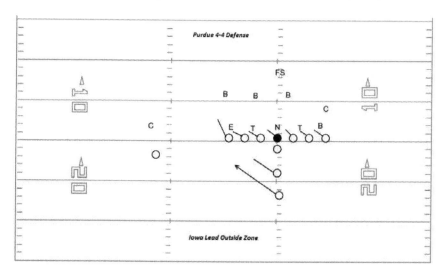

Three critical blocks allow this play to succeed. Tight end Henry Krieger Coble (#80) has a defensive end aligned across from him, but he ignores the defensive end at the snap and works immediately to the second level, to block outside linebacker Garcia. This leaves left tackle Boone Myers (#52) responsible for the playside DE, Robinson. Myers flows to the left at the snap, and when the defensive end angles to the inside, the left tackle quickly recognizes the movement from the defensive end and turns his hips back toward the middle of the field to pick up Robinson. Not to be outdone, Cox executes the third big block on the play, on middle linebacker Garrett

Hudson (#16). The middle linebacker identifies the play and scrapes to the hole, but the fullback neutralizes the threat in front of Canzeri:

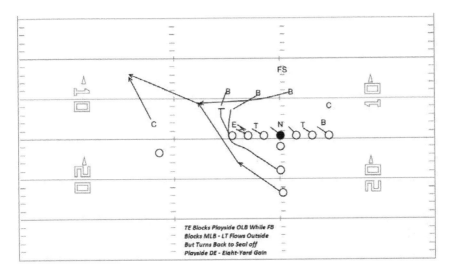

With the edge sealed, the running back gets into the secondary with the help of a strong stiff arm on weakside linebacker Danny Ezechukwu (#36) before Garcia and Ezechukwu are finally able to drag him down after a 7-yard gain.

Now facing 1st and goal at the 7, Canzeri checks out for a breather and is replaced by fellow running back LeShun Daniels Jr. (#29). Beathard remains under center with the same personnel personnel grouping in the game, in another tight i-formation, this time with the flanker split to the right side of the field. The Boilermakers adjust and bring on a 5-3 defense, and crowd the box with nine defenders once more:

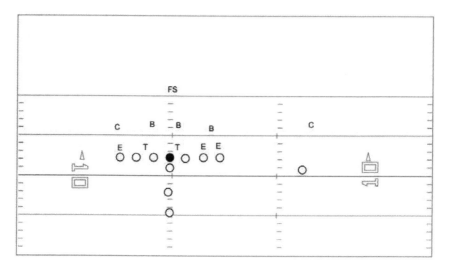

Having gained 15 yards on successive outside zone running plays, it's no surprise that Iowa runs it for a third consecutive play.

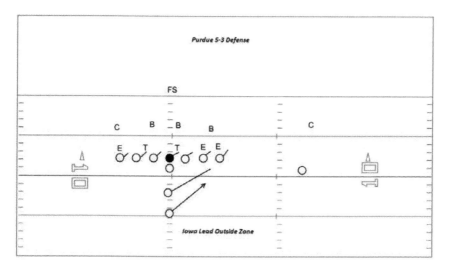

Only this time, the defense is ready. Purdue gets good interior pressure at the point of attack, with defensive end Evan Panfil (#95) able to attack the playside A gap. As the play flows to the right, Hudson again meets Cox in the hole, but this time it pays off as the cavalry is coming behind the MLB, in the form of defensive tackle Jake Replogle (#54):

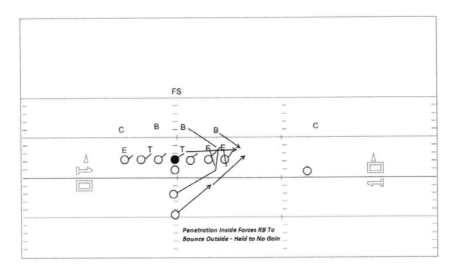

Penetration Inside Forces RB To
Bounce Outside - Held to No Gain

The defensive tackle and linebacker combine to hold Daniels to no gain.

On second down, the Hawkeyes return to the air. They put Beathard in the shotgun with a running back, a tight end, and three wide receivers on the field. Canzeri is in the backfield to the right of the quarterback. Smith is the single receiver to the right and shows a trips formation on the left with Hillyer and Krieger Coble on the outside of wide receiver Matt VandeBerg (#89). The Boilermakers revert to their base 4-3 because of the shift in offensive personnel, and slide Garcia to the outside over the tight end in the trips alignment, and bring Gregory down into the box lined up as a linebacker to the weak side of the offensive formation:

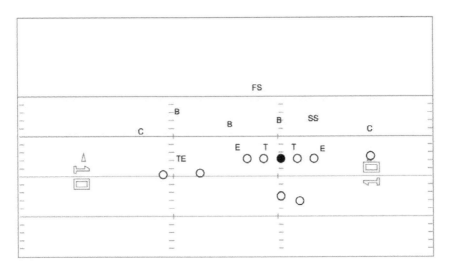

With only two defenders lined up over the trips, Beathard plays the numbers advantage and throws a swing screen to VandeBerg on the outside:

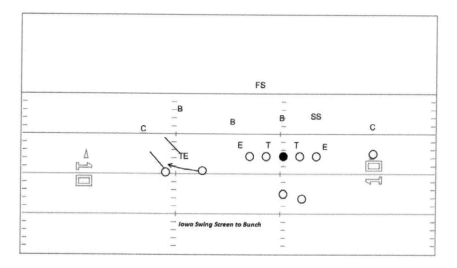

The play works as designed. The trio of receivers flow toward the sideline, with the tight end blocking the linebacker while Hillyer locks up cornerback Frankie Williams (#24):

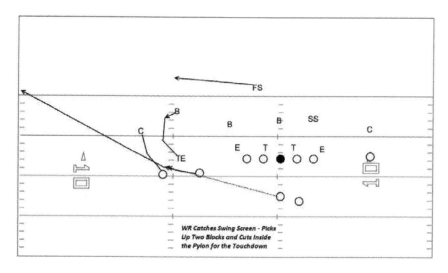

This creates enough of a crease along the sideline for the receiver, and VandeBerg squeezes himself inside the pylon for the score.

Even though the Hawkeyes missed the extra point, the short touchdown pass gave them a 20-0 lead early in the second quarter. They went on to a 40-20 victory against Purdue, securing the division title. This early touchdown drive illustrated the ability of Iowa to run its base offense and wear down an opponent, as the Hawkeyes had done throughout their season. They were able to use their outside zone running play to get the ball into the red zone, and exploit a numbers and personnel advantage with a simple swing screen pass for the score. The drive was a nicely crafted, and executed, bit of offensive football.

CHAPTER THIRTEEN

CARDINAL SUMMON THE ONE BIG PLAY

Do. Your. Job.

This is a mantra of the New England Patriots under head coach Bill Belichick. Following New England's Super Bowl XLIX victory, the coaching staff along with advisor Ernie Adams sat down with producers at the NFL Network to outline some of the inside information and stories behind the victory. During one segment, the head coach outlined that the three-word phrase was really a four-word phrase: Do your job, well.

On the final regular season weekend of the 2015-16 college football season, a number of important rivalry games were played, including a relatively recent but fierce annual matchup between Stanford and Notre Dame. In Stanford, Calif., the Notre Dame Fighting Irish needed a big road victory against Stanford to keep their national championship dreams alive. For the Cardinal, having secured a berth in the Pac 12 Championship a week prior with a victory against California, a win over Notre Dame would keep their own slim title hopes alive.

With under a minute remaining, Notre Dame quarterback DeShone Kizer appeared to score the decisive touchdown on a 2-yard run to give the Fighting Irish a 36-35 lead. They failed on the two-point conversion try, but kicked off with 30 seconds remaining on the clock and Stanford needing to at least get within field-goal range for a chance at victory.

After running back Christian McCaffrey (#5) returned the kickoff to the Stanford 27-yard line, the Cardinal offense lines up with quarterback Kevin Hogan (#8) in the shotgun with a single running back, tight end, and with three receivers in a bunch to the right and a single receiver split to the left. Notre Dame lines up with a 4-2-5 sub package in the game, and shows a prevent defense with defensive end Romeo Okwara (#45) lined up as a middle linebacker and only three down linemen. Behind the front four players, the defense puts linebackers Jaylon Smith (#9) and Joe Schmidt (#38) in the middle with a defensive back on each side, to cover the intermediate underneath zones. Behind these players lurk three additional defensive backs in a three-deep shell:

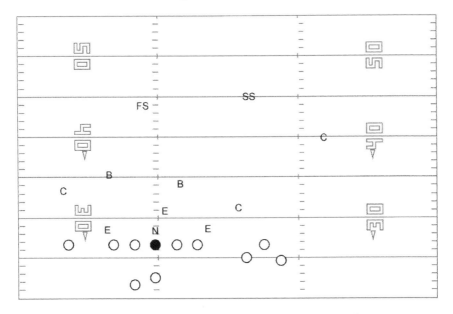

The Cardinal use a sail concept to the bunch side of the field, while the single receiver split out to the left runs a straight go route:

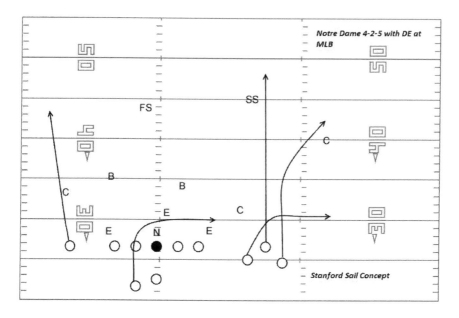

Notre Dame 4-2-5 with DE at MLB

Stanford Sail Concept

Hogan takes his drop, and the defense sends only three rushers after the quarterback with Okwara spying Hogan. Even with minimal pass rushers, defensive tackle Sheldon Day (#91) generates pressure off the edge to Hogan's right. As the quarterback looks to climb the pocket, defensive end Isaac Rochell (#90) reaches to swat the football:

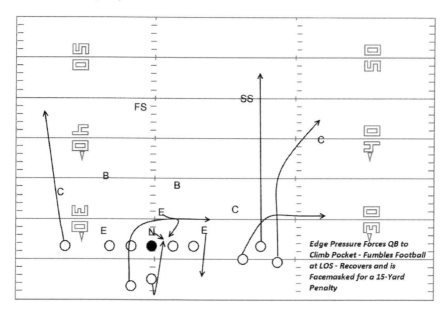

Edge Pressure Forces QB to Climb Pocket - Fumbles Football at LOS - Recovers and is Facemasked for a 15-Yard Penalty

The ball pops out, and Hogan falls on it before Okwara falls onto his back. The quarterback manages to somehow pick up a1-yard gain to the 28-yard line.

Cue the flag.

As Rochell tried to swat at the quarterback, he grabbed onto Hogan's facemask. The 15-yard personal foul penalty advances the football to the Stanford 43-yard line, and gives the offense a new set of downs. The offense takes a timeout, giving Notre Dame head coach Brian Kelly a chance to calm the rattled players on his defense after the penalty.

On the next play, Stanford lines up with the same offensive personnel group. The Cardinal put Hogan in the shotgun flanked by tight end Dalton Schultz (#9) and running back Remound Wright (#22). The offense has an inverted slot formation on the right, and split Michael Rector (#3) out wide to the left. Notre Dame stays with its 4-2-5 defense in a prevent alignment, dropping Okwara off the line of scrimmage and putting Smith and Schmidt in intermediate zones, and the secondary sets in a soft Cover 2 shell:

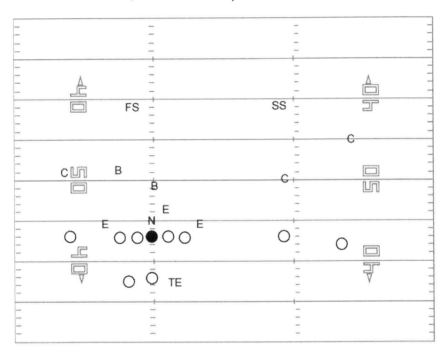

The Cardinal try a vertical concept with Rector running a go route, and Devon Cajuste (#89) running a deep post from his slot alignment. The receiver split to the outside, Francis Owusu (#6), runs a stop-and-go pattern:

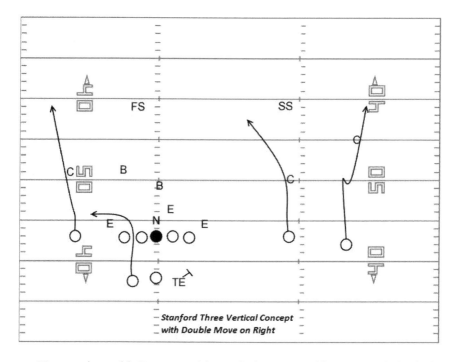

Stanford Three Vertical Concept
with Double Move on Right

Hogan tries to hit Rector on his vertical route, seeking to attack the hole in the Cover 2 scheme along the sideline:

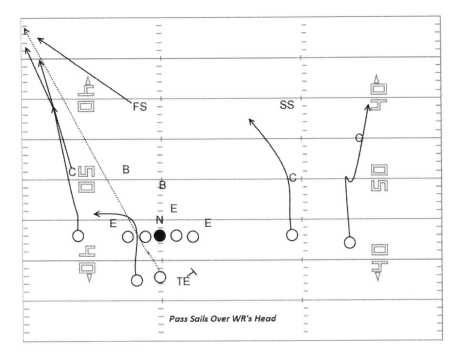

Pass Sails Over WR's Head

But the pass sails high, and out of bounds.

On second down, the Cardinal bring tight end Austin Hooper (#18) into the game, but stay with the same personnel grouping. Hogan sets in the shotgun with Wright to his left. The offense uses an inverted slot look to the right, with Cajuste on the inside and Rector split wide. Hooper and Owusu set in a pro formation on the left. Notre Dame stays with the same prevent formation used on the previous two snaps:

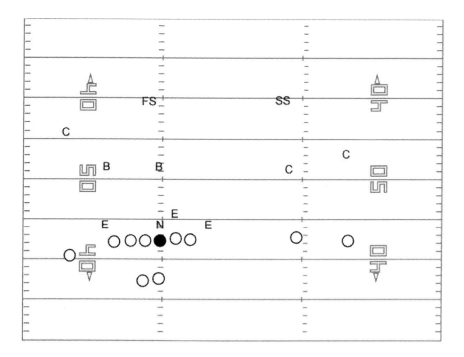

Here is the passing concept that the Cardinal run on this play:

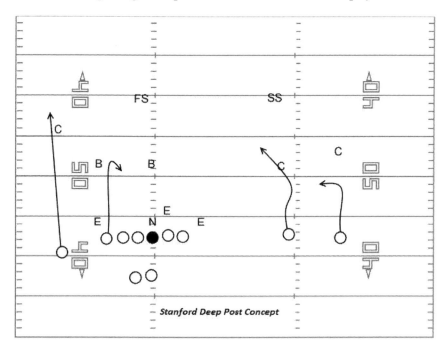

Stanford Deep Post Concept

On the pro side of the formation, Owusu releases vertically while Hooper runs a curl route right at the first down marker. From the slot side of the field, Cajuste runs a deep post while Rector runs a short in route. As the play develops, the curl route from the tight end occupies the two intermediate linebackers, Schmidt and Smith. Cajuste gets inside leverage on the slot defender, safety Matthias Farley (#41), and with the linebackers converging on the tight end, Cajuste gets behind the intermediate defenders and into the soft area of this Cover 2 scheme:

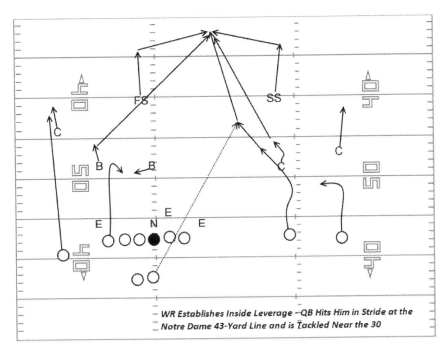

WR Establishes Inside Leverage –QB Hits Him in Stride at the Notre Dame 43-Yard Line and is Tackled Near the 30

Hogan delivers a strike, showing off his arm strength, and Cajuste reels in the pass at the Notre Dame 42-yard line. Farley jumps on the back of the WR and drags him down to the turf, but not before a 27-yard gain gets Stanford down to the Fighting Irish 30-yard line. The Cardinal quickly use their second timeout.

Looking to gain just a few more yards before attempting the field goal, the Cardinal line up for the next play with a jumbo formation and personnel grouping. Hogan is under center with an i-formation behind him, with McCaffrey the deep back and reserve offensive guard Brandon Fanaika (#71) in front as a fullback. Two more offensive linemen align as tight ends on the left, with guard David Bright (#64) on the wing and tackle Harrison Phillips (#96) on the end of the line. To the right, Schultz sets as an in-line TE on the end of the line. Notre Dame puts a 4-4 defense on the field and stacks the box, with six defenders on the line of scrimmage and 10 defenders in the box:

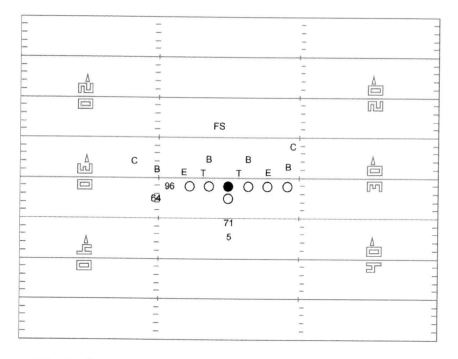

The Cardinal run a simple HB lead play through the left A gap, with right guard Johnny Caspers (#57) pulling under the center and into the hole as well:

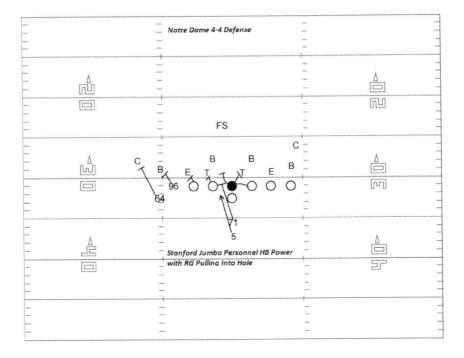

Notre Dame 4-4 Defense

Stanford Jumbo Personnel HB Power
with RG Pulling Into Hole

At the snap both Smith and Schmidt recognize the play and explode forward into the hole. But Fanaika surges forward as does Caspers. These four players collide in the hole, with the right guard taking on Smith while the reserve guard smashes into Schmidt:

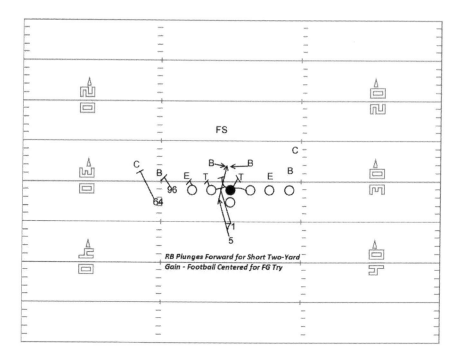

RB Plunges Forward for Short Two-Yard Gain - Football Centered for FG Try

These two blocks create enough of a crease for the back. McCaffrey plunges forward for a short 2-yard gain. But more importantly, he holds onto the football and keeps the ball centered in the middle of the field for the field goal try. The Cardinal burn their final timeout with 6 seconds left, setting the stage for Conrad Ukropina (#34).

Brian Kelly tries to ice the kicker, but when play resumes, the senior calmly drills the game-winning field goal.

In the end, it was Stanford's offense that did its job... well. Given new life with the personal foul penalty, Hogan and the offense were able to make the one big play they needed to get into field goal range. Consider the final offensive play of the game for a moment. It took two big blocks, from the starting right guard and from a reserve lineman aligned as a fullback, to clear the path and get a few more yards for the field goal try. In this sport, sometimes moments require players to step up and contribute in unorthodox ways. Asking Fanaika to line up as a fullback and clear the road on such a crucial play was asking a lot, but the lineman responded and delivered a crucial block, setting up the game-winning field goal. Bill Belichick would be proud.

CHAPTER FOURTEEN

MICHIGAN STATE PUNCHES ITS TICKET

In the final College Football Playoff standings released before conference championship weekend, the Big Ten had two teams in the top 5, with Iowa ranked fourth and Michigan State ranked fifth. As fate would have it, those two teams met in Indianapolis to decide the Big Ten Championship, with the winner virtually guaranteeing itself a spot in the playoffs.

The game was a tight, defensive affair, and with more than 9 minutes remaining in the game the Hawkeyes clung to a four-point lead, but were forced to punt. What followed was some of the most amazing football of the entire season – and a clear example of what is meant by the term "championship drive."

After an Iowa punt, Michigan State takes over at its 18-yard line, with quarterback Connor Cook (#18) under center and a personnel grouping of two running backs, a tight end, and two wide receivers on the field. The Spartans employ an i-formation in the backfield, with pro alignment to the left and a single receiver split to the right. The Hawkeyes have their base 4-3 defense in the game, with outside linebacker Ben Niemann (#44) down on the line of scrimmage across from the tight end:

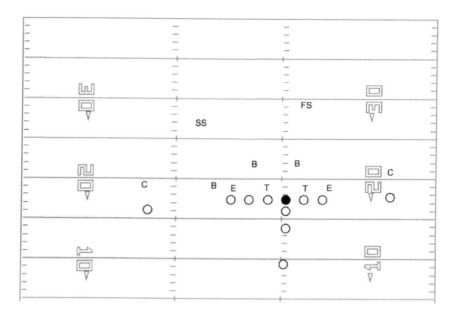

The Spartans run a power play to the right side, with left tackle Jack Conklin (#74) pulling in front of running back LJ Scott (#3), and leading him into the right B gap between the guard and tackle. Fullback Trevon Pendleton (#37) heads toward the left side, to replace Conklin and pick up his defensive tackle:

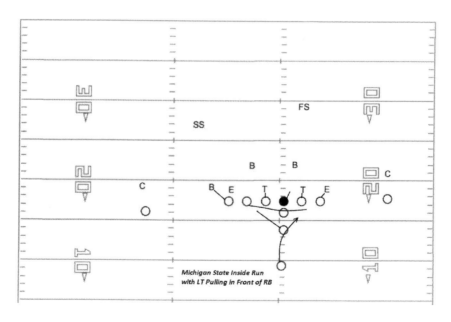

Michigan State Inside Run
with LT Pulling in Front of RB

Cook takes the snap, opens to his right and puts the football into the belly of Scott, who comes underneath the quarterback before bending his run to the right. He cuts behind his big right tackle, and then slices through a narrow crease to the inside of a tackle attempt by linebacker Cole Fisher (#36):

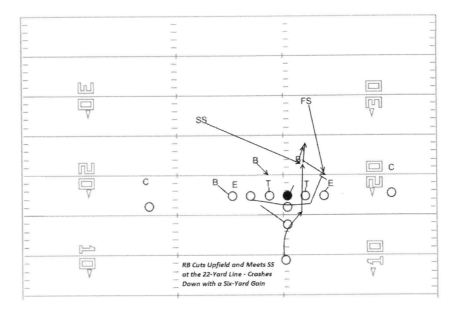

RB Cuts Upfield and Meets SS at the 22-Yard Line - Crashes Down with a Six-Yard Gain

After making the linebacker miss, Scott runs straight into strong safety Miles Taylor (#19). As these two players fight at the point of contact, a host of Hawkeyes join the party, finally driving Scott to the playing surface after a 6-yard gain.

On second down, the Spartans alter their lineup and put Cook in the shotgun with a personnel grouping of a running back, two tight ends, and two receivers. Scott stands to the right of the quarterback and Michigan State has a tight end on each end of the line. The two wide receivers align to the left, giving the Spartans a tight end trips look to that side. The Hawkeyes stay with their base 4-3, but walk Niemann out over the receiver in the slot:

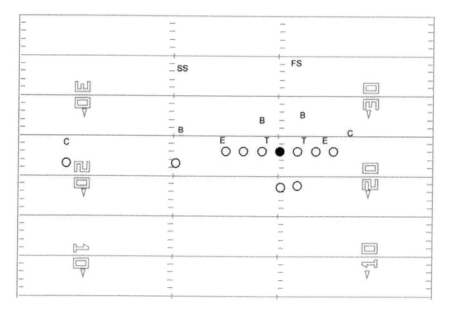

Cook looks to throw on this play, with these routes to choose from to attack the Iowa Cover 2 defense:

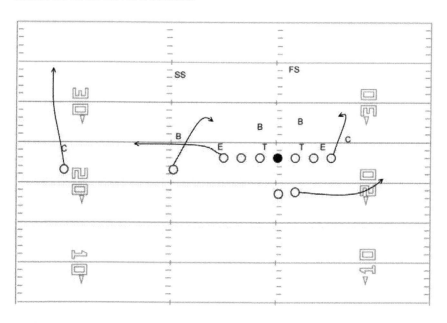

Aaron Burbridge (#16),the outside receiver, uses a straight vertical route. Macgarrett Kings Jr. (#85) runs a short snag route, cutting to the inside of the field. Tight end Jamal Lyles (#11), who begins the play on the left edge of the line, runs a quick flat route while his fellow tight end Josiah Price (#82) runs another curl. Scott executes a swing route cutting toward the right sideline.

Cook takes the snap and reads this play to the left side. Burbridge is matched up against cornerback Desmond King (#14), one of Iowa's leading defenders, and the cornerback is in great position along the receiver's outside release. Cook then brings his field of vision down to the shorter routes, first checking Lyles in the flat. But since the Niemann began the play in the slot, the outside linebacker is in perfect position to cover this route. Cook quickly snaps his eyes to his third read, Kings on the underneath curl route:

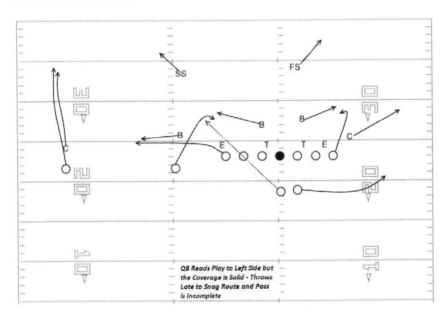

QB Reads Play to Left Side but the Coverage is Solid - Throws Late to Snag Route and Pass is Incomplete

The receiver has settled down into an underneath zone, but has middle linebacker Josey Jewell (#43) closing in on him. Cook's throw is slightly low and outside, away from the defender, and the pass falls incomplete.

The incompletion forces the first third down of the drive (but by no means the last). The Spartans line up with Cook in the shotgun and one running back and one tight end on the field. Scott stands to the left of his quarterback, and wide receiver R.J. Shelton (#12) comes in motion from the left to the right, and then back, before setting up in a wing to the left at the snap. Two Spartans receivers line up in a slot look to the left as well, with tight end Price on the right end of the line. The Hawkeyes adjust their lineup for the first time this drive, setting up with a 2-4-5 nickel defense that uses two defensive ends and four linebackers, and show Cover 2 man underneath. On this play, King shadows Shelton. Up front, Iowa puts all six defenders on the line of scrimmage in a two-point stance, employing a radar alignment:

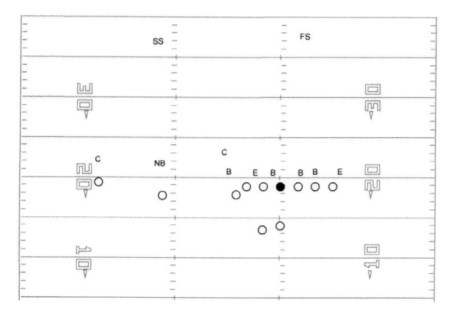

Of all the options in the playbook, the last one people were expecting was the tight end shovel pass:

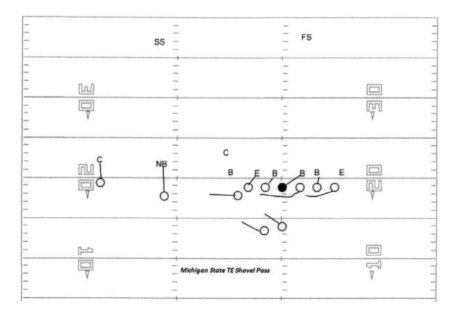

The design works to perfection. Cook takes the snap and shows a speed option play to the left edge. The linebacker to that side, Aaron Mends (#31), is unblocked off the snap, but before he can get to Cook, Scott loops around Cook and gets in the way of the redshirt freshman defender. This gives the quarterback enough of a window to flip the ball forward to Price, tracking down the line of scrimmage and following behind right guard Donavon Clark (#76), who is pulling in front of the tight end:

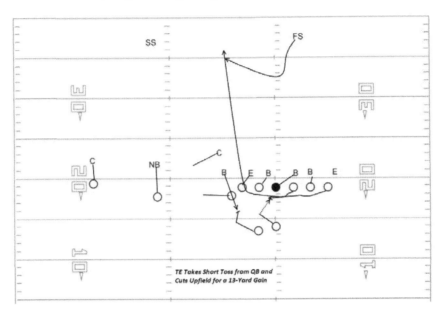

TE Takes Short Toss from QB and
Cuts Upfield for a 13-Yard Gain

The other critical block is thrown by Conklin at the point of attack. Jewell is in a two-point stance to the inside of the left tackle at the snap, but Conklin fires out of his stance and into the right shoulder of the linebacker. After the initial contact, the right tackle drives the defender up the field while Price cuts in behind this block and races into the secondary before being dragged down from behind by free safety Jordan Lomax (#27). The 13-yard gain moves the chains.

Armed with a fresh set of downs, the Spartans line up for the next play with two running backs and a tight end in the game in a weak i-right formation. Cook is under center and Pendleton is in the game as a fullback, staggered behind the left B gap. The offense has a pro formation to the right side of the field, and a single receiver split to the left. The Hawkeyes bring their base 4-3 defense back into the game, with Niemann again on the line of scrimmage, shaded to the tight end side of the field. The cornerbacks align in press coverage, and before the snap Taylor starts cheating into the box from his strong safety spot:

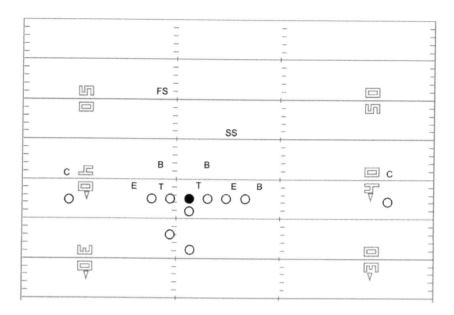

The Spartans throw on first down, employing a quick passing concept and a three-step drop from the quarterback:

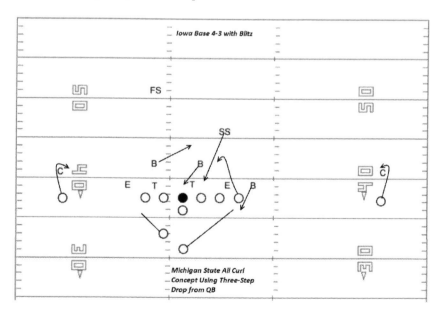

Both receivers run curl routes, while tight end Paul Lang (#83) checks the protection before releasing on a third curl pattern. The Hawkeyes bring pressure on this play, blitzing both Taylor and two linebackers, Jewell and Niemann:

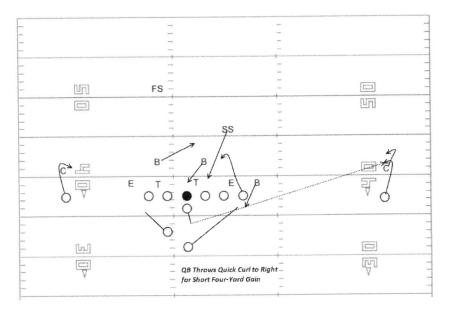

QB Throws Quick Curl to Right
for Short Four-Yard Gain

Cook executes a perfectly timed three-step drop, beginning his throw right as he hits his final step. He throws to the curl route on his right, run by Kings. The receiver gets enough separation from the defender and works back to the pass for the catch, but as the ball tracks toward the receiver it is clear there is a lingering issue with Cook's throwing shoulder. The ball is thrown with minimal velocity and starts to dip downward well before reaching the target. The play goes for a gain of 4 yards, but raises concern along the MSU sideline, as well as in the booth. Fox Sports color analyst Joel Klatt sounds the alarm about Cook's shoulder from above the field at Lucas Oil Stadium.

On second down, the Spartans' concern over Cook's shoulder is illustrated in their play calling. They line up in the wildcat with Cook split wide to the left. Burbridge stands in the shotgun ready to take the snap with Scott standing to his left. Price splits wide to the right in a receiver's alignment, and Lang aligns in a wing position outside Conklin:

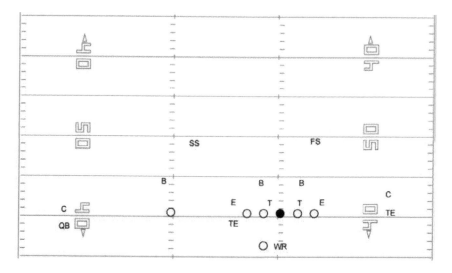

Iowa stays with its base defense and walks Niemann to the outside over Shelton, who is in the slot. The Hawkeyes show Cover 2 in the secondary, but drop both safeties down near the box, expecting a running play based on the formation. That is exactly what happens. Burbridge takes the snap and hands the ball to Scott, aiming for the right edge:

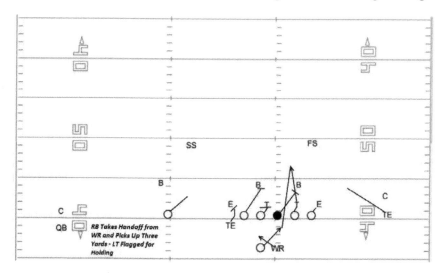

The Spartans use a zone design here, with Lang sealing off the backside defensive end while the rest of the offensive line flows to the right. They also employ a crackback block from Price, who cuts toward the middle of the field. The running back takes the handoff and cuts behind these blocks for a 3-yard gain. But there is a flag. Conklin, who worked to the second level off the snap, gets flagged for holding, pushing the Spartans back to their own 34-yard line.

Facing 2nd and 13, Michigan State stays in a wildcat formation, with Burbridge in the backfield to take the shotgun snap from center Jack Allen (#66), while Scott stands to the left of the receiver. Price sets to the outside on the right with Lang in a wing position to the left, and the Spartans put both Shelton and Cook to the outside on the left with the receiver in a slot alignment. As with the previous play, the Hawkeyes stay with their 4-3 base defense, walking an outside linebacker outside over Shelton and bringing both safeties down into the box:

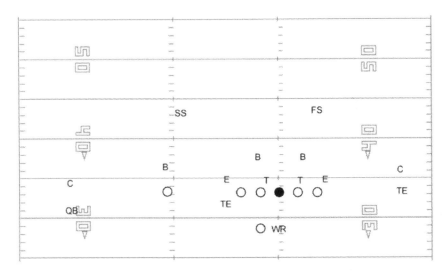

The offense uses some misdirection, based off of a speed option design. Burbridge takes the snap and cuts to the left edge with Scott trailing him. But Shelton pivots to his right and cuts between the two players, and takes a pitch from the receiver around the right edge. While the bulk of the offensive line blocks to the left to help sell the fake, the center blocks left initially before he peels around to the right in front of Shelton. Once more, Price cracks down to the inside as well:

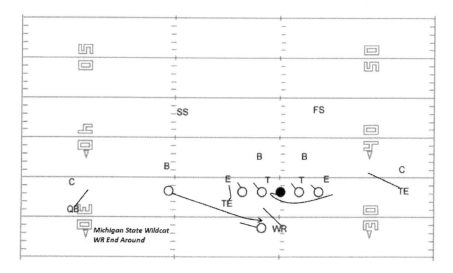

Jordan Lomax (#27), the free safety, appears to be the one defender not fooled by this play. He reads the misdirection perfectly, and crashes down toward the box in anticipation of the edge run from Shelton. But his path soon crosses with Price:

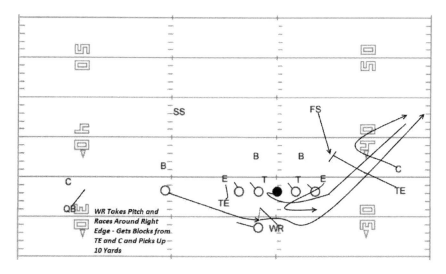

The tight end executes a crushing block on the free safety, securing the edge for Shelton's end around. The receiver then picks up Allen as the center pulls around the edge, and cuts right behind his big one-man convoy before being driven out of bounds at the Spartans' 44-yard line after a 10-yard gain.

Despite the solid gain on the previous play, the Spartans still need 3 yards to extend the drive. They line up with Cook back in the shotgun and Scott to the right of the quarterback, with a three receiver set and a running back and tight end on the field. Price is in a wing alignment on a left with slot to the outside, and the Spartans have a single receiver split wide to the right. The Hawkeyes stay with their base 4-3 defense, again walking Niemann outside over Shelton in the slot:

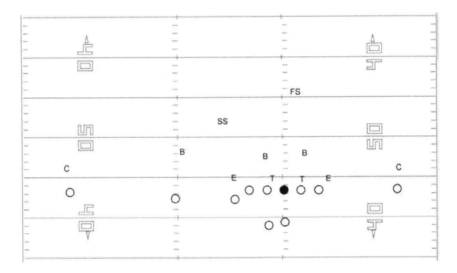

The offense runs a counter play, with Scott using a jab step to his left to help set the table for his blocking, before cutting to the right and taking an underneath handoff from Cook. Up front, Conklin pulls around from his left tackle spot to help out in front of the running back:

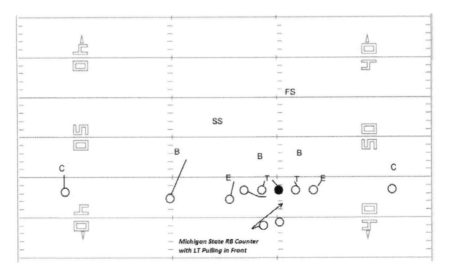

Michigan State RB Counter with LT Pulling in Front

Off the snap the defense gets tremendous penetration, led by defensive tackle Faith Ekakitie (#56) who drives into the backfield, as well as defensive end Matt Nelson (#96). These two defenders impede the ability of Conklin to peel around on his pull, and it allows the playside cornerback, Greg Mabin (#13), to read the play and attack the edge. The cornerback is in perfect position to stop this run at the line of scrimmage:

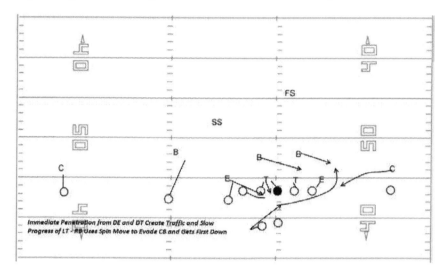

But just before contact, Scott employs a spin move, planting his left foot in the turf and twisting toward the backfield and around to the middle of the field. This juke is enough to avoid the tackle from Mabin. The running back then stumbles forward, crashing to the field just past the 47-yard line, enough for a first down.

Just shy of midfield now with just over six minutes remaining, the Spartans line up with Cook under center and move back to a two running back set, with a tight end and two receivers rounding out the personnel grouping. Pendleton has returned to the field, and sets as an upback in the i-formation, staggered to the left behind the A gap. The offense uses a pro formation on the left, and has a single receiver outside on the right. Iowa stays with its base defense, showing Cover 2 in the secondary and putting Niemann down on the line of scrimmage over the tight end:

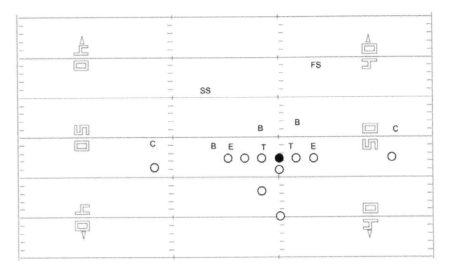

Michigan State runs another counter play to the right here, with Scott taking two quick chop steps to his left before cutting to the upfield behind Conklin, pulling once more:

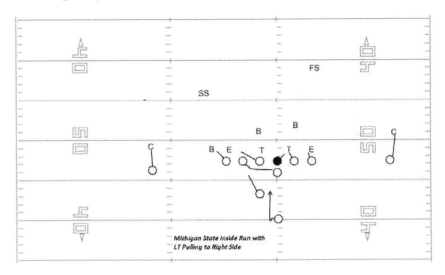

Michigan State Inside Run with
LT Pulling to Right Side

Off the snap the right tackle, Kodi Kieler (#79) looks to block Fisher, the playside outside linebacker. As he works to the second level, the defensive end slows him a bit with his left arm, preventing Kieler from having a quick burst ahead to the second level. As the left tackle turns the corner, he runs right into Nelson, the defensive end who has just slowed the right tackle. As these two massive players struggle on the edge, Scott tracks behind them with the football. Conklin wins the battle at the point of contact, but because Kieler was slowed in working to Fisher, the outside linebacker has established outside leverage and works around the right tackle:

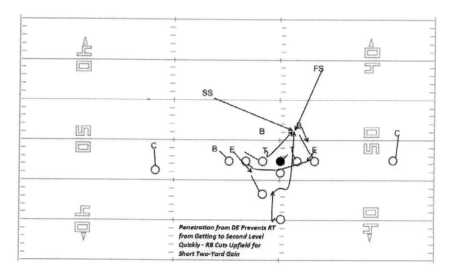

The work from Fisher forces the running back to cut back toward the middle of the field, where the rest of the defense is waiting. A host of tacklers bring Scott down, after a short 2-yard gain.

The Spartans line up for second down and return to a personnel grouping of three receivers, a running back and a tight end, with a trips look to the left including Price, who is on the end of the line, and Burbridge alone to the right, using a split just past the bottom of the numbers. The Hawkeyes stay with their base 4-3 defense, sliding Niemann out into the slot over Shelton:

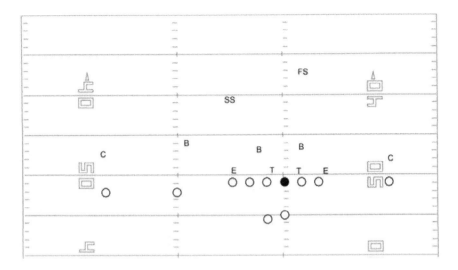

Cook takes the snap and looks to throw:

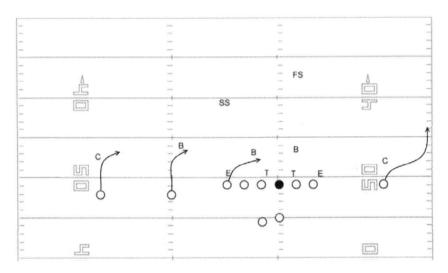

The Spartans use a double slant concept on the left, with both Shelton and Kings cutting to the inside. Price releases over the middle of the field on a shallow dig route, while Burbridge cuts vertically along the sideline. Cook throws a back-shoulder route to Burbridge on the right, who has Mabin draped all over him:

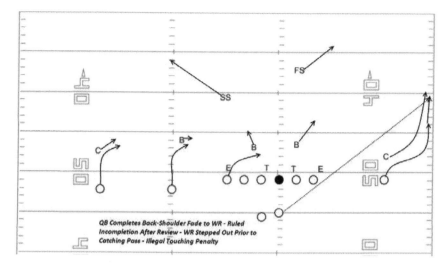

QB Completes Back-Shoulder Fade to WR - Ruled
Incompletion After Review - WR Stepped Out Prior to
Catching Pass - Illegal Touching Penalty

With the tight coverage, Cook's timing and accuracy are on display on this throw. He puts the football where only the receiver can make a play, and Burbridge twists back toward the throw to snare the football from the sky before crashing down in front of the MSU bench near the Iowa 45-yard line.

But there is another flag.

Upon review, it is determined that the receiver stepped out of bounds, and then came back into the field of play and was the first to touch the football. The illegal touching penalty negates the completion, and forces Michigan State into a third and long.

The clock stops for the review, and play resumes with a little over 5 minutes to play. Nearly 4 minutes have elapsed already on this drive, and while the Spartans have all three timeouts and could theoretically punt if their third down play fails, they are approaching four-down territory. The offense aligns with Cook in the shotgun and two running backs and three wide receivers on the field, with an inverted slot formation on each side of the field and Scott split wide to the right, outside of Burbridge. The Hawkeyes adjust their defense, bringing a 2-3-6 dime package onto the field. They show Cover 2 man underneath, with the defensive front in radar alignment. With four cornerbacks in press alignment, nine defenders are on or just off the line of scrimmage:

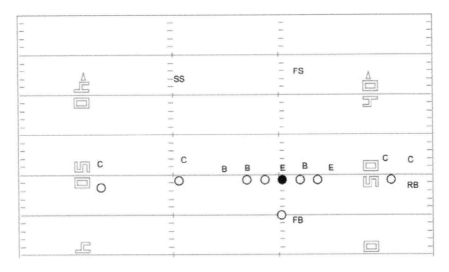

The Spartans attack vertically, with three receivers running vertical routes while Scott runs a curl along the sideline. Iowa blitzes all three linebackers and stays with its Cover 2 man underneath coverage:

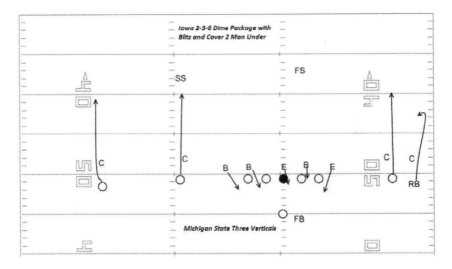

Needing a big play, Cook looks to the right at the seam route from Burbridge:

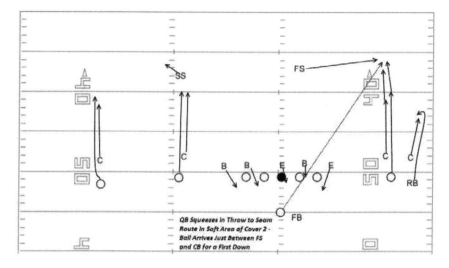

QB Squeezes in Throw to Seam
Route in Soft Area of Cover 2 -
Ball Arrives Just Between FS
and CB for a First Down

The cornerback tries to jam him, but the receiver gets enough of a step to the outside on Mabin to avoid the jam and get open as he releases vertically. Cook sees this and drops in a touch pass that arrives milliseconds before Lomax. As Gus Johnson described the throw, the QB "put it into a shoebox." Despite the tight coverage and narrow throwing window, Burbridge makes the reception for a 16-yard gain, giving the Spartans a fresh set of downs at Iowa's 34-yard line.

On the ensuing play, Michigan State takes to the air once more. The Spartans set their offense with the QB under center, changing the personnel to add two tight ends in place of two of the three receivers, and keeping both running backs on the field. Scott is the deep back behind Pendleton in an i-formation, and the Spartans split Burbridge to the right and put two tight ends, Lyles and Lang, to the left in a wing formation. The Hawkeyes put their base 4-3 defense on the field and show a two-high safety look, with Niemann and King both down over the two tight ends, and Mabin in press alignment over Burbridge:

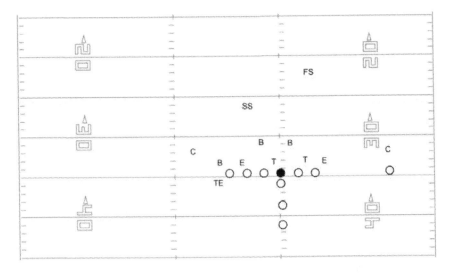

Cook works off of play action, taking the handoff and reverse-pivoting before faking a running play with Scott to the right side. Burbridge releases vertically, while Lang and Lyles run a dig and post combination (known as the Mills Concept). After faking a lead block, Pendleton swings into the flat:

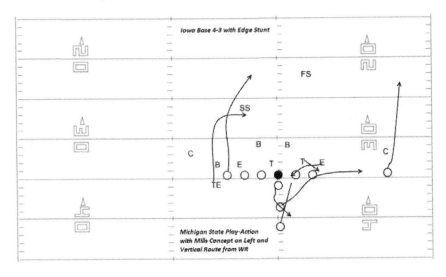

Iowa's coverage in the secondary is stout. Coming out of the fake Cook checks the two-TE side of the field, but both routes are blanketed by defenders. As he tries to work through his progressions, he is flushed from the pocket by defensive end Nate Meier (#34), who twisted to the right A gap on a stunt:

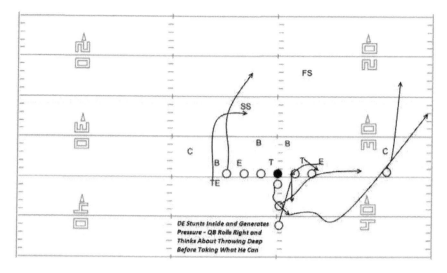

DE Stunts Inside and Generates
Pressure - QB Rolls Right and
Thinks About Throwing Deep
Before Taking What He Can

Forced to his right, Cook looks to hit Burbridge deep, but decides against this option, and just tucks the football, angling to the right sideline and out of bounds for a 7-yard gain. Rather than risking the aggressive decision, the quarterback wisely takes what he can, keeping the drive alive.

Now the clock is stopped with 4:44 remaining, and the Spartans have the football at the Iowa 27-yard line trailing by four. They line up for second down with Cook under center and a running back and two tight ends still in the game, with Burbridge split to the right and three receivers on the left in a bunch alignment, Lyles on the line of scrimmage and Lang lined up off the line, in the gap between Lyles and Conklin:

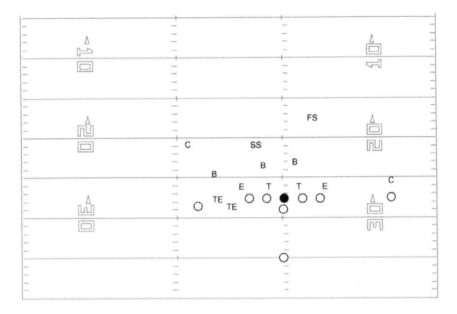

Iowa has its base 4-3 defense in the game, with Niemann down on the end of the line across from the bunch group.

The Spartans run Scott on the right edge using a power design, with both the center Jake Allen, as well as Lang, leading the running back to the right side:

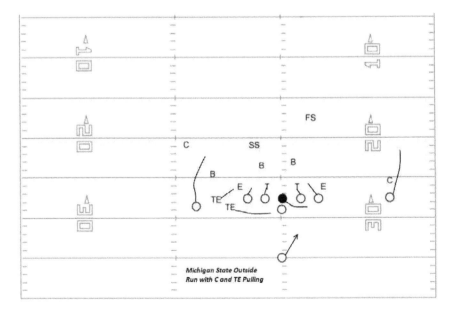

Michigan State Outside Run with C and TE Pulling

Allen excels on this play. Pulling around the edge is hard enough, but when you have to make sure of the properly executed snap before you race to the outside, the level of difficulty is raised. But Allen makes the snap, opens his hips to the sideline and angles down the line, where he encounters Meier. The defensive end has scraped down to the inside, but the center seals him off from the play, shoving him back toward the middle of the field. Following behind the center, and just in front of the ball-carrier, is Lang. As the tight end turns the corner he encounters Fisher. The outside linebacker has diagnosed the run and has spilled forward to try and set the edge. But Lang has momentum, and explodes into the linebacker's outside shoulder:

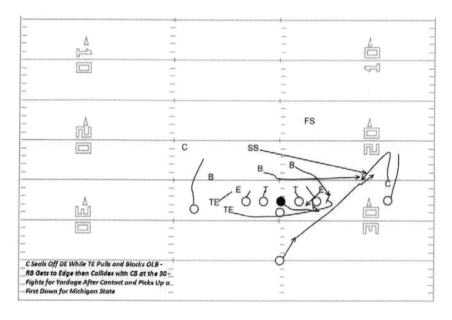

These two blocks give Scott an alley to the outside, but his work is not complete. Mabin explodes toward the back from the outside, and hurls himself into the thighs of the freshman ball-carrier. With the cornerback hanging onto his right ankle, Scott stays upright and absorbs one more blow to his back, a tackle attempt from Ekakitie. The defensive tackle has scraped down the line, and is in position to finish off the tackle. But using pure strength, Scott plunges forward with the defensive tackle on his back, falling to the turf at the 24-yard line. The tough 3-yard gain is enough to move the sticks once again.

When the ball is snapped next, just more than 4 minutes remain.

The Spartans line up with two running backs and three wide receivers on the field. Cook is in the shotgun flanked by the two running backs, with Pendleton on his left and Scott to his right. The offense has slot formation to the left, and a single receiver to the right. As they have for most of the drive, Iowa puts its base defense into a Cover 2 look, with Niemann, the outside linebacker, sliding over toward the slot formation:

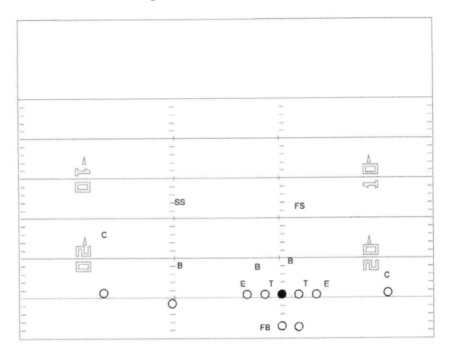

MSU uses a split zone design on this running play. The offensive line flows in unison to the left at the snap, while Pendleton cuts toward the right edge to block the backside defensive end, Meier. Scott takes the handoff from Cook and reads the blocking up front, working behind his fullback:

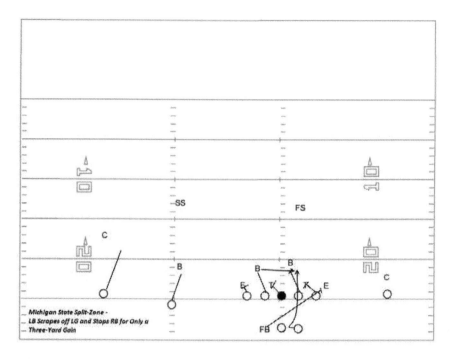

The blocking sets well, but as Scott cuts behind the block of Pendleton on Meier, the second level defenders flow to him, led by Jewell, to stop him after a short 3-yard gain. This is a very impressive play from the sophomore middle linebacker, who scrapes to the hole, works off the block from left guard Brian Allen (#65), and plunges into the legs of Scott, slicing the runner to the turf.

The clock stops for an injury, as Pendleton is shaken up after the collision with the defensive end. When the whistle blows again, the clock starts running with less than 4 minutes to play.

The Spartans head to the line of scrimmage and put Cook in the shotgun, changing the personnel grouping to a running back, a tight end, and three wide receivers. Burbridge is split to the right, while the offense puts the three receivers to the left. Price sets in a wing alignment while Shelton stands in the slot and Kings is wide to the left. Scott stands to the left of his quarterback. The Hawkeyes stay with their base 4-3, showing two high safeties, and once again Niemann is in the slot across from Shelton:

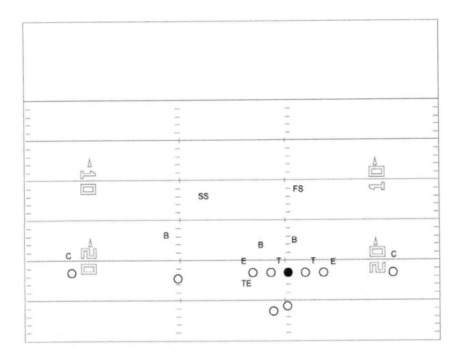

Michigan State gives Scott the football, heading to the right:

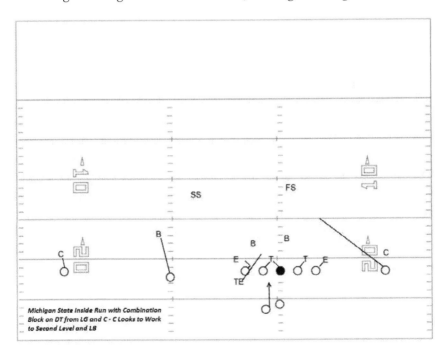

Michigan State Inside Run with Combination Block on DT from LG and C - C Looks to Work to Second Level and LB

This play begins with crucial execution over the football. The two Allens, center Jack and left guard Brian, execute a combination block on the defensive tackle who lines up in the gap between them. At the snap the center drives his right foot to the outside, giving him leverage on the left shoulder of the defensive tackle. Jack Allen then plunges ahead into that shoulder, while Brian Allen looks to help. With the center having stopped the forward momentum of the DT, he passes him off to the left guard and looks to the second level defenders:

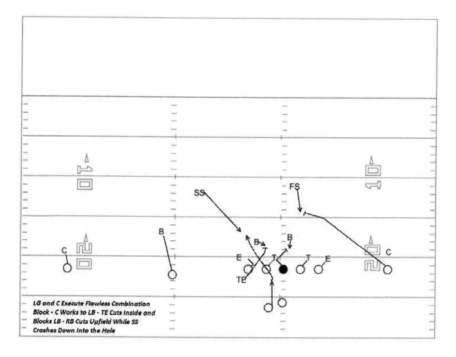

Scott follows his center, but after he crosses the line of scrimmage traffic builds in front of him. He looks to bend this run back to the left, where there is a crease thanks to blocks from Price to the inside and Conklin on the backside defensive end. But as Scott bounces into this narrow lane, he encounters the safety Taylor.

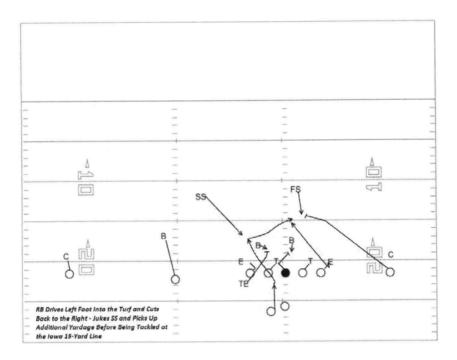

*RB Drives Left Foot Into the Turf and Cuts
Back to the Right - Jukes SS and Picks Up
Additional Yardage Before Being Tackled at
the Iowa 15-Yard Line*

Scott makes the defender, who is in perfect position for the tackle, miss. After bouncing to the left, he identifies the defender, sticks his left foot into the playing surface and cuts back to his right. He runs into Meier, who is hustling toward the play, and is dragged down. The 6-yard gain is not only a very impressive run, but it gives the Spartans a very manageable 3rd and 1.

Under 3 minutes remaining, and a potential playoff berth on the line.

Cook positions himself under center for the next play, with a heavier personnel grouping of two running backs, two tight ends, and a wide receiver. Pendleton returns to the field after taking a play off, and puts himself in a three-point stance in front of Scott, slightly shaded to the left side. Lang is in a wing to the left just outside Conklin, with Burbridge split to the left. The Hawkeyes have their 4-3 defense in the game, but Niemann is down on the line over Price on the right side of the offense, with Mabin on the line as well. Lomax is also down in the box, and at the snap Iowa has nine defenders ready for a running play:

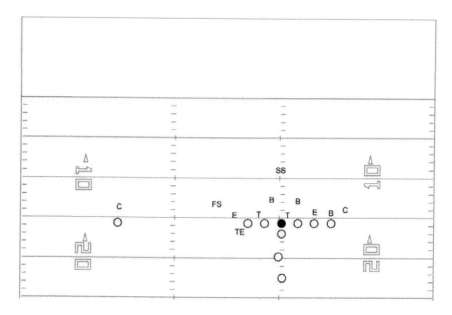

The running play is coming:

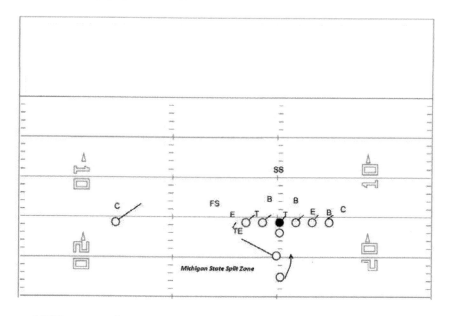

MSU uses a split zone scheme once more, with Lang and the rest of the offensive line blocking to the right while Pendleton cuts across to the left edge. The fullback and Lang throw the crucial blocks here. At the snap, right defensive end Parker Hesse (#40) explodes to the inside expecting an interior running play. Lang simply plunges himself into the right shoulder of the DE, riding him toward the middle of the field. Behind him comes Pendleton, and the fullback finds Lomax on the edge, the safety having read the play and collapsing into the potential hole to force this run to the inside:

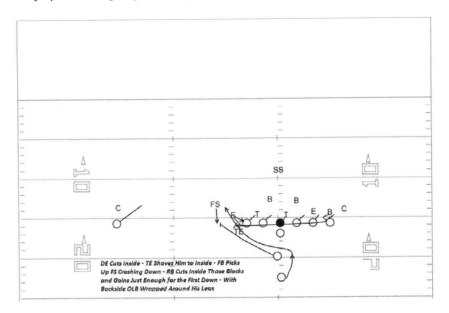

Even though the safety has a burst of momentum, Pendleton stands him up on the edge. Scott cuts to the inside of this block, but as he does he has a pair of hands wrapped around his legs. From the other side Niemann has bent around the edge, into the backfield and has hurled himself at the ankles of the ball carrier. Somehow, Scott stays upright and drags the outside linebacker past the line of scrimmage before he falls to the turf. Gain of two. First down.

The first down stops the clock while the chains are reset. When it starts ticking before the next play, it counts down from 2:48 remaining.

Cook lines up under center again with the same personnel grouping on the field, with Lyles the tight end to the right and Lang once more in a wing alignment to the left. Scott is behind Pendleton in an i-formation once more. The Hawkeyes stay with their base defense, putting Niemann on the line of scrimmage over Lyles on the right edge of the offense, and Lomax drifts down into the box yet again:

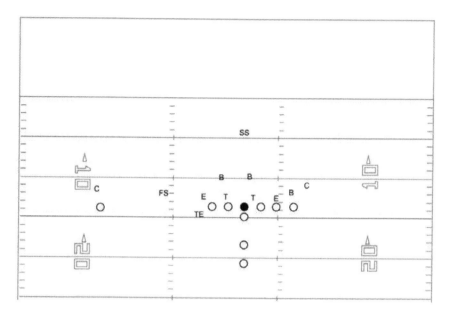

The Spartans try a run to the left edge:

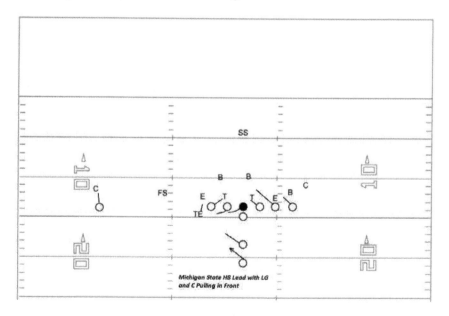

This play is a reminder about the team aspect of defensive football. As this run develops, Lomax crashes down along the left edge of the offense, and soon finds both Pendleton and left guard Allen flowing his way in this blocking scheme. The safety has no choice and gives himself up, crashing into both blockers in an effort to maintain the outside leverage and set the edge. His kamikaze mission succeeds, and it forces Scott to cut back toward the middle of the field:

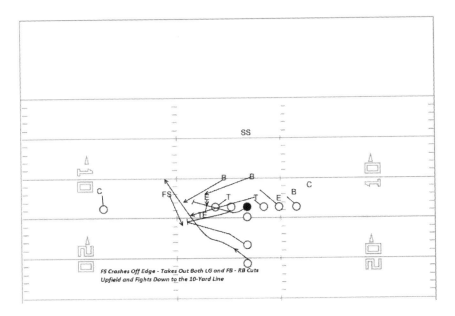

FS Crashes Off Edge - Takes Out Both LG and FB - RB Cuts
Upfield and Fights Down to the 10-Yard Line

As the running back cuts back to his right, he first encounters a tackle attempt from defensive tackle Jaleel Johnson (#67). The big defender has worked through the cutblock attempt of Clark and scraped down the line. But when he lunges at Scott's back, the running back brushes the DT away. He then absorbs a shot from Fisher, and is crumpled to the turf. But he picks up 3 yards for his work.

Iowa takes its first timeout with 2:09 remaining. If it was not clear already, the outcome of this drive decides the ballgame.

Facing 2nd and 7, the Spartans line up with Cook under center and a slight adjustment to their personnel. Reserve offensive guard Benny McGowan (#75) checks into the game and lines up at center, a spot usually occupied by Jack Allen. But the center shifts into a wing alignment, lining up between Lang and left tackle Conklin. Kings stands outside these two players in a flanker alignment. The Hawkeyes set their 4-3 defense with the three linebackers in standard positioning, and show Cover 6 in the secondary with King down in press alignment over Kings:

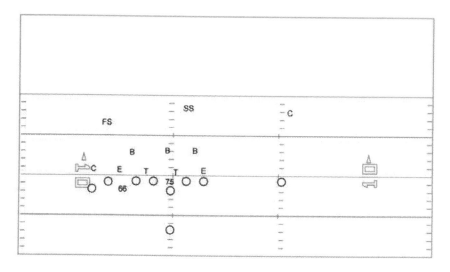

The Spartans use a power running play, pulling Clark, the right guard, to the left into the C gap behind Allen, and in front of Scott. Conklin and the right guard execute a double-team at the point of attack on the playside defensive tackle:

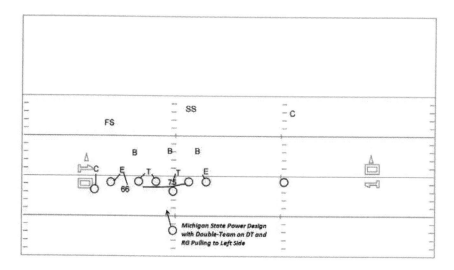

As Clark turns the corner he sees Fisher exploding down into the hole, and the guard twists the linebacker to the inside and away from the hole. Allen bursts forward from an unfamiliar position and looks to block Lomax, and twists him away from the play. Scott comes behind these two blockers and bursts ahead before he collides with Taylor, the strong safety:

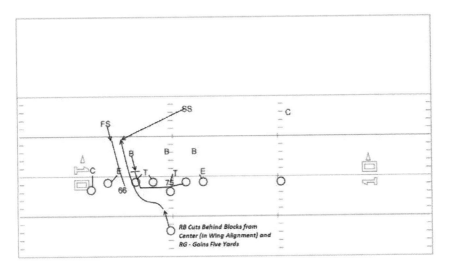

Taylor holds this to a 5-yard run, and Iowa takes its second timeout. 2:04 left in the game.

When play resumes, the Spartans need two yards for a first down, and five for the go-ahead score. Cook lines up under center and MSU uses the same formation and personnel as the previous play: McGowan at center, Allen in the wing alignment between Lang and Conklin, and Kings just to the outside of them. Iowa's 4-3 defense is in the game, with its linebackers stacked behind the defensive tackles and the backside defensive end, Meier:

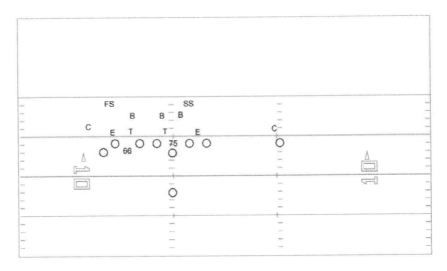

The Spartans run the same play, with Scott heading to the left side and Clark pulling in front of him. But this time the Hawkeyes are ready:

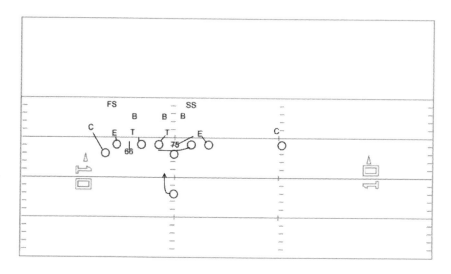

Prior to the snap defensive tackle Nathan Bazata (#99) aligns on the left, outside shoulder of Conklin. When the play begins the DT cuts to the inside and meets the left tackle head-on. Seeing this and the playside linebacker burst forward into the hold, Allen leaves Conklin isolated on Bazata and surges forward to meet the threat from Fisher, and shortly after Clark arrives to help. But as Scott enters the hole, Bazata disengages from Conklin – who may be looking to move to the second level and leave the defensive tackle behind:

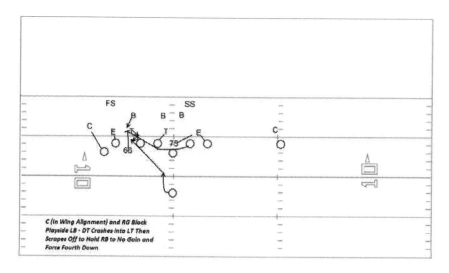

Bazata meets Scott in the hole and drives his right shoulder into the belly of the running back, stopping him at the line of scrimmage. No gain. Fourth down.

Iowa's final time out stops the clock with 1:59 to play.

McGowan stays on the field and shifts to right guard, giving the offense six linemen up front and an unbalanced look to the right. Cook stands in the shotgun with Scott to his left and Pendleton to his right, but before the play the fullback goes in motion and lines up as a receiver on the left. The two tight ends, Lyles and Lang, align on the right side with Lang in a wing alignment and Lyles on the end. Iowa's 4-3 defense sets up with Niemann on the line over Lyles, and Lomax drops into the box as well in a linebacker's alignment, just outside the left tackle:

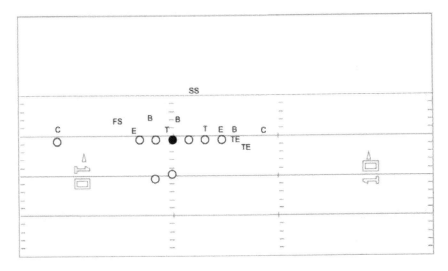

With the season on the line, the MSU coaches put the ball in the hands of their quarterback and fifth-year senior, and run a speed option play to the left side:

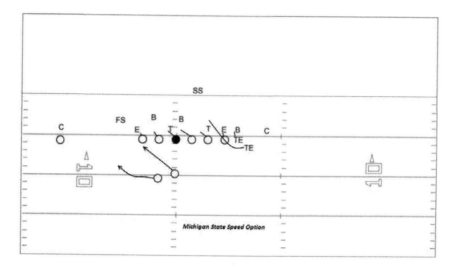

Michigan State Speed Option

Cook takes the snap and attacks the left edge. Lomax diagnoses this play immediately and cuts upfield in the direction of Scott, anticipating the pitch. Cook keeps the football and lowers his injured right shoulder toward the 3-yard line, the distance needed for the first down, and collides with the mass of bodies flowing to the football right at the line to gain two yards:

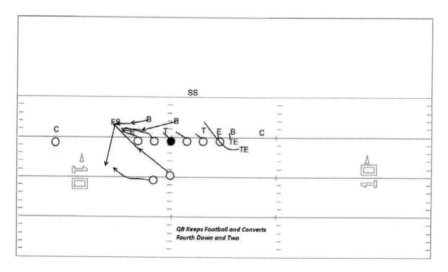

QB Keeps Football and Converts Fourth Down and Two

The first down was confirmed by a measurement.

On the next play, Cook lines up under center and Michigan State uses a jumbo package, with Pendleton and Scott in an i-formation, a tight end on each end of the line and Jack Allen as an up back, staggered behind Conklin. McGowan is handling the snap from the center position. Iowa brings on its goal line defense with six down linemen, three linebackers and two defensive backs:

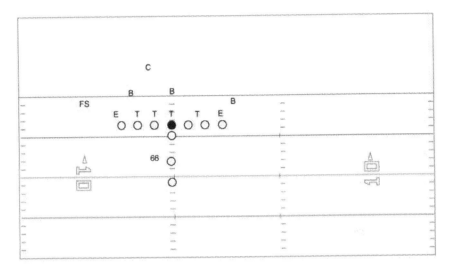

The Spartans run power to the left side, with Scott following Pendleton and Allen. Cook reverse pivots, taking the snap from McGowan, turning to his right first and wheeling around to make the handoff:

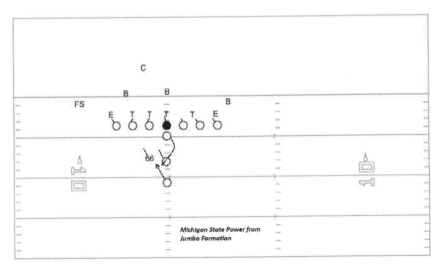

Michigan State Power from
Jumbo Formation

At the snap Lyles, the playside tight end, makes contact with Melvin Spears (#49), the defensive end across from him, before releasing to the flat to block Lomax. Allen follows behind the tight end, and finishes the job on the DE. But to the inside, three defenders identify and explode forward:

Fisher, King and Jewell:

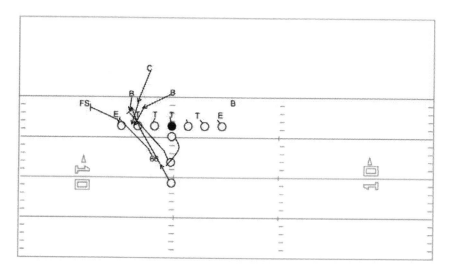

Pendleton rushes forward but can only block one member of this trio. He chooses Fisher. Left unblocked, both Jewell and King rocket into the hole, see the ball-carrier, and dive at Scott's ankles. The running back tries to cut to the inside and over these two players, but King's right shoulder just clips the left shin of Scott, tripping up the runner. The freshman running back plunges face-first into the turf – at the 1-yard line.

The clock continues to run.

Both teams use the same formation, alignment, and personnel.

Michigan State runs the same play:

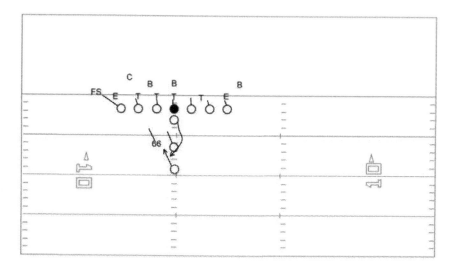

At the snap, Spears cuts to the inside aiming right for the block from the fullback. The defensive end and Pendleton come together in the backfield, a yard behind the line of scrimmage. Allen, bursting forward from his upback alignment, is forced to help out on this block at the point of attack. Scott takes the handoff from Cook at the 5-yard line, and seeing the traffic in front of him created by Spears, he bounces to his left – in the backfield – and tries to cut to the left edge:

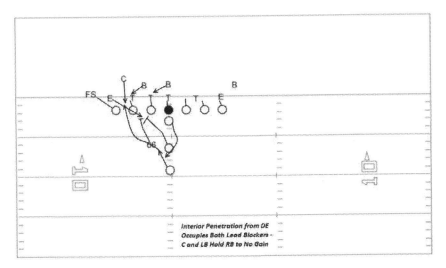

That's where he meets King.

The cornerback cuts behind the mass of bodies in front of him and wraps both arms around the knees of the ball-carrier. Scott has enough momentum for one final burst toward the end zone and lunges forward, but makes impact with the pile of humanity in front of him, specifically the back of Fisher. No Gain.

Michigan State burns its first timeout with 33 seconds remaining.

When the two teams line up, nothing has changed personnel-wise. Cook is under center with Pendleton, Allen and Scott in the backfield behind him. The Hawkeyes have six defensive linemen in the game, three linebackers and Lomax and King for defensive backs:

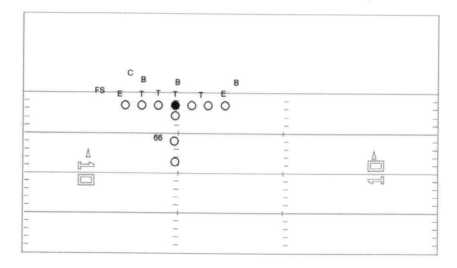

The Spartans, however, run a different play than the previous two snaps. Pendleton leads Scott to the right edge with Lang blocking down on the defensive end. After snapping the football, McGowan looks to pull in front of this play:

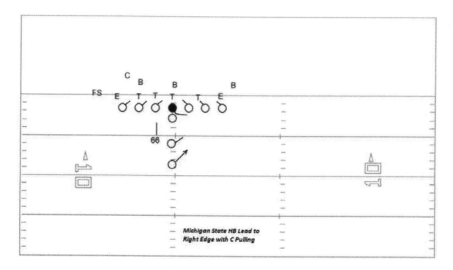

But at the snap, the left side of the Iowa defensive line gets great penetration, and this prevents McGowan from executing his pull block as he is stuck in the backfield. Lang does seal the edge, and Pendleton leads Scott to the right where Niemann is waiting. The outside linebacker surges forward and the fullback goes for the cutblock:

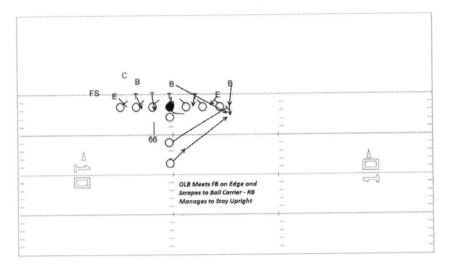

OLB Meets FB on Edge and
Scrapes to Ball Carrier - RB
Manages to Stay Upright

Niemann does a very good job using his hands here to control the blocker, and manages to stay upright. He and Jewell meet Scott in the backfield, at the 3 yard line, but they can't finish the tackle. Scott steps through these two defenders, where he then lowers a shoulder into Fisher, who has scraped down the line of scrimmage and meets Scott at the 1-yard line:

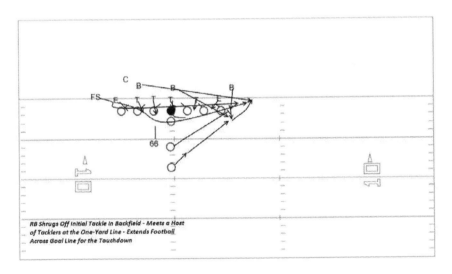

RB Shrugs Off Initial Tackle in Backfield - Meets a Host
of Tacklers at the One-Yard Line - Extends Football
Across Goal Line for the Touchdown

Jewell and Kings, with some later help from Lomax, seem to have the freshman running back stopped. But Scott keeps twisting his body, and he tries to turn around to the middle of the field and plunge into the end zone. That is when Spears, chasing this play down from the other side of the field, lunges towards the running back's legs.

That's also when Scott sticks his right arm, and the football, across the goal line for the deciding score with only 27 seconds remaining.

"It's only a championship drive if you can finish it."

Those were the words of color analyst Klatt prior to the play, and finish it the Spartans did. The drive began at their own 18-yard line with more than nine minutes left in the game, and on the next 22 plays the offense did everything possible to move the ball down the field, led by a quarterback with an injured throwing shoulder. They used the running game, they used the wildcat, they threw the ball when they could, they lined up linemen in the backfield, and brought in a reserve lineman to play center for a number of critical plays. All this while the Iowa defense did everything in its power to end the drive. On almost every play the Hawkeyes had one or more defenders excel. But in the end, the offense did its job. The Spartans finished the drive, and punched their ticket to the playoffs in the game's final seconds.

CHAPTER FIFTEEN

CLEMSON PULLS AWAY IN THE ORANGE BOWL

The Clemson Tigers earned their spot in the National Championship game with a 37-17 victory against the Oklahoma Sooners in the Orange Bowl. Trailing 17-16 at halftime, the Tigers took the lead on the opening drive of the third quarter when Wayne Gallman capped off a 12-play drive with a 1-yard touchdown run to make the score 23-17.

The Sooners were forced to punt and the Tigers missed a field goal on the next two possessions. Then Oklahoma went for it on fourth down in Clemson territory and the Tiger defense held Samaje Perine to no gain.

Clemson took over possession on their own 30-yard line with 5:28 remaining in the third quarter. Four official plays later the game was all but over.

On first down Clemson's offense lines up with quarterback Deshaun Watson (#4) in the shotgun and Gallman (#9) standing to his right. The Tigers have one running back and one tight end along with three receivers, using dual stack-slot formations. Tight end Jordan Leggett (#16) and wide receiver Charone Peake (#19) split wide to the right and receivers Hunter Renfrow (#13) and Artavis Scott (#3) go to the left. Oklahoma has a 3-4 defense on the field, with linebacker Eric Striker (#19) cheating toward the line of scrimmage and fellow LB Devante Bond (#23) aligned across from Leggett. The secondary shows Cover 1:

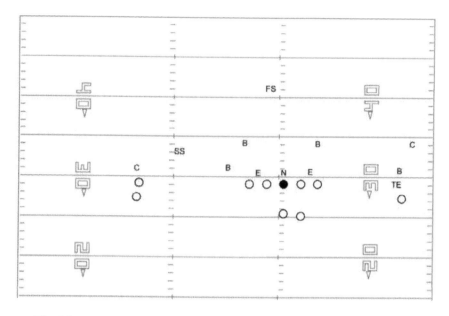

The Tigers run an inside zone read on this play. They set up a bubble screen look to each slot formation, but when Watson takes the snap he turns to his right and eyes the edge defender, linebacker Dominique Alexander (#1):

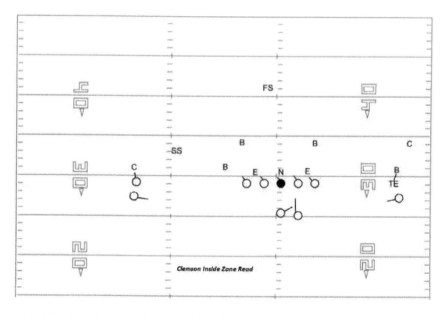

With the offensive line blocking in unison to the left, the quarterback reads Alexander and decides whether to keep the football or hand the ball off to Gallman. For their part, the Sooners blitz both Striker and strong safety Steven Parker (#10) off the opposite edge.

As Watson turns to his right to read Alexander, the linebacker slides toward the line of scrimmage, maintaining outside leverage. This is a signal for the quarterback to hand the ball off:

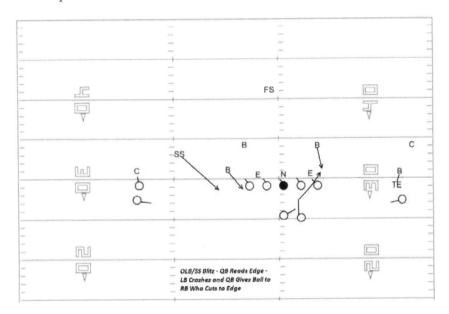

Gallman takes the ball and immediately bends to the outside, toward the incoming linebacker. But just as the two players nearly collide, the running back uses a skip-hop move to the outside, and avoids the tackle:

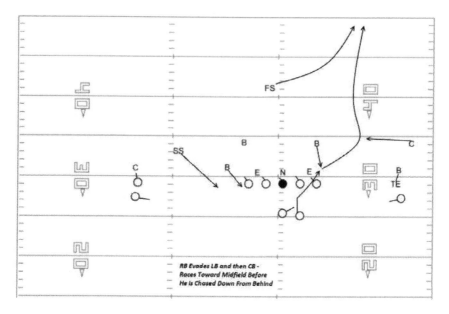

*RB Evades LB and then CB -
Races Toward Midfield Before
He is Chased Down From Behind*

Gallman then puts another juke move on cornerback Zack Sanchez (#15), cutting to the inside, before being tackled from behind by Bond. But the 21-yard gain moves the football into Sooners' territory.

Without a huddle the offense heads straight to the line with the same personnel, putting Watson in the shotgun and Gallman to his left. They again use trips formation to that side of the field, with Leggett lining up next to the tackle and Renfrow and Scott to the outside. Oklahoma stays with its personnel as well, putting both Striker and Bond near the line, while showing Cover 1, with the cornerbacks and the strong safety showing off-man technique:

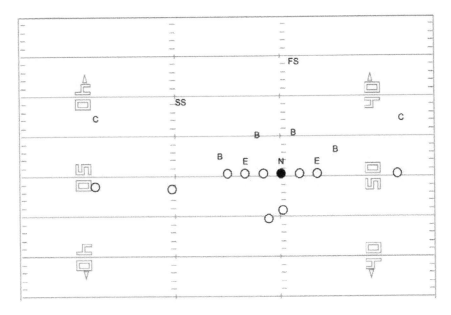

At the snap Watson again puts the football in Gallman's belly to read the defense, as they set up a bubble screen to the left side:

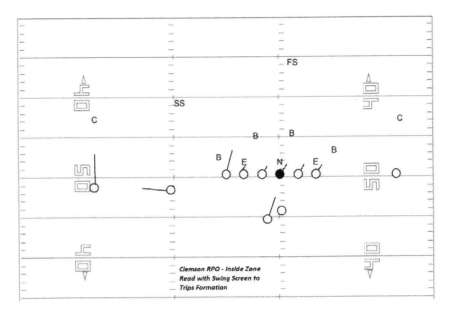

Striker stays home, anticipating a run. The quarterback reads this and swings the football to Renfrow on the outside:

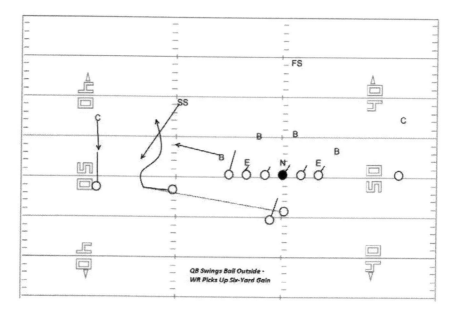

QB Swings Ball Outside -
WR Picks Up Six-Yard Gain

Scott throws a solid block at the point of attack on cornerback Jordan Thomas (#7). Renfrow catches the football and starts upfield, where he encounters Parker. The wide receiver tries a spin move inside to avoid this first tackle attempt, but at the 45-yard line Renfrow nearly runs into Striker. With a second spin move to the inside, the receiver avoids this second tackle attempt. He stumbles forward to the Oklahoma 43-yard line for a gain of 6, setting up a 2nd and 4 play with nearly 5 minutes left in the third quarter.

On the next play the Tigers again line up with a single running back and tight end in the game. Leggett deploys to the right side, with Renfrow and Scott in a stack to to the outside of the tight end. Peake is a single receiver split to the left. The Sooners stay in their 3-4 base defense and put Parker in press alignment over the stack slot, with Sanchez playing off coverage:

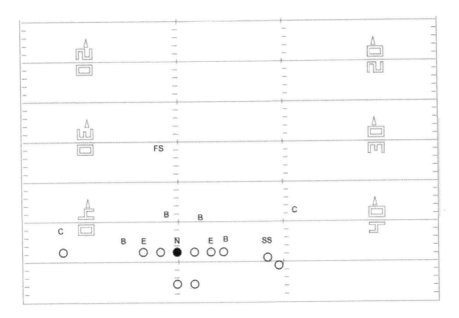

The Tigers run a drive concept, with Scott running the underneath crossing route while Renfrow runs a deeper in-route. On the outside, Peake runs a straight go pattern:

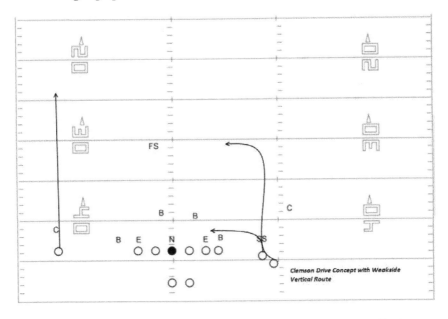

Clemson Drive Concept with Weakside Vertical Route

Watson takes the snap and sees free safety Ahmad Thomas (#13) jump the dig route from Renfrow. Recognizing this, the quarterback takes a deep shot:

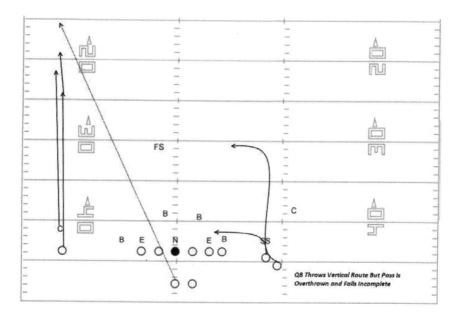

QB Throws Vertical Route But Pass Is
Overthrown and Falls Incomplete

The pass is overthrown and falls incomplete. However, a yellow flag flutters onto the field. Parker lined up in the neutral zone across from Renfrow, and is guilty of a violation. The 5-yard penalty puts the football to the Oklahoma 38-yard line, and gives Clemson a fresh set of downs.

On the next play, the Tigers make a substitution, bringing Leggett to the sideline and replacing him with Stanton Seckinger (#81). The reserve tight end lines up on the left edge next to left tackle Taylor Hearn (#51). Renfrow, Peake and Scott align in a trips to the right. Watson is in the shotgun with Gallman to his left. The Sooners stay with their 3-4 personnel, and put Bond on the line over Seckinger. Striker walks outside over the middle trips receiver, while Parker stands across from the inside trips receiver:

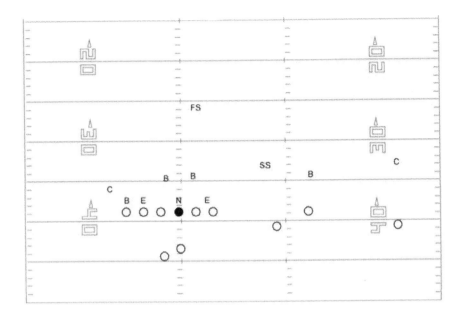

Clemson sets up a bubble screen to the trips formation, but Watson takes the snap and then executes a quarterback draw. He follows Gallman to the left, while left guard Eric Mac Lain (#78) pulls to the edge:

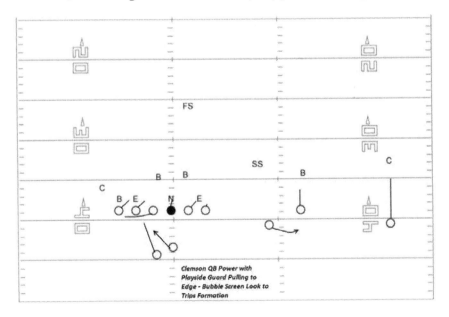

Clemson QB Power with
Playside Guard Pulling to
Edge - Bubble Screen Look to
Trips Formation

Alexander reads this play perfectly from his linebacker spot, crashing forward toward the hole. The linebacker collides with Gallman just past the line of scrimmage, forcing Watson to cut inside. There the quarterback meets both Bond and defensive end Charles Tapper (#91), who have scraped off their blocks:

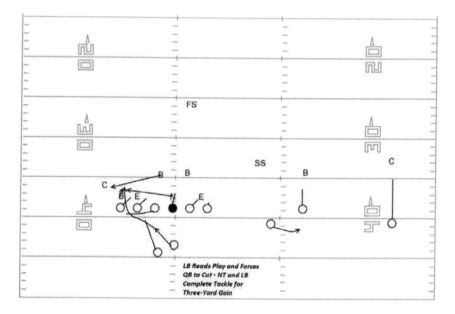

These two players bring Watson down after a short 3-yard gain.

Facing second down, the Tigers again hurry to the line without a huddle. Watson stands in the shotgun with Gallman to his right, a tight end, and three receivers in the game. The offense uses trips right with the TE on the line and Renfrow and Scott to the outside. Receiver Trevion Thompson (#1) checks into the game, and is a single receiver to the left. Oklahoma stays with its 3-4 defense, putting Bond on the line of scrimmage outside the left tackle. The secondary shows Cover 1 before the snap:

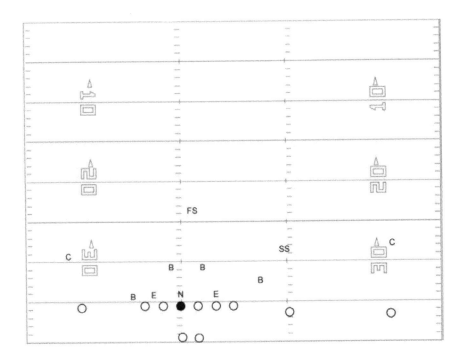

Clemson rolls Watson to the right on this play, with Thompson running a slant pattern and Scott running a short curl. Renfrow, from his middle trips alignment, runs a deep out route:

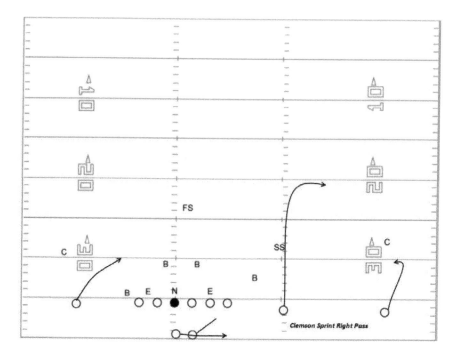

The Sooners have a bit of a surprise in store for the offense:

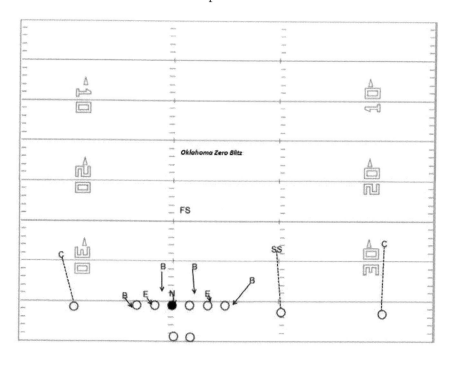

Off the snap they blitz and play straight man coverage in the secondary. This leaves Parker isolated on Renfrow. As Watson rolls to his right, he spots the redshirt freshman receiver with a step on the strong safety:

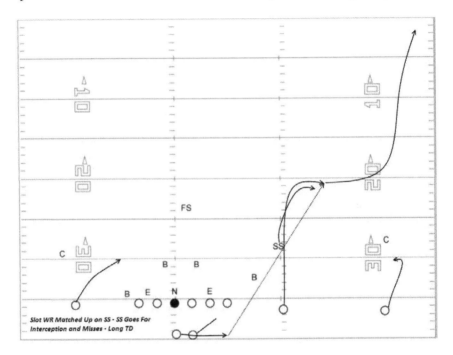

Slot WR Matched Up on SS - SS Goes For Interception and Misses - Long TD

Parker tries to cut under the route to make the deflection, but whiffs on the attempt and the ball sails safely into Renfrow's hands. Because of the straight man coverage, the free safety Thomas is behind the play, and not in position to prevent the 35-yard score.

The touchdown and extra point extended Clemson's lead to 13, putting the game and accompanying ticket to the National Championship beyond doubt. The drive began with stopping the Sooners' offense on a short-yardage play. Building off that momentum the Tigers' offense raced down the field in five plays, to the joy of the Clemson faithful and the dismay of the Sooners fans.

CHAPTER SIXTEEN

ROLL DAMN TIDE

In the first semifinal game the Clemson Tigers and the Oklahoma Sooners were locked in a close battle until the third quarter, with the Sooners enjoying a one-point lead at halftime. In the night's second game, this was not the case. After Michigan State and Alabama held each other scoreless through the first quarter, the Crimson Tide halted a promising Spartans drive early in the second quarter, and forced a punt. Shortly thereafter, the SEC champions scored all points they would need on the night.

Following a touchback on the punt the Crimson Tide take over on their own 20-yard line. They line up with quarterback Jake Coker (#14) in the shotgun with running back Kenyan Drake (#17) to his right. Wide receivers Calvin Ridley (#3) and Richard Mullaney (#16) align to the left in an inverted slot, with the freshman Ridley inside. The third receiver, ArDarius Stewart (#13), splits to the right with tight end O.J. Howard (#88) in a wing alignment just outside the tackle. The Spartans have their base 4-3 defense on the field showing Cover 4 in the secondary, and walk outside linebacker Darien Harris (#45) up to the line on the right, shaded toward the inverted slot formation:

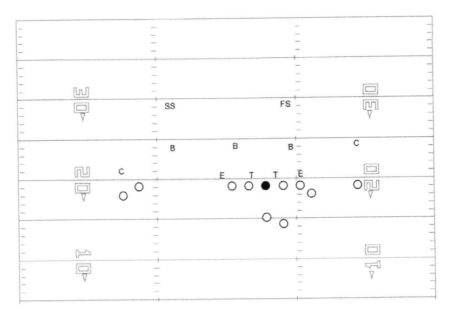

Just prior to the snap, Drake uses deep motion to the left side, which causes Harris to widen outside:

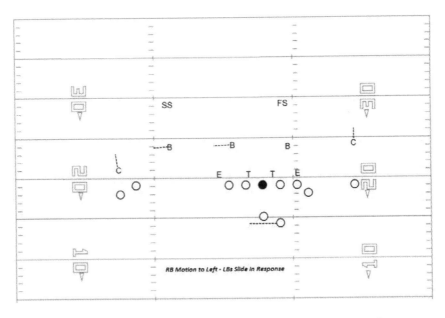

At the snap, Drake runs a swing route to the left side. Ridley runs a corner pattern, while on the backside Stewart runs a deep comeback and Howard releases into the flat. Mullaney is the primary target here, and he is running a post, completing Alabama's divide concept:

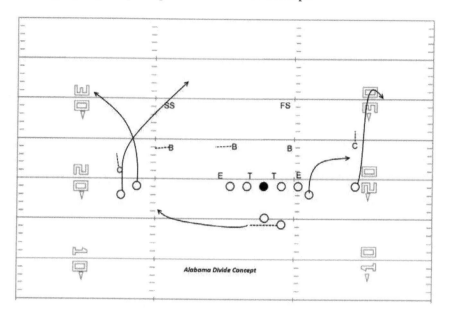

Alabama Divide Concept

Against the Michigan State Cover 4 scheme, the primary receiver breaks open:

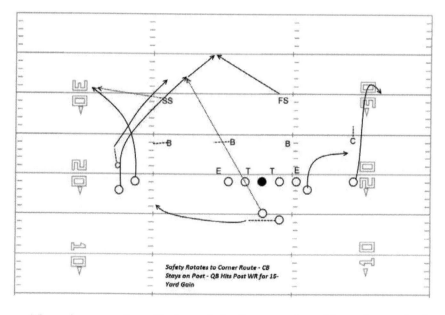

Safety Rotates to Corner Route - CB
Stays on Post - QB Hits Post WR for 15-
Yard Gain

The swing route from Drake and the flat route from Howard cause both underneath linebackers to widen, opening a throwing lane for Coker to find the post pattern. Against this coverage scheme – with both receivers releasing vertically – the safety stays on Ridley, the inside receiver, and covers the corner route. This enables Mullaney to establish inside leverage on cornerback Jermaine Edmondson (#39). Coker hits the receiver in stride for a 15-yard gain and a fresh set of downs.

With the ball at the 35-yard line, Alabama stays with one running back and one tight end, but brings in Heisman Trophy winner Derrick Henry (#2). He stands behind Coker in the pistol formation. The Crimson Tide again use an inverted slot to the left, with Ridley inside of Mullaney. Howard shifts onto the line of scrimmage – next to the right tackle in a three-point stance – while Stewart sets as a flanker to the right side. The Spartans stay with their base 4-3 defense, and once more show Cover 4:

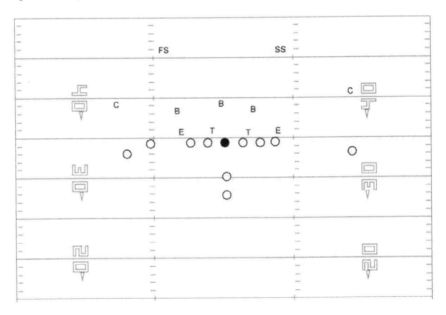

Just prior to the play, Mullaney comes in motion from left to right. The offense executes a split zone running play, with the offensive line blocking to the left and Mullaney responsible for handling the backside edge defender:

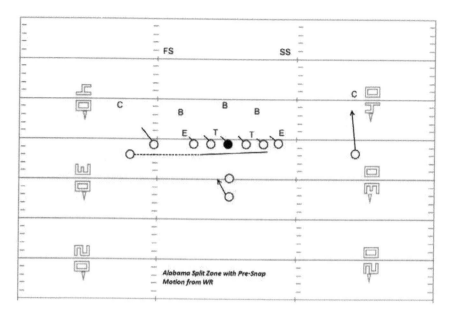

Alabama Split Zone with Pre-Snap Motion from WR

Coker turns to his left and gives the football to Henry, who is aiming for the left side. The offensive line fires out to the left. After snapping the football center Ryan Kelly (#70) is tasked with blocking defensive tackle Malik McDowell (#4). The big defensive tackle begins the play in a 1 technique between the center and guard, lined up on Kelly's left shoulder. McDowell beats Kelly to the outside and knifes into the backfield:

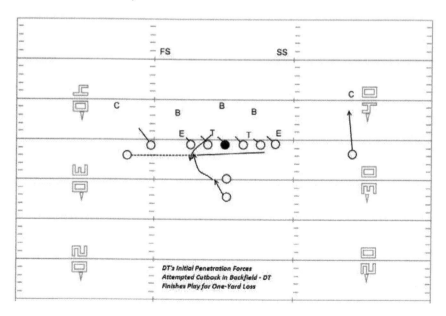

DT's Initial Penetration Forces Attempted Cutback in Backfield - DT Finishes Play for One-Yard Loss

Henry tries to cut back, but the defensive tackle wraps him up for a 1-yard loss.

Now facing second and long, Alabama lines up with Coker in the shotgun and the same personnel group. Henry stands to the left of the quarterback, while to the outside Mullaney and Ridley set up in another inverted slot, Mullaney inside. Howard and Stewart align in a pro formation, with the wide receiver using a short split from the tight end. Michigan State stays with its base defense, and shows Cover 2 with Arjen Colquhoun (#36) in press alignment over Ridley:

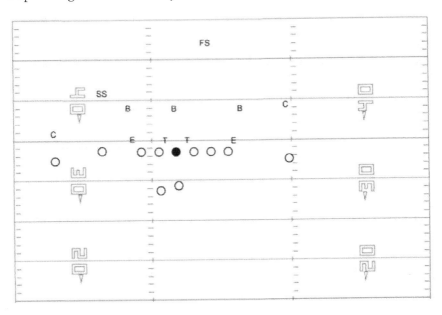

Prior to the play, Stewart comes in motion from the left. In response, the Spartans adjust their defense to Cover 1, with safety Montae Nicholson (#9) dropping down to cover Mullaney. The offense sets up a designed route for Stewart in the flat. Coker takes the snap and fakes the inside zone run to Henry. Mullaney executes a crackback block to the inside, while the motion man releases into the flat on a short out route:

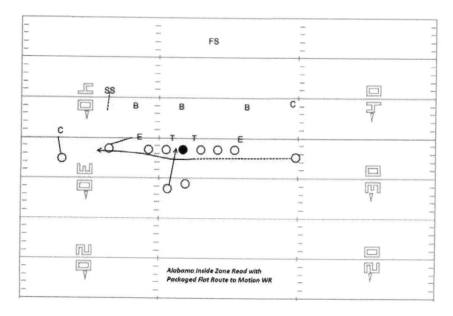

Alabama Inside Zone Read with
Packaged Flat Route to Motion WR

Mullaney delivers a solid block on the edge, and the run action draws Nicholson to the inside. This opens up the space for the quarterback to swing the football to Stewart outside:

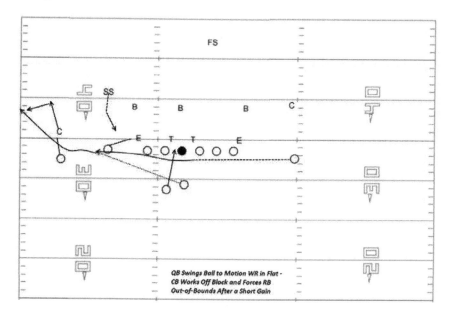

QB Swings Ball to Motion WR in Flat -
CB Works Off Block and Forces RB
Out-of-Bounds After a Short Gain

The wide receiver secures the pass and cuts upfield before being forced out of bounds by Colquhoun at the Crimson Tide 38-yard line.

Looking at 3rd and 7, offensive coordinator Lane Kiffin puts Coker in the shotgun with Henry standing to his right. The offense stays with one back and one tight end, putting Mullaney and Ridley in an inverted slot right, with Mullaney inside. Howard and Stewart line up in pro formation on the left.

The Spartans adjust their defense, rolling with a 3-3-5 nickel. They place linebacker Chris Frey (#23) on the line over the TE, and they show a very soft Cover 1 scheme in the secondary. The defenders are aligned in off-man technique, giving each receiver about 8 yards of cushion before the play. They also show an interior blitz pre-snap, with the middle linebacker over the right guard:

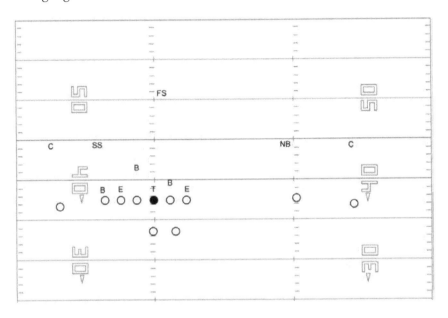

The three receivers all run curls right at the sticks, with Howard releasing on a post route:

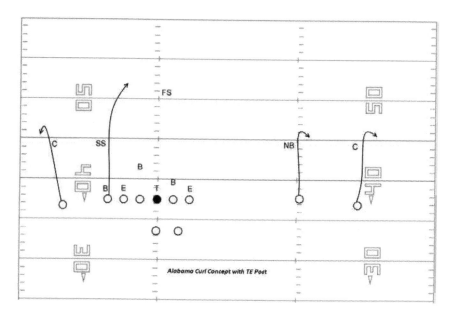

Alabama Curl Concept with TE Post

With the cushion afforded him by the coverage, Stewart releases vertically and then stops right at the first-down marker. Coker's timing on the throw is perfect:

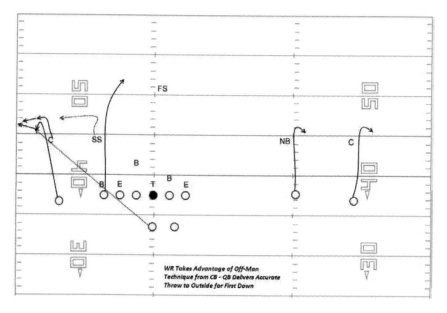

WR Takes Advantage of Off-Man Technique from CB - QB Delivers Accurate Throw to Outside for First Down

The ball arrives just after the receiver's break, thrown high and to the outside, away from the interior defenders. Colquhoun and Nicholson try to recover, but cannot prevent the completion. The 11-yard gain is enough for a first down.

Following the completion, ESPN commentators Chris Fowler and Kirk Herbstreit question the cushion given to the receivers, and continue to wonder (as they had been most of the quarter) when the deep vertical shot was going to come. They would not wait long.

Coker stands in the pistol on the next play, with Henry a few yards behind him. Howard sets in a wing to the left, with Stewart outside of the tight end. To the right Ridley and Mullaney align in an inverted slot, with Mullaney split wide toward the sideline. The Spartans stay with their base 4-3 defense and show Cover 4 again. They walk Harris outside toward the slot, but he stays inside of Ridley:

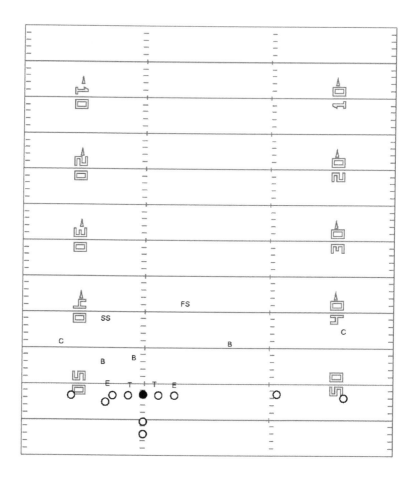

Howard stays in to help with pass protection, as the three receivers release vertically. Stewart and Mullaney run deep comeback routes while the freshman wide receiver goes deep:

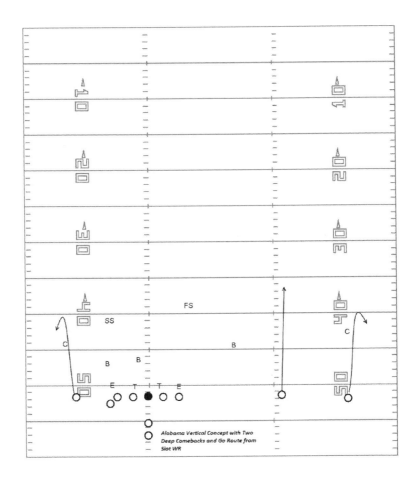

Alabama Vertical Concept with Two Deep Comebacks and Go Route from Slot WR

In this Cover 4 scheme, Ridley gets matched up on safety Demetrious Cox (#7). With the linebacker shaded to the inside, the receiver gets a free release, and a full head of steam to erase the cushion, before he blows by the safety:

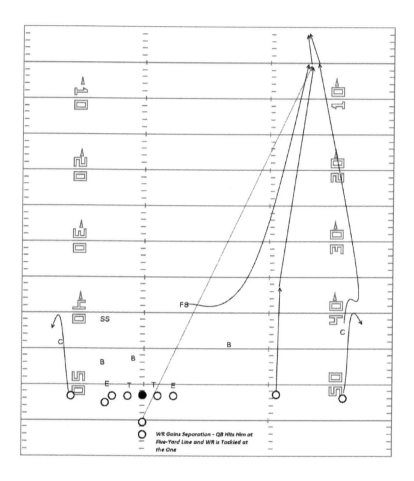

WR Gains Separation - QB Hits Him at
Five-Yard Line and WR is Tackled at
the One

Coker uncorks the throw, the freshman reels in the over-the-shoulder pass, and Ridley is tackled at the 1-yard line for a 50-yard gain.

The Crimson Tide waste no time celebrating, and head to the line and snap the football quickly, giving the ball to their Heisman-winning back. Henry gets stuffed for no gain, but the quick play caught the Spartans in the midst of a substitution. The infraction moves the football half the distance to the goal, which is inches closer, and it remains first down.

It's hard enough to stop a back like Henry in a short yardage situation, but it's nearly impossible when the offense puts two huge lead blockers in front of him. Kiffin brings in a jumbo package for the next play, placing Coker under center and three "backs" in a strong i-formation. Henry is the deep back, and in front of him stand defensive end A'Shawn Robinson (#86) and defensive tackle Jarran Reed (#90). The Spartans counter with their goal-line package:

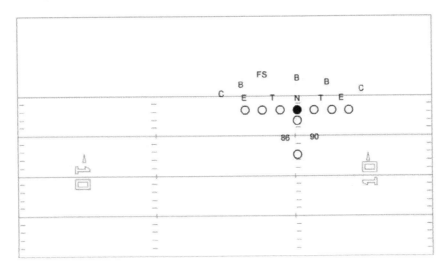

Coker turns to his right and hands the ball to the running back, who is aiming for the right A-gap and following the two big lead blockers:

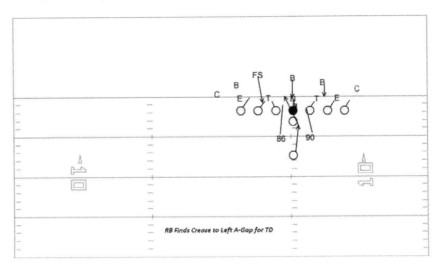

Henry finds a crease behind Robinson and plunges into the end zone for the first score of the night.

The short touchdown run gave Alabama all the points it needed to secure the victory. The Crimson Tide tacked on a field goal later in the quarter for a 10-0 lead at the half, and then exploded for 21 points in the third quarter to put the game out of reach. With their defense pitching a shutout, the game was never really in question after this touchdown drive.

CHAPTER SEVENTEEN

ROLL DAMN TIDE, REDUX

We end nearly where we began.

This book has covered a number of touchdown drives, from a number of different schools. We have seen different offensive styles, different offensive schemes, and different means of finishing a drive. We have seen spread offenses throw the football all over the field, pro-style offenses rely on a mix of the passing and the running attacks, and even a 22-play march that encompassed nearly the entire fourth quarter of the Big Ten Championship Game. But all of these drives had one basic thing in common:

Possession of the football.

Alabama and Clemson met out west on January 11 to decide the national champion. After an eight-play Alabama drive resulted in a short field goal to tie the game at 24, the Crimson Tide lined up to kick off with just more than 10 minutes remaining in the game:

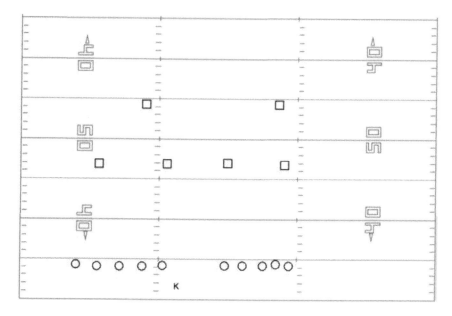

Notice the alignment of both the kicking and the receiving teams. Alabama uses its regular kickoff personnel and formation, and Clemson, which has been tight with its receiving alignment throughout the night, has only four men up front, leaving a massive area of the field uncovered before the kick. Kicker Adam Griffith (#99) approaches the football, and simply pooches the football into the air toward the right side:

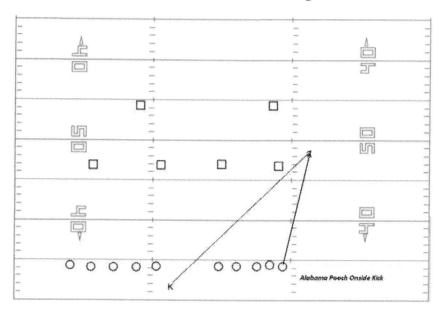

Starting cornerback Marlon Humphrey (#26) runs under the football, much like a wide receiver tracking a pass over his shoulder, and catches the ball on the fly to give the Crimson Tide one extra possession in the game.

They quickly capitalized.

Facing first and 10 at midfield, Alabama lines up with one running back and a pair of tight ends, placing both tight ends in a wing trips formation to the right and a single receiver split to the left. Quarterback Jake Coker (#14) stands in the shotgun with Heisman Trophy-winner Derrick Henry (#2) standing to the left of the quarterback. Clemson lines up with its 4-2-5 nickel defense on the field, and shows Cover 2 man underneath with both cornerbacks and the nickelback in press alignment:

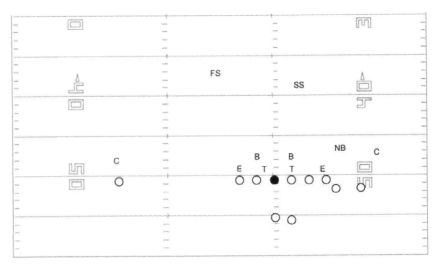

Alabama tries a counter run to the left side, pulling right guard Alphonse Taylor (#50) to the left side in front of the running back. Tight end O.J. Howard (#88) also comes across the formation as a lead blocker, from his starting point on the right. Henry freezes, for a moment, to let the blocking develop, before bursting forward to take the handoff aiming for the left side:

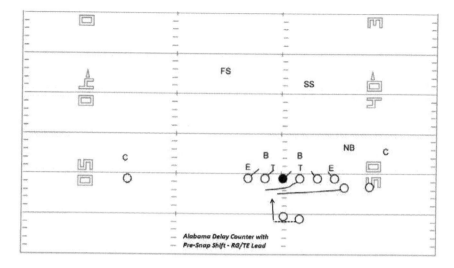

The blocking scheme tasks left tackle Cam Robinson (#74) with leaving defensive end Shaq Lawson (#90) unblocked, with the tackle heading immediately for the second level and Taylor executing a trap block on the defensive end. But Lawson is too quick for the blocking scheme, and beats the right guard to the outside. Henry takes the handoff and is quickly met by Lawson, but steps to the inside and then angles to the outside to avoid the tackle in the backfield:

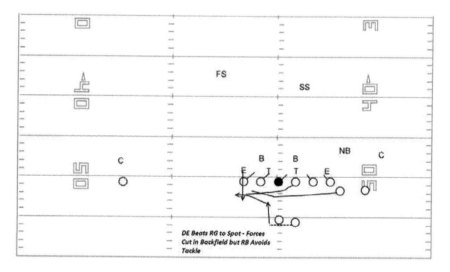

Henry still has work to do to even get back to the line of scrimmage, and he doesn't get there. Linebacker Ben Boulware (#10) splits through the line, to the inside of Howard's block. The linebacker lunges for Henry's legs, but the running back steps through the tackle attempt and continues toward the outside:

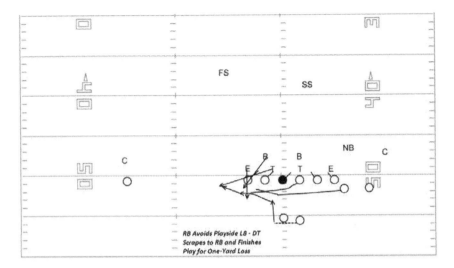

RB Avoids Playside LB - DT Scrapes to RB and Finishes Play for One-Yard Loss

Finally, defensive tackle Carlos Watkins (#94) finishes the play, dragging the Heisman-winner to the turf for a 1-yard loss.

Facing second and long, the Crimson Tide adjust their lineup, taking Henry off the field and replacing him with running back Kenyan Drake (#17). Drake stands to the left of Coker in the backfield, and the offense lines up with trips to the right and Howard alone as an in-line TE to the left:

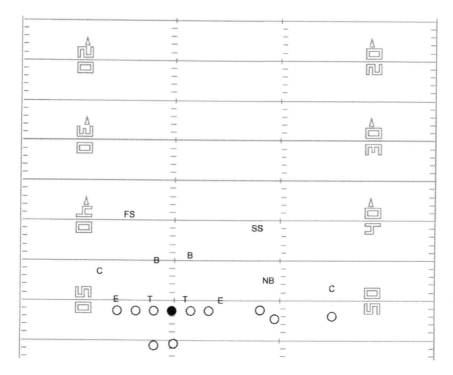

The Tigers stay with their 4-2-5 nickel defense, and again show Cover 2 before the snap with both safeties around 10-yards deep.

Offensive coordinator Lane Kiffin calls for a vertical passing concept, using a double-in design on the trips side of the field, and two vertical routes on the backside, with both Howard and Drake releasing vertically:

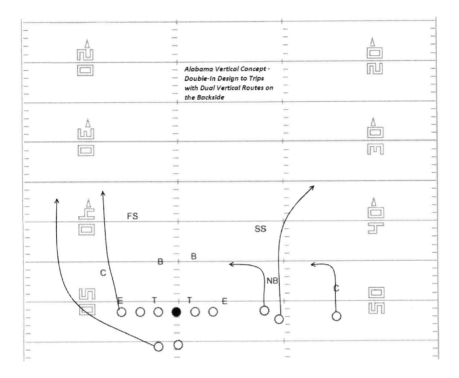

Here is what Clemson does for coverage:

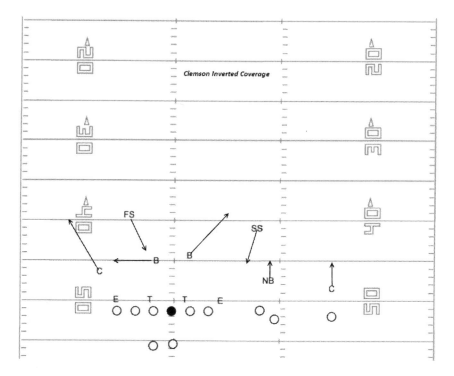

This almost looks like an inverted Cover 6, with both safeties dropping down into underneath zones, one cornerback covering a deep half-field, the middle linebacker dropping with the inside trips receiver, and the secondary using Cover 4 concepts on the trips side of the formation. For reference, here is a diagram of an inverted Cover 6 scheme from a lecture given by John Donovan, the former offensive coordinator at Penn State:

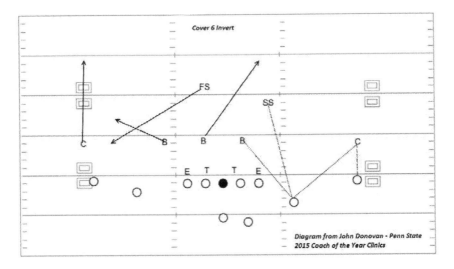

Cover 6 Invert

Diagram from John Donovan - Penn State
2015 Coach of the Year Clinics

At least, that's what the coverage looks like. Neither Kirk Herbstreit in the booth, nor the collective of coaches watching the play on ESPN's film room feed, were convinced this was nothing more than a blown coverage. Whether it is by design or a missed coverage, the result is the same:

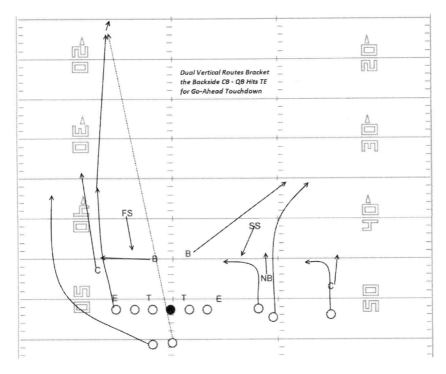

Dual Vertical Routes Bracket
the Backside CB - QB Hits TE
for Go-Ahead Touchdown

Both Drake and Howard release vertically, and cornerback Cordrea Tankersley (#25) drops into the deep outside zone and tries to split the difference between the two routes. But the tight end has inside leverage, and with the middle linebacker rotation to the other side of the field, Howard is wide open. Coker hits his tight end in stride for the go-ahead touchdown.

If anything, this drive illustrates the importance of stealing possessions, and giving your offense one more chance each game to put together a championship drive. This has become a trend recently in football, at all levels. Teams like the New England Patriots, Minnesota Vikings, and Green Bay Packers like to defer at the coin toss and try to execute a "two-for-one," where they score before halftime and then receive the second-half kick. Here, the Crimson Tide stole an extra possession with the onside kick, and they used it to put together a quick, two-play drive for the go-ahead score. It was the extra possession they needed to cap off the season with their fourth national championship in seven years.

ABOUT THE AUTHOR

After a decade of practicing law in the Washington DC area, Mr. Schofield began a second career as a writer with InsidethePylon.com. He lives in Maryland with his wife and two young children.

34330496R00178

Made in the USA
Middletown, DE
17 August 2016